The
CHINA
Cloud

*America's Tragic Blunder
and China's Rise to Nuclear Power*

by WILLIAM L. RYAN *&* SAM SUMMERLIN

Little, Brown and Company   *Boston* • *Toronto*

Published simultaneously in Canada
by Little, Brown & Company (Canada) Limited

PRINTED IN THE UNITED STATES OF AMERICA

For Edythe

W.L.R.

For Cynthia, and for Dolly and Irl

S.S.

This is a flower that blooms in adversity.

TSIEN HSUE-SHEN

The Chinese nation will never be insulted again.
We have stood up! Let the world tremble!

MAO TSE-TUNG

ACKNOWLEDGMENTS

This book treats a subject both fascinating and frustrating; a theme crucial to our time and yet one shrouded in secrecy.

The authors have relied on facts and judgments marshaled by those scientists, scholars, journalists and other sensitive observers who have been directly concerned with Red China's rise to nuclear power. Many are mentioned in the pages of this book.

Particular acknowledgment is made to those who conducted research and interviews.

We are especially indebted to Paul Green Houston, who manifests the literary heritage of his late father and of the playwright whose name he bears; to Ann Novotny and Susan Hartung of Research Reports, New York City, who assembled a remarkable collection of data on China's nuclear age; to Leon Pearle, whose imaginative sleuthing helped make it possible to re-create the past; and to Stanley Hart and John Starr, an editor and an agent who led us along the rocky road to publication.

Many others merit our gratitude for their contributions: Alice Langley Hsieh of the Rand Corporation; Dr. Chu-yuan Cheng of the University of Michigan; Jim Miller, Graham Berry and John Dart of Caltech; Professors Frank E. Marble, Duncan W. Rannie, Homer J. Stewart, Frederick Lindvall, Horace N. Gilbert, Theodore Wu, Carl Anderson, E. C. Watson and William R. Smythe of Caltech; Dr. C. C. Lin of M.I.T.; Tom Henshaw of Boston; Frank Bristow of the Jet Propulsion Laboratory; Dan Kimball and William Zisch of Aerojet-General; Robert

ACKNOWLEDGMENTS

E. Wick, formerly of the FBI; former mayor Fletcher Bowron, attorney Max F. Deutz, Police Captains Charles Stanley and Joe Stephens, and Mrs. Dorothy Healey, all of Los Angeles; Robert Gibson of the Los Angeles *Times*; and, in particular, four men whose patient recollection of their roles in this drama made it possible to relive the past: Grant B. Cooper, Sidney Weinbaum, Allan G. Juhl and William Ward Kimple.

Appreciation is extended to those who told us how it was in China: Tanio Matsuno of *Asahi Shimbun*, Tokyo; Charles F. Lynch of the Southam News Services; Charles Taylor of the Toronto *Globe and Mail*; Koji Moriwaki and Roy Matsuura of *Chugoku Shimbun*, Hiroshima; Henry Hartzenbusch and Shinobu Higashi of the Associated Press, Tokyo; Forrest Edwards, Associated Press, Hong Kong; Steve Aug of the Associated Press, Washington, and Al Wall, formerly of AP, Washington.

In final tribute, this book could never have appeared without the assistance of Joyce Thompson, Tina Marshall, Janice Ellertsen, and Mary-Rose Rogers.

W. L. R. and S. S.

CONTENTS

The CHINA CLOUD

PROLOGUE

The ancient ghosts of Lop have reappeared, this time not to haunt caravans plodding across vast wastes of sand, but to taunt the people of China and their rulers. The echoes of their mockery disturb the dreams of the mighty Russians and the powerful Americans.

In the thirteenth century, Marco Polo traversed the forbidden desert on his journey to Cathay.

"The town of Lop," he wrote, "is situated . . . near the commencement of the Great Desert of Lop . . . To travel it in the direction of its length would prove a vain attempt, as little less than a year must be consumed, and to convey stores for such a period would be found impracticable. . . .

"It is asserted as a well-known fact that this desert is the abode of many evil spirits which amuse travelers to their destruction with the most extraordinary illusions. . . . It is said . . . that some persons in their journey across the desert have seen what appeared to be a body of armed men advancing towards them and, apprehensive of being attacked and plundered, have taken flight. . . .

"Marvellous, indeed, and almost passing belief, are the stories related to these spirits of the desert which are said at times to fill the air with the sounds of all kinds of musical instruments and also of drums and the clash of arms." [1]

The air over the Desert of Lop once again is filled with the sound of the clash of arms — nuclear arms. Somewhere not far from Lop Nor — Lake Lop — the Communist People's Republic of China produced the key which opened the door to the Nuclear Club.

The Lop Nor area is in westernmost China, in Sinkiang (New Frontier) Province, which now goes by the name of Sinkiang-Uighur Autonomous Region (Hsin-Chiang Wei-Wu-Erh Tzu-Chih-Ch'u.) Lake Lop's ancient salt-encrusted bed is on the eastern fringes of the vast Takla Makan Desert of drifting sands and towering dunes, bleak, desolate and uninhabitable except for sparse settlements along the banks of the Tarim and other smaller rivers which fight their way desperately through to the lake-marsh region. The desert is the center of the great basin of the Tarim River, which meanders for a thousand miles eastward from the area between the Tien Shan and Kunlun mountains. Historically, the basin was a highway, the principal route for caravans between east and west. In the mid-1960s it became Communist China's highway to nuclear power.

As explosion succeeded explosion, the world watched tensely. Did the entry of China into the Club bring humanity closer to the day of nuclear Armageddon? The possibilities seemed awesome, especially the possibilities of miscalculation and of nuclear war by accident.

China, a land of calamity, is also a land of paradox. To a puzzled world, the most fascinating of all the paradoxes is the spectacle of that vast nation, despite years of political and economic chaos and the dangerous confusion of the Great Proletarian Cultural Revolution, marching steadily forward in the nuclear weapons field at a pace which astonishes Americans and the rest of the Western nations.

The spectacle is all the more alarming in the light of what China is — a painfully backward nation of 750 million or more people, its population growing at a rate of 15 million a year. More than a half billion of that population are chained to the earth, the enormous peasantry, most of whom still scratch out a living with tools and methods which differ little from those used by their ancestors.

Prologue

China's Communists dominate a country a third larger than the United States, but the bulk of the people must live in the provinces of the eastern and central regions. The rest of the land is sparsely settled, much of it uninhabitable, cruel and inhospitable. China is poor and backward by the standards of Western civilization. Yet the Chinese were the people who invented gunpowder and who were experimenting with rockets before the civilization of the West had wholly emerged from the era of the crossbow.

More than four hundred years ago, while Leonardo da Vinci was sketching a flying machine with oars for wings and pulleys for power, a Chinese was dreaming of jet flight. Wan Hu, an inventor, constructed a weird contraption: a chair on two wheels to which he lashed black-powder rockets. Wan went aloft clutching two kites, one in each hand. Legend says that the daring inventor managed to fire the rockets. But Wan Hu came to an untimely end. When the fire and smoke of man's first attempt at rocket flight cleared away, Wan Hu, his chair and his kites had disintegrated.

The outside world, the world which cultivated Chinese regarded as barbarian and unworthy of notice, knew nothing of Wan Hu's explosion into the pages of China's history. China was far away, insulated, mysterious but by no means terrifying. Four centuries later, it was a much different story. When China began exploding her way into the nuclear age, a frightening picture emerged. It was a picture of great civilizations utterly unable to comprehend one another.[2] It was a picture of two worlds — the haves and the have-nots. It was a picture of a have-not nation smashing its way into an exclusive club of the haves and demonstrating to the world of the have-nots what total concentration on power could accomplish.

China has, with its nuclear explosions, reemphasized a claim to the leadership of the have-not world. The nations which like to call themselves advanced are uncomfortable.

Even in the mid-1960s, desipte the riotous "Great Proletarian Cultural Revolution" and a titanic power struggle at the top,

China has been looked upon by much of the rest of the world — however mistakenly — as a nation unified in one enormous collective under a regime seized by a Messianic complex, evidently convinced she must save the rest of civilization for its own good, even if much of it must be destroyed in the process of salvation.

To awed onlookers, it seems virtually a foregone conclusion that Communist China, with its vast and soaring population, must inevitably engage in some form of imperialist expansion. China is exploding with people, many of them underfed, underclothed and sullenly angry with themselves and the rest of the world. The anger of the peasantry lifted communism to power in old China. Its Communist rulers are aware of the potentialities of that anger. To divert it from themselves, the leaders could well feel impelled to take long risks.

Probably China would eventually have become a nuclear power without any significant outside help. She has made it with astonishing speed, however, because of the help of two great nuclear powers, the United States and the Soviet Union.

In the case of the Americans, the help was unintentional. It was extended at a time when it was assumed that China always would be a safe and grateful ally. In the case of the Russians, the help was political expediency, a response to the insistent demands of a "fraternal Communist nation" which could be expected to remain a fraternal ally indefinitely, in spite of the long record of obvious strains between the two.

Both the Russians and the Americans would have reason to regret deeply having extended such help.

China's bomb was a boomerang for all concerned, probably including the Chinese themselves. Were it not for the bomb, there is a good chance that China would have suffered much less than she did in the era of Communist rule. The bomb was costly. It ate up much of the wealth which could have gone toward alleviating the economic — and thus the political — woes of a crowded and hungry nation.

Were it not for China's bomb, it is likely that the Soviet

Union's relations with its big Communist neighbor would have been at least tolerable and Moscow's painful problems with the world Communist movement might have been at least delayed, if not avoided. The bomb intruded itself into China's internal and foreign policies alike and had a strong influence on what proved to be a turbulent decade for world communism. The history of that decade, after Nikita S. Khrushchev exorcised the ghost of the dictator Stalin, has provided excellent reasons for believing that China's nuclear weapons program probably is more responsible than any other single factor in the long and bitter quarrel between Moscow and Peking which has led the two steadily toward a final break and an irreparable split in the Communist world.

Behind all the ideology, the role of the nuclear weapon in the feud has been clearly discernible from the outset. It was the bomb issue which prompted Peking eventually to describe Moscow's leadership as China's "Enemy No. 1." [3]

Many factors, of course, are involved in China's internal and external political wars: questions involving national interest, military posture, territorial conflicts, ancient woes and phobias, the clash between the ruling Communists and the Chinese intellectuals, massive economic problems. The debate over ideology seemed at times a curtain of words whose purpose was to hide other things that were going on. [4]

The "Great Proletarian Cultural Revolution" in China had Peking's leaders at one another's throats. Chairman Mao Tse-tung seemed intent on pulling to pieces the structure of the party he had so laboriously built, if doing so should prove necessary to protect his leadership and his niche in history. Yet, for all of that, the nuclear research continued, under the guidance of scientists insulated as far as possible from the storms of Chinese politics.

This is the story of some of those scientists. It is the story of how China blasted her way into the Nuclear Association and then quickly lifted herself out of the status of apprenticeship to full membership by wedding her bomb to a missile long before Westerners thought it possible. Much of this is the story of one man from Shanghai and his treatment at the hands of the Americans to whom he had contributed so much.

It is also the story of an era, of a state of mind which caused Americans to cringe at labels. It is a story of how nations, in their pursuit of their own narrow aims, are persuaded for the sake of an elusive factor known as "security" to act against their own best interests.

No one can say precisely how many Chinese scientists were trained in the United States in techniques related to nuclear energy and then carried their knowledge home to China. The figure most widely accepted is eighty or more, who studied on campuses from Pasadena to Cambridge, from Princeton to Berkeley. Many of the eighty-odd were considered brilliant. But they represented only a tiny proportion of the Chinese who studied in the United States. Many remained in America after communism took over their native land.

Of those who returned — and they were key men — some may have been pawns of intrigue, lured home by propaganda and threats from Peking which played upon deep Chinese feelings of family loyalty. Several became discouraged or even frightened by the atmosphere in America at the beginning of the decade of the fifties. Some may have been convinced Communists all along. In any case, the point to remember is that they went home from America, and had they not gone, the Chinese would have had a severe shortage of the senior scientists necessary to produce nuclear weapons.

By an ironic twist of fate, many — including the celebrated missileman from Shanghai — had come to the United States on scholarship funds contributed by America from its share of Boxer Rebellion indemnities.

Twelve years before Tsien Hsue-shen, the missileman, was born, the aging Empress Dowager Tz'u Hsi staged a coup d'etat for conservatism as China reeled into the twentieth century in turmoil and despair. The Empress imprisoned her nephew, the twenty-seven-year-old Emperor Kuang Hsu, who had planned to assassinate her most loyal henchmen and throttle her reactionary followers. The young ruler's reformers were caught and executed, and most of his reformist decrees were annulled.

This conservative assault sparked a violent reaction. Unrest swept all China. A fever of hatred spread through the nation against all foreign devils who had preyed upon China for years. For a century, below the surface, China had boiled with a deep hatred for the foreigners who had moved in on her ancient and proud civilization and considered it their God-given right to do with the country as they pleased, to divide it into spheres of influence, exploit it, humiliate it.

The Boxer Rebellion erupted in 1899. With the warrior motto, "Protect the country, destroy the foreigner," the Boxers stormed into Peking in 1900 and laid siege for fifty-five days of terror to the missions there. The Empress Dowager called for death to all foreigners. An international force broke the rebellion in August of that year, and the Empress was vanquished. Leaders of the Boxer Rebellion were slaughtered. The foreign masters banned the import of arms and ammunition for another five years. China was prostrate at the feet of the powerful invaders.

Defeated, the Manchu regime agreed to create a sector, for foreigners only, in the heart of Peking and to pay indemnities to thirteen foreign nations. The United States, eight years later, decided magnanimously to set aside its share of the indemnities for scholarships to assist Chinese studying in America.

But China never forgot. It was the power of superior weapons which had made the foreigner the master of the country once again. The British, the French, the Japanese, the Russians, the Germans and the Americans, all deemed barbarians, had shared in the spoils. China learned the bitter price of failing to modernize its forces against the outsiders.

The hatred persisted and grew after communism took over. "Old China hands" — the missionaries, journalists and the like, including many of the exploiters themselves — almost invariably profess love for China and its people and an unflagging faith in the notion that the foreigners are loved in return. It was not true in the past. It was even less true under communism.

More and more under the Communists, China has retreated into a shell of isolation and suspicion, as apart from the rest of the world, in many respects, as ever the old Middle Kingdom had been. Its leaders evidently are certain that the Chinese are targets of a nefarious plot of the Americans and the Russians to contain them and their ambitions. This attitude is shared by both sides in the great struggle for power and for the right to determine China's future path.

"We cannot overemphasize the huge morale boost and the importance of sheer prestige China feels from having the bomb," said a high-ranking Sinologist in the U.S. government, after China's H-bomb explosion. "After years of ignominy and having to accept battleships, booze and bibles forced on them by foreigners, after suffering heartaches and burning in their bellies from all that, the bomb is a tremendous symbol of emancipation from second class status." [5]

China still has not forgiven the battleships, booze and bibles, nor has China ever given up the idea that most of Asia by right belongs in her sphere of influence. A China in such a state of mind, and with a nuclear arsenal, will present a constant menace to her neighbors and, indeed, to Western civilization, in spite of all the trouble and turmoil going on inside the country.

Even should China one day turn away from communism, there would be little likelihood of turning back the clock as far as nuclear potential is concerned. China thrust her foot in the door and forced the door open. No regime would voluntarily discard her nuclear capability.

There is likely to be a long and intense contest between the Chinese and the Russians for allies, a cold war of their own not unlike the East-West cold war that persisted throughout the 1950s.

Prologue

The effects on United States policy — in fact on the whole future of the United States — of what China has done and will do in the nuclear arms race will be enormous. The world never will be the same. For good or evil, it will be transformed by the explosions which promoted China to the level of an atomic power.

I

THE CLOUD

I

THE CLOUD

1

Precisely at 3 P.M., Peking time, October 16, 1964, a great fireball seared the autumn sky over the Sinkiang region, casting an eerie purple glow across the bleak flats of the Takla Makan Desert. Prevailing winds wafted a poisonous mushroom cloud over Mongolia and eastward toward Japan.

Scientists at stations from the Orient to the Aleutians to Maryland watched, transfixed, as seismograph needles scratched erratically up and down. Other delicate instruments recorded electromagnetic impulses of distant nuclear thunder.

American U-2 spy planes prowled the skies high over the China mainland, their sensitive nose scoops sucking in radioactive debris which would reveal the mysteries behind the explosion. An American spy satellite streaked high over the barren northwest of Communist China. Its powerful eyes probed the area of Lop Nor, two hundred miles below, and the desolate sands of the Takla Makan Desert.

Thousands of miles away, a U.S. space engineer pushed a button which triggered an intricate maze of cameras aboard the circling satellite. Powerful lenses searched out the fiery secrets of Takla Makan and recorded on film the fateful story of that day.

Halfway across the globe from Lop Nor and worlds away from China, only a few lights burned in Washington. Most Americans were sound asleep when telephones jarred the predawn quiet of the Pentagon and the White House. The telephones carried the message. A fifth nation had just detonated an atomic bomb.

2

At Peking Airport, Liao Cheng-chih fidgeted nervously as he squinted into a brilliant autumn sky. The plane bearing an important guest would appear at any moment. Liao may have wished it would be involved in a convenient accident and never reach Peking.[1]

Liao's whole demeanor had changed abruptly. He was standing bareheaded in the open, under the balmy October sun, his baggy blue suit flopping in a brisk breeze. He had been enjoying an exchange of banter with Japanese correspondents, who, along with him, were awaiting the arrival of an extreme leftist from Tokyo, a man who long had been a pliant and useful echo of Red Chinese notions.

The correspondents noted the sudden change and wondered. Soon they would surmise the answer to this minor mystery. The change had come about when Liao's easy give-and-take chatter was interrupted by a diffident young Chinese official in a blue "national suit." He seemed a highly nervous young man.

The stranger gave Liao a signal. Liao left the cluster of correspondents and welcome-delegation members, put his arm reassuringly around the young man's shoulders and drew him off to a quiet corner for a brief, secret talk. When he rejoined the waiting group, Liao's equine face also wore an expression of tension.

Liao Cheng-chih was an important person. He was a secretary of the Communist party Central Committee, chairman of the Afro-Asian Solidarity Committee, president of the China-Asia Friendship Society and also of the China-Japan Friendship Society. In fact, except for a few clerks in offices which housed scores of friendship societies, Liao in himself was practically the entire China-Asia Society and the whole China-Japan Society at the same time. Such societies were merely lists of names, each much the same as any other; titles were juggled from time to time according to which leftist luminary from abroad had to be honored and impressed at any given moment.

But the job of impressing important visitors was serious business. Now, on October 16, 1964, Liao was awaiting the arrival of Tomomi Narita, secretary general of the Japanese Socialist party and a delegation of his Socialists from Tokyo. The Japanese Socialists were important to the Chinese Communist party. They had taken an extreme left and extreme anti-American line and had even described the "U.S. imperialists" as the common enemies of China and Japan.

The jet appeared in the distance, descending from the northeast above the Great Wall. Liao marched out to the strip with his retinue as the doors of the plane opened to disgorge the visiting Japanese Socialists. Liao stepped up briskly, shook hands with Narita and then, after a few murmured words of welcome, stepped back to permit his guest to dominate the stage with an arrival statement. Narita read it with all the stilted formality which seems so dear to the extreme leftist heart. He laid heavy stress on the line: "We oppose nuclear testing by any country."

Liao Cheng-chih nodded. A discussion of nuclear testing would be the main item on the agenda of the Socialists' meeting with the Chinese Communists.

Formally and politely, Liao replied to Narita's statement. Liao did not mention nuclear weapons. China's first atomic blast had already gone off, just three hours before the Japanese visitors arrived. The Japanese visitors could not have known that. But, thanks to the young Chinese official who had interrupted Liao's conversation with the correspondents, Liao had known it. He would have some explaining to do.[2]

3

It had been a hard day for the Japanese correspondents in Peking. Not only had they been duty-bound to see that Narita got safely to Peking, but they had been required to file reams of news dispatches on the Peking reaction, public and probable, to the fall of Khrushchev. Late that night, three of them relaxed in Room 460 on the fourth floor of the Hsin Chiao Hotel.[1]

The Hsin Chiao was one of Peking's better hotels. Designed originally for tourists, the six-story concrete hostelry was a permanent residence for correspondents and various diplomatic mission members, including a number of Russians still lingering there on assignments. The establishment boasted some creature comforts such as Western-style plumbing which sometimes worked.

The Hsin Chiao gloried in one elevator, red wall-to-wall carpeting in the corridors and adequate service, including if one wished it, room service. It had two dining rooms, one for Chinese food and one for Western. The Western food was not authentic though the menu offered a large variety of choices. Women worked as waitresses, but there were no chambermaids. All the cleaning, room service and other such chores were handled by bellhops, industrious and respectful young men ordinarily, who worked hard and said little.

Room 460, on the floor which other guests called Newspaper Row, was occupied by Churo Nishimura, the Peking correspondent of Tokyo's *Yomiuri*. All rooms assigned to journalists and diplomats contained a single bed, a desk, several simple armchairs and a small table. White lace curtains adorned the windows. A carpet with a purple flower design covered most of the floor.

With Nishimura that night were Tonio Matsuno, the Peking

Bureau Chief of *Asahi Shimbun,* and Eiichi Suga of *Sankei Shimbun.* Nishimura had been having a difficult time. It had been his turn that month to man the telephone for all nine Japanese newsmen and to go to the Foreign Ministry Press Department for announcements. The press office called correspondents any time, day or night. No announcements could be made by telephone. The Japanese had to travel to the ministry to pick up official handouts and, as Matsuno put it, "the Chinese government didn't give a damn whether it was midnight or not." The correspondents worked out a rotation system for their own protection.

The relaxation didn't last long. Suddenly, Nishimura's telephone shrilled. Matsuno, closest to it, picked up the receiver.

"*Wei?*" (Hello?)

A high-pitched voice said matter of factly: "This is the Press Department. There is a very important announcement. Please come immediately to the Foreign Ministry."

The words "very important" got quick action. The three tumbled out the door and split up to alert others on the floor.

In an instant, the corridor was a jumble of correspondents. Some dashed for the elevator. Others raced down the stairs. None knew for certain what the announcement would be. All had their suspicions. There had been predictions from Washington. They had been debating the possibilities for weeks.

The newsmen dashed out of the hotel without hats or coats, in search of taxis. At that hour — just past 11 P.M. — the streets were dark and almost deserted. Only a scattering of East European cars were visible. Few pedestrians were out. No bicycles or horses were in sight.

A thin, silvery moon hung over the Chungwen Gate and the ancient castle walls hard by the hotel. Matsuno and Suga found the taxi lot empty. But they had a stroke of luck. Charles Taylor of the Toronto *Globe and Mail* had been entertaining guests at a restaurant after his busy day, keeping in touch with the Foreign Ministry by telephone. He arrived back at the Hsin Chiao just in time to receive the urgent call. He dashed out and hailed a Czechoslovak Skoda-4 taxi. On his way he spotted the two Japanese frantically hunting transportation. He ordered his driver to slow down, opened the door and yelled, "Get in here, quickly." The little car puttered along the asphalt road past Tongtang Park, now dark and eerily quiet. The driver – a man this time, though many Chinese cab drivers are women – remained stolidly silent for the whole six minutes of the trip to the Foreign Ministry.

The three correspondents scrambled out at the Ministry building and rushed up the stairs, ignoring the luxurious reception room with its thick carpeting and artistic pottery. Sometimes a correspondent would be ushered in and given fragrant Chinese tea and cigarettes manufactured for foreigners. There would be no such frills at this hour of the night. The writers went directly to the room where official statements were issued.

A low-ranking bureaucrat in the blue serge suit affected by virtually all Chinese government functionaries met the newsmen. By his hand was a stack of mimeographed statements, of the kind usually issued in English, Russian, French and Japanese, as well as in Chinese. This night there would be only English and Chinese.

The young bureaucrat had no more authority than to pass out the papers. Ordinarily the functionary would perform such a chore without a trace of change in facial expression. This time he was grinning broadly, as if finding it difficult to suppress excitement. He watched the correspondents' faces as they scanned the handouts. The key words jumped out at the newsmen: ". . . exploded an atom bomb."

In seconds the correspondents were out the door and down the stairs with the biggest Chinese story of the decade. They hurtled back into their taxis, dashing to the Hsin Chiao to write their accounts.

The news already was reaching the people of Peking. A *bao wei*, the Chinese version of an extra, was on the streets, a one-page broadsheet edition of *People's Daily*, printed only on one side of the paper. It was being distributed – free of charge – from trucks roaming from street to street. The extra carried the biggest banner headlines the correspondents had seen in China: red characters three inches high proclaimed that China had exploded an atomic bomb.

People's Daily carried the same formal announcement given to the correspondents. It began: "China exploded an atom bomb at 1500 hours on October 16, 1964, and thereby conducted successfully its first nuclear test.

"This is a major achievement of the Chinese people in their struggle to increase their national defense capability and oppose the U.S. imperialistic policy of nuclear blackmail and nuclear threats.

"To defend one's self is the inalienable right of every sovereign state, and to safeguard world peace is the common task of all peace-loving countries.

"China cannot remain idle and do nothing in the face of the ever-increasing nuclear threat posed by the United States. China is forced to conduct nuclear tests and develop nuclear weapons." [2]

That phrase was designed to ease the fears of such people as the Japanese Socialists. Peking then tried to demonstrate that China in truth was peace-loving.

"The Chinese Government hereby formally proposes to the governments of the world that a summit conference of all the countries of the world be convened to discuss the question of the complete prohibition and thorough destruction of nuclear weapons, and that as a first step, the summit conference should reach an agreement to the effect that the nuclear powers and those countries which will soon become nuclear powers undertake not to use nuclear weapons, neither to use them against non-nuclear countries and nuclear-free zones nor against each other."

The statement then quoted the Mao Tse-tung cliché about the A-bomb being a paper tiger.[3]

"We believe in the people. It is the people who decide the outcome of a war and not any weapons. The destiny of China is decided by the Chinese people and the destiny of the world by the peoples of the world and not by the nuclear weapons."

China, of course, had more people than any other country in the world.

The Ministry statement ran on for 1,200 words. It expressed an ardent desire for prohibition of nuclear weapons and claimed if this had been done, "China need not have developed the nuclear weapon."

"But this position of ours has met the stubborn resistance of the U.S. imperialists. The Chinese Government pointed out long ago that the treaty on partial halting of nuclear tests signed by the United States, Britain and the Soviet Union in Moscow in July, 1963, was a big fraud to fool the people of the world."

Many of Peking's hopes for its atomic achievement were political, and the statement betrayed this.

"The mastery of the nuclear weapon by China is a great encouragement to the revolutionary peoples of the world in their struggles and a great contribution to the cause of defending peace.

"The Chinese Government hereby solemnly declares that China never at any time or under any circumstances will be the first to use nuclear weapons."

Thus, Peking could justify calling the bomb — as its propaganda would do before long — the "peace bomb" as well as the "people's bomb" and the "freedom bomb." [4]

At the hotel, the correspondents found the normally unsmiling help — bellhops and waitresses — chattering happily about the bomb. They typed their stories and dashed out again, into the same taxi for the run to the telegraph office. There is no night telephone communication between Peking and Tokyo.

The fifteen-minute trip to East Changan Boulevard showed the newsmen how swiftly the word had spread. Near Tien An Men, the Gate of Heavenly Peace, there was no more midnight quiet. People were milling about everywhere while men on trucks distributed the extras of *People's Daily*. Most took the news without undue excitement.

But that was not the case with the visiting Japanese Socialists.

Unable to believe this timing, a reporter who had accompanied the Socialists from Tokyo ran all the way from the Peking Hotel to the Hsin Chiao to seek explanation of the mystery from his colleagues.

It seemed incredible to the Japanese Socialists that Communist China would choose for its first atomic test the very day their delegation was arriving to talk about its abhorrence of all atomic testing. No one could believe for a moment that the arrival of the Japanese Socialists had even a vague connection with the timing of the test.

But there was a great deal of speculation among foreigners in Peking about the question of timing. They had, in fact, expected the first Chinese test two weeks before, on October 1, Communist China's national day. Washington had publicly predicted that date as a likely time, and possibly for that reason, or for others, the blast was delayed.

Just a day in advance of the Chinese test, Nikita Sergeyevitch Khrushchev had been forced out in the Soviet Union as premier and party chief. The event, indeed, appeared to the Japanese correspondents to have contributed much to Liao Cheng-chih's happy frame of mind at the airport before he had been brought the message about the test.

What better time for Communist China to jar the nerves of the hated Soviet revisionists, to say nothing of the nerves of the rest of the world? This could have been crediting the Chinese with a readiness capability they might not have possessed at the time. Was the timing just another coincidence? Perhaps.

The banquet the next night of the China-Japan Friendship Society was a joyless affair. The Japanese who were there noted that there was no lively chatter of voices in animated conversation. Scarcely any of the guests had anything to say, and the Chinese glumly paid attention to their food.

Liao Cheng-chih, in his capacity as president of the society, was host to the visiting Japanese Socialist delegation, and he sat with

Tomomi Narita, the star guest, at his right, exchanging only a few occasional polite words now and again, but obviously knowing he was getting nowhere in his efforts to warm up the occasion.

The visiting Japanese were not feeling cordial. Their faces displayed their bruised feelings as Liao Cheng-chih arose to make his formal address. It was an exercise in futility. He tried to make the best of a bad situation. He referred to the test of the day before as "a great achievement of the Chinese people" and a victory for "Mao Tse-tung's thinking." He could see his guests staring down at their wine glasses, as if the idea of listening in itself was a bit too much. Liao finished lamely and sat down.

Stony-faced, Narita arose to reply. He fixed his gaze upon the uncomfortable Liao Cheng-chih and intoned:

"Our anti-bomb movement is making great efforts to oppose nuclear tests by any country and is supported in its earnest desire for peace by the Japanese people, the only nation to suffer an atomic bombing.

"Today, before the banquet, we expressed our opposition to the test, and at the risk of being impolite we repeat our opposition now."

Liao was obviously shaken. He tried to shrug it off. Once again, he was on his feet.

"Mr. Narita spoke out to reflect the wishes of the Japanese people," he said. "But please note that China made the test to meet the wishes of six hundred and fifty million Chinese people. I propose that our Japanese Socialist friends study the Chinese statement on the test. We must find a point we can share in common.

"This, I believe, is the fight against American imperialism. We both attack it squarely. You Japanese Socialists can attack them on the flank while we build our nuclear weapons to oppose them directly. By playing our respective roles, we can conform with each other and strengthen the fight for peace." [5]

But the breach had been accomplished. In the past the Japanese Socialists were one with the Chinese in statements condemning nuclear weapons, and thus in describing the Americans as common enemies. But to support China after a nuclear test could be political suicide in the only nation which knew firsthand what atomic bombing meant.

4

A withered old patient in Hiroshima's Atomic Bomb Hospital shook his head in despair.

"Not again . . . not again . . ."

The news of China's atomic blast reached the hospital at a bad psychological moment. The patients had all but forgotten their troubles that night of October 16. They had been deeply absorbed in a long television program about the Tokyo Olympic Games. The program had lasted until almost midnight, and the news came as the program ended.

The old man, who had been in the hospital for the whole nineteen years since the atomic bomb was first used in anger, hung his head and sighed.

"Every one of us prayed so hard . . . don't test it . . . don't test it!"

5

In Nagasaki, the second city to suffer an A-bomb attack, there is another Atomic Bomb Hospital which has an Association of

Atomic-Bomb Patients. There were about a hundred and sixty of them at the time China tested her first device.

"They learned the news in the morning," said Kakuyoshi Okida, the association's president. "The hospital rooms were heavy with grief. Everyone must have been recalling that tragic day nineteen years ago . . ."

The association's Council of Patients convened that morning and sent out two protests, one to Peking, and one to the Japanese Government, although there was little the Japanese Government could have done.

6

Ten years before China's first atomic blast, there had lived in the town of Yaizu in Japan a fisherman named Kuboyama. He had been one of the crew of twenty-three on a fishing boat called the *Lucky Dragon*. The *Lucky Dragon* had been unlucky enough to be in the closed fallout area when the United States conducted its Bikini Atoll test in March, 1954. The *Lucky Dragon* was subjected to a rain of fine ash for several hours. All twenty-three crew members were hospitalized with burns. Kuboyama died of his. Amid a storm of shocked protest, the United States paid an indemnity of two million dollars.

Now the man who had been chief of that crew, Yoshio Misaki, wrung his hands.

"To think," he wailed, "that in a place so near us they have developed that devil's weapon."

And Mrs. Aikichi Kuboyama, widow of the dead crew member, heard the news with a display of anguish.

"This test has turned the world's desperate cry for a test ban into something as meaningless as bubbles of water," she lamented. "I regret to report this sad news to the grave of my late husband."

As she spoke, Widow Kuboyama looked truly exhausted.

7

American leaders quickly reassured the U.S. public. China's bomb had been a "primitive" device. After all, it was just one explosion and there had been in the world up to that time 485 others — 330 by the United States, 126 by the Soviet Union, 24 by Britain and five by France. Secretary of Defense Robert S. McNamara judged that the Chinese device was not yet a weapon as such, but a crude affair which had to be scaled down and refined.[1]

Americans were told it might be a long time before China became an efficient nuclear power. After all, where was the delivery system? Could China really marry a nuclear warhead to a missile in the near future? She could not have much potential. She might use up her atomic fuel in one or two blasts and that would be that. There would be no real stockpile to worry about for a long, long time.[2]

Three weeks in advance of China's debut, Secretary of State Dean Rusk had issued a statement predicting the Chinese explosion. This had helped prepare Americans for the news and keep nerves calm. Rusk had assured the U.S. public that "the detonation of a first device does not mean a stockpile of nuclear weapons and the presence of modern delivery systems."[3]

The tendency in the United States at that moment — after years and many varieties of predictions about it — was to downgrade the Chinese potential. Typical of many reactions had been that of one respected scientific journal which said it was estimated that Red China would "not have an effective delivery system such as missiles to threaten anyone until the mid-1970s . . . so long as China is unable to take the bomb beyond her own backyard, most observers feel, there is no immediate cause for alarm."

Said President Lyndon B. Johnson: "Its military significance should not be overestimated. Many years and great efforts separate testing of a first nuclear device from having a stockpile of reliable weapons with effective delivery systems." [4]

Americans had become accustomed to the notion that China, after all, was backward. They couldn't have known at that time that China was well on her way to marrying the nuclear weapon to a missile within two short years. And they did not know at that moment how sophisticated and advanced that first China bomb had been. The jolt was yet to come.

But some in America were quick to voice concern.

"The sands of time may bury us if we do an ostrich act on the significance of Red China's nuclear debut," commented Dr. Ralph Lapp,[5] who had been an important figure in America's Manhattan Project which developed the first A-bomb. His warning would take on added meaning before long.

Past comments by Russians had indicated that Soviet officials were not deluding themselves about China's potential. The Russians, who had given the Chinese significant help until they suddenly found their difficult allies progressing too fast, expected the worst. A glum one-line report relayed the news of the first Chinese blast to the Soviet public, which at that moment was preoccupied with the backlash of the anti-Khrushchev plot.

Americans hardly could be expected to remember that the United States itself had contributed a great deal to the program which would make the Chinese achievements possible so swiftly. The sardonic truth was that the two nations most appalled by China's rapid nuclear progress were the two which had given the

Chinese the most help, each at a time when it had considered the Chinese reliable and grateful allies. The Russian help probably sprang from a naïve belief that China could not afford to act as anything else but a Communist friend. Russian help might place a lien on China's allegiance. Much of the American help was the result of what many in responsible places regarded as sheer stupidity.

In the mid-1960s, Americans had all but forgotten the era of hysteria which began early in 1950, grew into a wave of fear and suspicion with the outbreak of the Korean War and lifted Senator Joseph McCarthy to international fame as a man who could find subversives under every American bed. The atmosphere in America at the depth of the cold war was largely responsible for persuading the United States to chase back to Red China a number of key men. Their knowledge put an atom bomb on the snout of a Chinese rocket, brought forth a hydrogen bomb and pointed China's military on the road to IRBMs and ICBMs (intermediate range and intercontinental ballistic missiles).

In China, the scientists remembered clearly — men like Tsien Hsue-shen, the missile specialist, and Chao Chung-yao, the atomic physicist. They had reasons to hate the United States after once having loved it. Perhaps now they would savor the bittersweet taste of revenge. Perhaps now they could say to one another, let the *kwei lo* — the white devil — sweat it out, both in Russia and the United States.

For Chao and Tsien and other Chinese scientists, 3 P.M., October 16, 1964, was a time for remembering both Russians and Americans. They and their colleagues could remember the Russians and their superior attitudes and how they tried to interfere when the Chinese scientists were progressing too swiftly. They could remember the Americans with their hysteria and witchhunts. Chao could hark back to his escape from the clutches of the U.S. law and his flight to his native China with a wealth of experience and secrets stored up in his head from his association with nuclear experiments in the United States. Tsien could remember how he had spent five years in a lonely limbo, condemned and rejected by the Americans to whom he had contributed so much. Largely, perhaps, it had been because he was careless in the selection of his friends.

Chao and Tsien could reflect with grim satisfaction that it was their return to China, along with scores of other talented Chinese, which had been in large measure responsible for the speed and sophistication of the Chinese nuclear program and for the ultimate wedding of warhead to missile. Now let the witch-hunters in the United States ponder the fruits of their super-patriotic zeal and passion for total security.

A few in the United States would, indeed, remember those days: days of fear and suspicion, days when the mere attachment of a label — pinko, red, left-winger, crypto-Communist — was enough to incite opportunist politicians, eager for the scalps of foreigners. Some in the United States would remember wryly what, in that time of confusion and exorcism of ghosts, a member of the federal government had said of Tsien: "I'd rather shoot him than let him leave this country. He knows too much."

But go Tsien did. So did Chao. So did other talented sons of China, who, between 1930 and 1950, made their marks on some of America's most prestigious campuses. They took with them huge stores of bitterness and rich funds of information.

For Chao Chung-yao, the physicist who once was an official observer at the American bomb test at Bikini, and some of his Chinese colleagues, the saga of their stay in the United States ended with their escape from U.S. authorities desperate to stop them. Some other Chinese students and scientists just vanished unnoticed from the American stage.

H. S. Tsien — as he called himself in the United States — intended to become an American citizen and pursue his research on behalf of his foster-fatherland. An FBI knock on his door shattered that dream.

But the story of the gentle genius of rocketry from Shanghai began long before Tsien Hsue-shen even dreamed of going to the

United States. It started at the outset of a violent era in American history. It was colored by the Great Depression, by the vast bloodletting of World War II and by the global political war which followed it.

Tsien Hsue-shen was a boy of ten in China, being prepared by his proud, scholarly father for an academic career, when, half a world away in St. Louis, Missouri, a husky young veteran of World War I was casting about for a vocation commensurate with his special talents. Perhaps if the man from St. Louis had not been so captivated by dreams of California, things would have turned out much differently. But William F. Hynes made a decision. He would go west. And fifteen years later, the young man from China also made a decision. He, too, would go to California.

The mills of the gods were grinding. Tiny bits and pieces of history's jigsaw were falling slowly into place.

II

DESTROY THE FOREIGNER

8

It was time, the foggy and patrician Warren Gamaliel Harding had counseled, for America to get "back to normalcy." But if the America of a few years before were to be considered the norm, then "back to normalcy" was an impossible goal. If normalcy meant a return to America's age of innocence, the Republican standard bearer of the 1920 Presidential campaign was asking Americans to believe in a dream world.

World War I, that War to Make the World Safe for Democracy, had destroyed old ways forever. From rubbled and bleeding Europe came new ferment, new political ideas. In enormous, backward and prostrate Russia, a system its leaders chose to call communism had taken hold. Americans worried about strange and terrifying creatures called the Bolsheviki. Cartoonists pictured the Bolsheviks as wild-eyed fanatics with bushy hair and thick black beards, brandishing bombs and threatening the American way of life.

Under President Harding and Prohibition, Americans reeled drunkenly into the Roaring Twenties, unable to grasp the idea that world leadership suddenly had been thrust upon them. Old shibboleths died hard. God was in His Heaven and all was right with the world, so far as middle- and upper-class Americans were concerned. They seldom bothered to contemplate their own backyards. To suggest that anything might be wrong with America was un-American and unpatriotic.

Bill Hynes was patriotic. He had been only seventeen years old when he enlisted in the United States Army in St. Louis. By the time the war came he had a lieutenant's commission. By the time the war was over, he was minus his right thumb, lost not in battle but in an army motorcycle accident. Mustered out in 1919, Hynes was restless. Out west was the golden promise of California.

The young six-footer headed there and eventually found his niche and his vocation in the Los Angeles Police Department. His army background served him well. His air of an officer's authority, his self-assured manner and the zeal he displayed pushed him up quickly.

Like so many others of his time, Hynes was fascinated by the Bolshevik ogre. He saw the Communists as potential troublemakers and a threat to the American way. He detested the very word "Communist." His superiors, noting all this and the ardor he showed as an officer, tapped him to turn in his pistol and his badge and to immerse himself in the netherworld of the Communists.

For many in those days of intellectual myopia in America, communism was anything to the left of Calvin Coolidge. The terms Socialist and Communist were synonymous; a man who called himself a worker probably was a Red, and the whole trade union movement was suspect. To Bill Hynes and his superiors, the rowdy, radical International Workers of the World — an already moribund left-wing labor movement — was no different from the bomb-wielding Bolsheviks of the editorial cartoons. Bill Hynes made a special target of the "Wobblies."

Hynes bluffed his way into the strike committee of the Wobblies and became its secretary. He infiltrated so deeply that he became editor of the *IWW Strike Bulletin*. He bided his time, and the moment for action came when the Wobblies called for a nationwide strike in 1923. It was a quixotic thing at best for the IWW to attempt, with its miniscule organization, but to the authorities of southern California, the Wobblies represented the threat of foreign ideas.

Bill Hynes played his part deftly. The strike in southern California was smothered. Casting off his masquerade, Hynes — to whom all Wobblies were Communists — testified against the ring-leaders. His contribution to the final destruction of the IWW in southern California was considerable. It brought torrents of threats and abuse from the left.

Unimpressed by the threats, Hynes carried on as before, single-mindedly, with his personal vendetta against the Communists. In the police department, his colleagues nicknamed him Red. It had nothing to do with his hair, which was sandy, darkening and thinning to a widow's peak. It was instead a tribute to his one-man war against the Communists, waged from the battlements of his Los Angeles Police Department "Red Squad."

Hynes, solidly built and commanding in appearance, with his strong, prominent nose and piercing gray eyes, won both popularity and respect among his fellow police officers. He rose to the rank of captain, and some of the younger men looked on him as a model of what a good, tough police officer should be — a bear for work and a man who did not know the meaning of fear. He was one of the department's most proficient poker players, but had few other diversions. He was what his superiors called a dedicated officer. Because of that, they liked to show him to the recruits, and he often addressed the police academy.

It was during a talk at the academy in 1924 that Red Hynes first met William Ward Kimple. That was, in its way, a historic meeting. Kimple had wanted to be a traffic cop. But Hynes was searching for promising material. Kimple's second choice had been work with the intelligence unit, and something about the lanky, alert-looking young man attracted Hynes.

Hynes called Bill Kimple into the Red Squad office. How would Kimple like police intelligence work? It would mean giving up his badge and gun and sinking himself in the ranks of suspect organizations. He would start by infiltrating what was left of the Wobblies after their 1923 disaster. If Hynes had any doubts about the assignment, the lean, asthmatic Kimple soon resolved them and became Captain Hynes's good right hand, undercover.

It was not easy to win the confidence of suspicious left-wingers of the day. He immersed himself in the personality of a threadbare, free-lance automobile mechanic, angry at his lot and at all capitalist oppression.

It would have been a dreary, unrewarding life but for Hynes and the zeal he inspired. Kimple greatly admired Hynes as a police officer. And then, there was always Clara. She was a help and an inspiration. Clara, the widow of a police commissioner, had been a secretary in the police department when Kimple first met her. They were attracted to one another and she was more than willing to help him. He found her both clever and daring, and she had more success than he in earning the trust of the left-wingers.

Bill Kimple and Clara were in love, but the Police Department refused to let them get married. They were too valuable as they were. Hynes frowned on the idea of marriage because, in his view, the Communists of the day would not approve of it. Before Russia's Communists reverted to Victorian morals under Stalin, the Communists of the Bolshevik days had made much of the notion of free love, and had ridiculed the rite of marriage as a bourgeois superstition.

Since Bill Kimple disliked writing reports, Clara took over for him. She proved expert. Hynes one day called Kimple into his office.

"Who in hell is writing those reports?" Hynes demanded. Kimple told him. "Well," snapped Hynes, "bring her in here."

Hynes was impressed by Clara — so impressed that he put her on his unit's payroll, not as a policewoman, but as an informant.

Kimple felt he was not making significant progress with the Communists because party members from New York were running the Red show in southern California.

"Most were New York Jews," he would say in later years, "and I couldn't get into the party. But then a Communist leader came out from New York and we drove her around."

The woman Communist leader from New York was instantly impressed by Clara, who had been posing as an ardent member of the IWW. To the Communists, the IWW was beneath contempt, just a bunch of fuzzy-minded petit-bourgeois reformists.

"Clara," the woman said to her, "you're not a Wobbly. You're a Communist."

This seal of approval from eastern headquarters was enough for the party branch in Los Angeles. The Hollywood unit took Clara in as a full member, with the party name of Clara Osvald. That was in 1927, when America was singing happily to the accompaniment of a rampaging bull market on Wall Street. Clara's friendship with Bill Kimple, alias Bill Ward, enabled him a year later to become a full member. They told Kimple that since he was attending all the meetings with Clara and listening in on everything, he might just as well leave the ranks of mere "sympathizers."

A short time thereafter came Black Friday, the day the bottom fell out of the bull market. The wonderful nonsense of the Roaring Twenties was at an end. Panic gripped the nation. Banks and businesses failed in appalling numbers. Farms went under. The plight of America, still largely unaware of its growing position in world leadership, sent a wave of shock around the globe. The Great Depression was about to begin.

From then on, Captain William F. Hynes and his Red Squad would have their hands full. A crisis of unemployment and breadlines plagued the nation. The Communists of the Los Angeles area, like those in the rest of the country, were out to win over those out of work. Kimple reported regularly to his superior officer on their tactics. Kimple recalled later:

"If the lights were turned off somewhere, the party would turn them on again. If they turned off the water, the party would turn it on again. They were all for the rights of the working man."

Red Hynes savored doing battle with the Communists. In fact, Hynes's outfit was a good deal more than an anti-Communist unit. By the reckoning of many who came in contact with it, the Red Squad also engaged in preventing strikes and battling organized labor.

For Hynes, the Communists always were the main targets. His men would infiltrate a meeting which Communists were suspected of running. One of the undercover agents would pick a fight and start an uproar. This would be the excuse for the Red Squad to charge in with billy clubs swinging. Some heads would be cracked. Some would be carted off to hospitals, others to jail.

Whenever the Communists met outdoors in Los Angeles in those desperate depression years, the Red Squad would move in, flailing right and left. Scores would be arrested each time.

The Communist candidate for the presidency of the United States in 1932, William Z. Foster, had a taste of the Hynes technique. The Red Squad not only interrupted a Foster speech in the downtown Plaza, but battered members of the audience, seized the presidential candidate, carted him off to custody and then invited him in no uncertain terms to get out of Los Angeles. He did.

To Bill Kimple (Ward), this use of force was no more than the simple duty of the police. "When radicals defied the law, they had to be met with the force to make them obey the laws, Communists included," he would say in later years, looking back on it all.

"If they had let him have his way, Hynes would have killed the Communist party in California. Red would walk into their meeting places, break up rallies, seize their records, arrest them on any grounds he could find — even for spitting on sidewalks. When Red Hynes burst into a meeting, all the Communists turned pale. Even the Negroes turned white."

Hynes had a reputation for roughness which possibly was out of proportion to what he deserved. The Communists even then were adept at labeling even ordinary police work as "police brutality," and at rallying enough unsuspecting sympathy from respectable sources to cause trouble for the police. Indeed, there had been one Congressional investigation of charges of "police brutality" in Los Angeles.

Hynes got the blame, but he had defenders who claimed he did not deserve his reputation for ruthlessness. These friends agreed he often failed to fit into the legend built around him. He was, they insisted, more inclined to be meek than to be tough, and even to be averse to all-out violence.

For some it was difficult to picture this man in the role of hard guy. With his colleagues, Hynes was an amiable, good-natured man with a quick sense of humor. He talked rapidly and gave the impression of knowing what he was talking about. He appeared to have few of the ordinary vices such as heavy drinking or gambling. His poker-playing, expert though it was, had been for low stakes. He had quirks which hardly fitted in with his reputation for inspiring terror. He had a passion for chocolate-covered, marshmallow-filled cookies, washed down with quarts of coffee. He also had a habit — it was a fetish with him — of stuffing his wallet only with absolutely new, bank-fresh bills. To his neighbors, Hynes was a God-fearing, everyday middle-class public servant who lived well but not showily in a desirable residential area. If he had personal problems, he kept them to himself.

Whatever the case, the life chosen by Hynes and Kimple was a lonely one. For twenty years they would play their small but significant part in fashioning one segment of a complex net. It was woven bit by bit, sometimes by accident, sometimes by design. Eventually the net would be cast into a murky American sea of suspicion and hysteria to catch whatever victims might blunder into it.

9

A revolutionary spirit was abroad in the land in the dark days between 1929 and 1933. Millions were hungry, running out of hope. The breadlines lengthened, and the number of men selling apples on city streets increased. The ranks of those the newspapers called the jobless swelled from day to day, and across the country there was an angry, ominous muttering with overtones of rebellion. Franklin Delano Roosevelt's New Deal muted the sound of revolution, but the darkest of the depression years already had left their mark. Among intellectuals, radical ideas were a mark of distinction. On campuses of the nation, every idea that came from the left was dissected and examined. Any educated American over the age of eighteen and under thirty was likely to consider himself a budding revolutionist whose ideas could save the country and the world. Few hesitated about discussing communism or any other ism that came along.

It was a fashion in those days among young liberals to denounce the police. Often they would look on at one of the raids and shout "Cossack!" at the policemen. The police, in turn, had little love for the liberals.

There was one celebrated incident of a journalist known for his liberal views if not for his sobriety. The police had been watching for him to slip up, and finally he did. Not entirely sober, he was involved in an accident. The police demanded he walk a chalk line, which he managed, unsteadily but defiantly. "Repeat this sentence," he was told. "She sells seashells on the seashore."

The journalist looked his official tormentor in the eye, and with perfect diction replied: "She sells seashells on the seashore and you sons of bitches get your cut."

That was the academic atmosphere when Tsien Hsue-shen arrived in the United States. Tsien was all scholar, and already at twenty-five, a scientist. He knew about things political only from hearsay and discussion, but he had a detached view of the world and looked at its troubles with a scientist's cold logic. To the dismay of many a scientist, however, scientific logic never mixed well with world politics. And H. S. Tsien walked unsuspectingly into a hidden trap.

10

Even when Tsien was a small boy in his native Shanghai, his proud and scholarly father, Tsien Chia-chih, was certain the lad was marked for greatness. The elder Tsien and his wife, Chang Lang-dran, struggled and sacrificed to get their boy into a high school for especially talented youngsters in Peking, the capital which Tsien grew to love and frequently called "the grandeur of Old China." Young Tsien attended Chiaotung University, and won a Boxer Rebellion fund scholarship (see Prologue). Under a student visa he arrived for the first time in the United States and a new world in September, 1935, prepared for two years of study with the option of an extension for an additional year. Massachusetts Institute of Technology in Cambridge was the school of his choice.

Throughout his first year in the United States, it is doubtful that H. S. Tsien paid much attention to any kind of politics. He was far too busy concentrating all his energies on taking a Master of Science degree in aeronautical engineering. Tsien had only one diversion in those days, and it was a passion with him. He loved classical music. The slight, five-foot-seven figure of the young Chinese became a familiar sight at the concerts of the Boston Symphony Orchestra under Serge Koussevitzky in that 1935–1936 season. It presented twenty-four weekly concerts and young Tsien missed not one of them.

"It was my only form of entertainment," Tsien would recall later.

It was a lonely life, but Tsien did not see it that way. He was utterly absorbed and fascinated by the challenging new field of aerodynamics. After a year at M.I.T. he was awarded his Master's degree and now decided to travel west to see a man he had not yet met, but whom he had idolized from a distance. Once in California, Tsien wasted no time in looking up his hero, and once under the spell of Dr. Theodore von Kármán, he had little hesitation in deciding to stay on at the California Institute of Technology in Pasadena. That decision meant that eventually the paths of H. S. Tsien, the young scholar from Shanghai, and William F. Hynes, the avid Communist-hunter from St. Louis, would cross.

To the nonscientific world, the name von Kármán meant little. Until he died at eighty-one in 1963, von Kármán was to those outside the scientific community an obscure Hungarian Jew who taught at Caltech. To the scientific world, however, von Kármán was a shining beacon. His genius, more than that of almost any other, had probed the mysteries of wind and space and left a heritage of conquest which would permit men to hurl missiles across undreamed-of barriers.

Von Kármán's aeronautics department at Caltech attracted scientists from all parts of the world. As many foreigners were studying in it at any given time as Americans. Only those with the rigid discipline of which people like Germans, Japanese and Chinese are capable would qualify to study under him, and he naturally attracted men of distinction. Tsien had the qualifications and von Kármán took to the young Chinese immediately. In his memoirs, von Kármán wrote:

> One day in 1936, he came to see me for advice on further graduate studies. This was our first meeting. I looked up to observe a slight short young man, with a serious look, who answered my questions with unusual precision. I was immediately impressed with the keenness and quickness of his mind, and I suggested that he enroll at Caltech for advanced study.
>
> Tsien agreed. He worked with me on many mathematical problems. I found him to be quite imaginative, with a mathematical aptitude which he combined successfully with a

great ability to visualize accurately the physical picture of natural phenomena. Even as a young student he helped clear up some of my own ideas on several difficult topics. These are gifts which I had not often encountered, and Tsien and I became close colleagues.

He was quickly noticed by other professors on the campus. I remember that Professor Paul S. Epstein of the Physics Department, a great theoretician, once said to me: "Your student H. S. Tsien is in one of my classes."

"*Ja*, he is good," I replied.

"Tell me," Epstein said with a twinkle in his eye, "do you think he has Jewish blood?" [1]

Once again, for Tsien it was a lonely life except for his science. Again his only diversion was music. He almost never missed the performances of the Los Angeles Symphony under Otto Klemperer at the Philharmonic Auditorium, to which he would drive from Pasadena in a second-hand jalopy he had acquired.

He had virtually no social life in those early days at Caltech, apart from frequent visits to the home of von Kármán, but it didn't matter to him at all. Pasadena was unfriendly to Chinese, probably even more so than it was to Negroes who dared try to make their homes within its palmy confines, but Tsien was the sort of man who would hardly notice. His whole life was wrapped up in working with von Kármán, and he told acquaintances on the campus that he intended to devote his years to continuing along the path his idol had blazed.

The flow of Chinese students into the United States was fairly small at that time, and there were only a handful at Caltech. Tsien knew few, if any, of them intimately. He was only vaguely aware, for example, of the presence of another extraordinarily brilliant Chinese who had made his mark in physics at Caltech in the ten years before Tsien had arrived there. The man was Chao Chung-yao, who had gained a solid reputation on the campus for his work on basic fundamentals of atomic research. It had taken him only four years from his arrival in 1926 at the age of twenty-four to win his Ph.D. *magna cum laude*.

Like Tsien, Chao was deadly serious about his work. He was not much for the social life, though he managed to mix better with Americans of nonscientific turn of mind than did Tsien. Like his compatriot, Chao neither drank nor smoked, and like Tsien, his only diversion, apart from a bit of tennis with campus acquaintances, was classical music. Like Tsien, Chao also could feel lonely in a state which could be hostile to Orientals. Tsien and Chao would play leading roles in the unfolding drama of history in the making.

11

The arrival at Caltech from Texas of an irrepressible young graduate student meant that before long Pasadena would echo to explosion after explosion. The good burghers were more mystified than frightened. Many a citizen of Pasadena was sure madmen were at work, lunatics who inevitably would blow themselves to bits.

It had taken Frank J. Malina a bit of time to get started. He had arrived from Texas A & M in 1934, eager to write a Ph.D. thesis on rocket flight, a subject in which he believed passionately at a time when others derided the whole idea. Young and full of enthusiasm for his vision, he finally approached the great von Kármán and laid before him a plan to experiment with rocket flight, on the theory that it would be the key to future travel in space.[1] Other educators were amused and even shocked at the notion, but von Kármán was impressed by Malina's earnestness.

Malina's partners in this far-out enterprise were two other young men who were not Caltech students but extraordinary technicians in their own fields. One was Edward S. Forman, who had long been tinkering with rocket engine ideas. The other was an incredibly talented self-taught chemist, John W. Parsons, who was doomed to a mysterious and explosive end. They were joined by another budding rocketeer named A. M. O. Smith, whom they called Amo for short.

The tiny band set to work with little more to support them than their own firm belief in their mission. They had no money to buy materials. They were forced to comb the junkyards of the Pasadena area for bits and pieces of metal, tubing and other items necessary to their experiments. But they did persuade Dr. von Kármán to grant them the use of Caltech's aeronautics laboratory and to stand by and advise them from time to time.

It was inevitable that young Tsien should come in contact with Frank Malina, given their common interest in rockets and aerodynamics. Malina was a fellow student of Tsien's in the Department of Aeronautics, and Tsien soon became friendly with him, pleased by Malina's love of classical music. The two attended many symphony concerts together.

One day in class, Tsien approached Malina and showed him a copy of an article Malina had written in a magazine on the subject of rocketry. Tsien's curiosity was piqued. They began an animated discussion of Malina's ideas. Malina outlined for the young Chinese his dreams of rockets which could soar miles into space and Tsien listened avidly.

"If you're interested in rockets, why don't you join our little group?" Malina asked Tsien.

Tsien needed no urging. He leaped at the idea.

For some time, the rocketeers worked in their own backyards and scarred the areas around their homes with the marks of rocket experiments gone awry. Malina himself dubbed the group "the Suicide Squad." [2] With von Kármán's permission, the group moved into the aeronautics laboratory after school hours, but one experiment with a propellant misfired. The entire laboratory was engulfed in acrid fumes. That caused considerable grumbling among students and faculty, so the crew moved to a concrete platform outside the lab.

One day, two enormous explosions shook the laboratory. Shrapnel from the second explosion smashed into a wall and gouged a gaping hole. It was just above the chair in which Malina would ordinarily have been sitting, as chief of the experimenters, had he not been off on a random errand. If he had been at his accustomed post, the young rocket enthusiast surely would have been killed.

That did it. Caltech admonished the group to perform its dangerous experiments away from the campus. Students derided Malina's Suicide Squad. But Malina, Tsien, Parsons, Forman and Smith cheerfully accepted their exile to the rocky ravines shadowed by the Sierra Madre. They also accepted yet another member, and he brought with him the gift of some financial support. Weld Arnold, a student whom the rocketeers dubbed Wild Arnold, shared their belief in rocketry and offered to donate a thousand dollars. He wanted to serve as photographer for the program. He delivered five hundred dollars, but soon thereafter was called away from Caltech. He had made his mark however. His was virtually the only monetary support the hardy group ever received.

Before long, the Suicide Squad began to break into California newspapers. The noise they had made alone would have been enough to attract attention. But the idea of rockets was beginning to stir imaginations, particularly in view of disturbing news from Europe. Benito Mussolini's controlled Fascist press had been saying that Nazi Germany was experimenting with rockets which one day could be fired against Britain.

Newspapers in California early in 1938 carried stories about Malina and his experiments with motors using gaseous oxygen and ethylene, and of his predictions that a rocket would be developed in time which would soar a hundred miles above the earth into space. Eventually, the crew worked also with smokeless powder as a propellant, after a long series of experiments with liquids. The Suicide Squad borrowed from the ideas of Dr. Robert H. Goddard, who was working on liquid propellants near Roswell, New Mexico, his experiments financed by the Guggenheim Foundation. The Squad confidently predicted the development of a rocket which would be fired in stages until the third and final stage would coast almost free from air resistance.

After a long period of struggle without any money, there was good news. Frank Malina was tapped by Dr. von Kármán to accompany him to Washington. His group might be getting a bit of recognition.

Malina, Tsien, young Parsons with his utterly uninhibited imagination, and the others had been plugging away doggedly, certain that they were on the track of something important. General Henry H. (Hap) Arnold, Chief of the Army Air Corps, learning of their work, appeared at the Caltech laboratories to have a look. What he saw and heard about the Suicide Squad convinced him that the idea was worth pursuing further. By this time, some American planners were convinced war was imminent, that the nation should look for sizable scientific contributions to the military.

Malina and von Kármán took off for Washington to talk with Arnold about what a newly organized committee under the sponsorship of the National Academy of Sciences might do to help the Air Corps.

To Arnold, what had been going on at GALCIT — the Guggenheim Aeronautical Laboratory of the California Institute of Technology — under von Kármán's direction had been impressive. Von Kármán had never lost faith in the Suicide Squad and had continued to support and encourage their work, badly hampered by lack of funds.

Dr. Tsien and Dr. Malina had amassed a large amount of data from their theoretical studies of the thermodynamic characteristics of a rocket motor, while Parsons and Edward Forman, the rocket engine enthusiast, had worked on the idea of a smokeless powder propellant. From the start, they had hoped that the government might take notice and come through with some money.[3]

In Washington, the Academy's committee discussed with von Kármán and Malina some of the things General Arnold had in mind: such matters as improving visibility for pilots by de-icing processes, and the possibility of rocket-assisted takeoff for planes.

At the time, the prevalent attitude toward rocketry was cynicism. Dr. Jerome Hunsaker, head of the Guggenheim Aeronautics Department at M.I.T., cracked: "We'll take the problem of visibility and von Kármán can take the Buck Rogers job." [4] The very word "rocket" was in such bad repute that the Caltech group dropped it and substituted the word "jet."

Von Kármán had so impressed the committee that in January, 1939, the Academy accepted his offer to assign the rocket researchers at Caltech to studying jet-assisted takeoff, and a thousand dollars was earmarked by the Academy for the work.

Now GALCIT Project No. 1 could be launched. When it was, more funds became available. That summer, the Academy granted Caltech a ten-thousand-dollar contract for basic studies of jet propulsion problems. Caltech leased land on the west bank of the Arroyo Seco for the experiments.

But Malina, Tsien and company had wider horizons. Their dreams were far out in space. In time, they were sure, motors fathered by their ideas would power a rocket a thousand miles above the earth and hurtle a vehicle through space at eleven thousand miles an hour, and they enthusiastically explained it to their friends.

The space age was within the reach of the Suicide Squad. But America was too preoccupied with the gathering shadow of a nightmare to take any notice.

12

My name is Samuel Hall
And I hate you one and all
God damn your eyes!

The singing rose in a melancholy and somewhat discordant attempt at harmony. All across Los Angeles in those days when war clouds were gathering in Europe, there were gatherings like this.

The Communist party, though small in numbers, had units and branches throughout the country which had attracted people from all walks of life: doctors, lawyers, motion-picture writers, scientists, scholars and, of course, the run-of-the-mill malcontents. In many of the units, some of the participants had only a foggy idea of what the politics were all about. Some were engaged in a game of follow-the-leader, flattered at the notion that they had been accepted as intellectuals. Some, true intellectuals, cared little about the politics of the others so long as the conversation remained at a high level. Apparently, this was the case in what the Communist party chose to call Professional Unit 122, Pasadena Section. The unit included a number of lonely and highly talented nonconformists, some of whom cared little whether the evening was just a gathering or in fact a meeting. Each of them, for one reason or another, was embraced by his own private gloom. For some it looked as if the world — or at least a good part of it — was coming apart.

On such evenings, Dr. Sidney Weinbaum drew a sort of wry pleasure and even a feeling of relative security from the often morose though always literate conversation. He enjoyed the company of those who could share his forebodings and listen sympathetically to his dimly defined views of how the world might be saved from cataclysm.

Dr. Weinbaum was a brilliant research fellow in chemistry at Caltech, who was also noted for his work in applied physics. He was a specialist in the application of quantum mechanics to molecules, in the crystalline structure of electrons, and in the physics of solids and heat conductivity. For him, what was happening in Europe foretokened the worst for all the world. In 1938, Adolf Hitler already had taken over Austria, and Mussolini was pledging total support to the strutting Nazi Fuehrer. In Spain, an agonizing civil war had been turned into an international laboratory for a new World War. In China, Japan's Imperial Armies had ravaged Tsientsin and Nanking, seized Shanghai and Peking. In America, the effects of the Great Depression still oppressed a big segment of American life.

The gatherings were at least a solace, a comfort. Dr. Weinbaum would listen, brooding, to some of the readings from books brought along by one or another guest as "discussion material."

They discussed such phenomena of American capitalism as the career of William Randolph Hearst, millionaire founder of the newspaper empire. They talked about Karl Marx and socialism and communism. They listened to readings from leftist and ultra-leftist writers and nodded agreement.

They were all intellectuals at these meetings. They were all, in their own opinions, liberals. They were willing to listen to all ideas, discuss all ideas. Some listened and nodded because, probably, they felt it was expected of them, although they would have been shocked if anyone had called this conforming.

H. S. Tsien often was a member of one of these groups. He liked discussion; he wanted to provoke people into saying meaningful things, and he was eager to talk about China.

None who knew him well in those days ever doubted that he retained an abiding love for his homeland and a deep pride in his Chinese ancestry. Close friends and intelligent people with whom he came in contact never affronted him on that score. Perhaps if

Pasadena had been a different sort of town, perhaps if its citizens had been a little less race-conscious, the story of what happened to H. S. Tsien might have had a different ending.

Tsien and two of his scientist friends groped their way down the aisle of the darkened movie house, their faces reflecting the flickering light from the screen. With hushed "excuse-me-pleases," they edged into a row in the center of the house. Citizens of Pasadena to the right and left of them peered at the young Chinese with undisguised hostility.

Tsien saw a man near the aisle raise his arm and signal an usher. There was a whispered conversation. The usher looked in Tsien's direction and nodded. He understood. He edged into the row in back of Tsien and his friends and tapped the Chinese on the shoulder.

"I beg your pardon, sir," said the usher with exaggerated politeness. "Would you mind moving to another part of the house?"

"Why?" Tsien and his friends wanted to know. The usher explained. The people sitting next to them objected to having a Chinese nearby. Tsien and the two other scientists moved — right out of the theater. But Tsien never forgot the incident, nor could he ever forget Pasadena's attitude toward Chinese.

It was little wonder, then, that Tsien sought out the company of people who accepted him for what he was and did not judge him only by the color of his skin. There was a strong bond between the young Chinese and Dr. Weinbaum, as there was between Tsien and young Malina. Tsien was a proud man, and for those who avoided him because of his race, he had nothing but scorn.

It was during the early days of the Suicide Squad that Tsien first met Dr. Weinbaum. Tsien and his new campus friend, Malina, both were avidly interested in the same areas of scientific development. They attended classes together at Caltech. Eventually, Tsien had a cubby-hole office assigned to him as a sort of private den for study and there he often met and studied with Malina, pondering problems of aeronautics and rocket propulsion. The favorite diversion of both Tsien and Malina was music. It happened that Sidney Weinbaum, too, was a passionate music-lover. Malina was a close friend of Weinbaum, and inevitably all three — the Chinese, the Ukrainian-born chemist and the young genius of rocketry from Texas — got together for excursions to the Philharmonic Auditorium to hear the Los Angeles Symphony.

Tsien developed a deep fondness for Weinbaum, intrigued by the chemist's Ukrainian penchant for scattering proverbs in English with a heavy Russian accent. Weinbaum, eleven years senior to Tsien, came to the United States in 1922 by way of the Ukraine and Kharkov Institute of Technology. At Caltech in 1924 he took a Bachelor of Science degree, and then left the institute to work for four years as a chemist in private industry. He became a United States citizen in 1927 and married in 1928. A year later he returned to Caltech as a research assistant, and in the same year won a doctorate in physics, *cum laude.*

Tsien had more than a passing interest in Weinbaum's work at Caltech, especially in the degree that it related to his own research. He had a large measure of respect for the older man's talent. He began to drop in once in awhile at the Weinbaum home. He knew he would have an interesting evening at the Weinbaums' with their lively conversation and their good library of classical music.

Young John Parsons wondered about Tsien's peregrinations from one home to another for weekly gatherings. At some of these gatherings there were likely to be people known as "inner-circle intellectuals," and Parsons suspected that at least some of them were card-carrying Communists. Occasionally, he dropped a hint to Tsien on the subject, but Tsien had heard many such hints and even warnings, and he was not inclined to pay much attention. He saw nothing wrong with evenings of talk. Tsien could talk about almost any subject, and did so with a quick sense of humor which endeared him to his friends.

Once in awhile Tsien would find Frank Malina and his wife,

Lillian, at such a gathering, or Jon Dubnoff, a biochemistry student, with his wife, Belle. Sometimes Frank Oppenheimer, the brother of the famous physicist Robert Oppenheimer, would be on hand. Frank Oppenheimer's contribution to the evening often would be a piccolo solo, to which Dr. Weinbaum rippled an expert accompaniment on the piano. They would talk about socialism and communism. Everybody argued.

The nucleus of this group was what the Communist party called Unit 122. From the weight of the evidence, it seems unlikely Tsien ever knew there was such a thing.

The unit probably was born in 1936 or 1937. The deliberately tangled records of the Communist party make it unclear just who set it up and when. Some of those who took part in the gatherings knew the party had a hand in them, and some did not. Sometimes the gatherings would provide convenient observation posts for party functionaries to note whether the conversation of this or that guest made him a likely prospect for party membership.

Those who gathered under the dubious auspices of Unit 122 made up an odd assortment. Several were physicists. One was a chemist, one a graduate student, one a movie-set designer, and one, of course, was Frank Malina, the lively scholar who was sure one day he could send a rocket to the moon. There were other Communist party units all over Los Angeles County, but in terms of brainpower, there were few, if any, which could match Unit 122.

Tsien liked the gatherings because there were likely to be people present who would speak sympathetically of his native China, then being trampled under the Japanese military boot. Tsien repeatedly told his friends he considered himself a sort of ambassador of China in the United States and wanted to act accordingly so as to reflect no discredit on his native land. He dressed immaculately and carried himself with unfailing dignity. He was gentle of manner, except for his sharp impatience with nonsense.

With Weinbaum, his conversations often were about the meaning of science in general, where it was headed, what were its relationships to society. Much of their talk was on the theoretical level. Naturally, when science and its prospects were projected into the future, politics had to come into the discussions.

"If political things were discussed, if socialism was discussed, the question was: what did it mean?" Weinbaum has told the authors. "What was the theoretical basis?"

It all seemed innocuous enough, especially in those days when Germany was the main enemy of the democracies and Russia was a potential ally. Russia could be forgiven for a lot of things — even for Stalin and his blood purges — in view of the greater menace of Hitler. To some, the payment of ten or even twenty-five or fifty cents per session was nothing more than a contribution for the coffee and cake and perhaps the sip of wine which was served. Some, however, knew the money represented payment of dues to the Communist party. Some let themselves be talked into subscribing to the *Daily Worker* or the *People's World*, paying little attention to the hammer-and-sickle emblems. Others knew it was for the Red cause. Some felt it their duty to carry party cards and use fictitious names. Others could not recall, later on, ever signing anything, nor could they recognize the false names listed on party documents alongside their own.

Each fall, the Communist party would stage a recruiting drive in the county, rounding up "sympathizers" and urging them to become full party members. The party was no select conspiracy in those days. It wanted numbers.

A good prospect could be judged at something like a kaffeeklatsch. His response to classical music and to profound literature was considered a fair party test. Above all, the party wanted intellectuals in its ranks. Was he shocked at the introduction of far-left ideas or did he show interest?

But many an intellectual, always conscious of the fact that he was one, would rather have been caught reading the comics than gag at the ideas the recruiters threw at him. The party recruiters could make it look like a mark of distinction to be accepted into the fold of those who really knew what was wrong with the poor old world. They were snobs.

So recruiters attended gatherings and eyed the prospects. When a likely one was found, any party member could fill out an application in the prospect's name. It wasn't even necessary for the prospect to know it had been done. He would find out when the proper time came.

Once a recruit was registered, he was supposed to be given a membership book which would provide a record of his dues payments. The functionary collecting the dues either would mark "paid" in the book or affix dues stamps to it.

The dues secretary in Los Angeles in the late 1930s was none other than Clara Osvald. Clara and now Bill Kimple had the confidence of the party, for Bill, too, had become a functionary. Since 1935 he had held the job of assistant membership director. He had worked his way up by small services to the party. Posing as an automobile mechanic, he made himself useful on occasion by patching up an old wreck for use in enterprises such as protest demonstrations.

William Ward Kimple, by this time, had been officially declared dead. His mother, never suspecting the truth, collected on his insurance until the day she died. As Bill Ward, Kimple remained on the inside of the party, keeping Bill Hynes and the Red Squad informed. For example, Hynes learned the Communist party had one member who was a telephone linesman and who had volunteered to tap any line in the country the party wanted to monitor. Knowing this, Kimple was careful about talking with his chief by telephone.

In his role as assistant membership director, Bill Kimple knew all about the recruiters and their work. He had access to the registrations they turned in. Records of the registrations had to be sent to the state membership director in San Francisco. It was Kimple's party job to make records of the registration on three-by-five cards. Bill and Clara together often would go from unit to unit visiting members and checking up to see that all party membership dues were paid.

In all his years as an undercover police operative inside the

Communist party, Bill Kimple had never laid eyes on Tsien. Tsien was, by the same token, unaware of the existence of either Kimple or Hynes.

"I was very good friends of Frank J. Malina and knew Sidney Weinbaum and Jon Dubnoff quite well," Tsien would recall later, speaking in awkward English.

"I often went to his (Weinbaum's) house and sometimes without calling them first through the telephone and tell them that I was coming and when I went to their house quite often I found they have already people in their house which at that time I took just for friends, and since there is no sign that I can recognize any formal meeting I naturally stayed in the house at what you shall say a social gathering." [1]

Tsien made such visits perhaps once a week, just "dropped in," as he put it, likely as not, uninvited. He knew some who were present as people from Caltech, but often there would be persons present whom he would not recognize at all. There were similar gatherings, too, at the home of his closest friend, Frank Malina, and some at the Dubnoff home. In fact, he was more often at Malina's home than at any other, since the Chinese and Malina shared a common understanding of rocketry.

Mostly, the gatherings were what the argot of the day called bull sessions. They would talk, as Tsien put it, about "issues of the day in the newspapers, and I particularly participated when questions about China were discussed."

"Very often," he recalled, "my opinions were solicited because I was Chinese . . . I do not recall that communism as a principle or philosophy was discussed as such in the meetings. The inferences of communism, I am quite sure, were discussed — mentioned . . . as a force in the political scene of the world — they always argued. I don't believe in any of these discussions there was a uniform unanimous opinion. There was always somebody against something . . . these discussions were no more organized and systematic than you meet a man in the street and discuss the issues of the day with him."

Sometimes, he would go to the homes of others with Weinbaum. As he explained it: "The Sidney Weinbaums at these times do not own a car and I being a friend of them very often take him to places he has to go, if I happen to be at his house, and when I took him to a certain place, naturally — if the host saw me there and asked me in for to stay awhile — sometime I was busy, I refused, sometime I did."[2]

Sometimes Tsien found himself puzzled by his friends and acquaintances and their penchant for reveling in the gloomy folk song: *My name is Samuel Hall / And I hate you one and all / God damn your eyes.*

Such gatherings, whether of Professional Unit 122 or otherwise, still were going strong late in December of 1938 when Bill Kimple paid a visit to a house on Boyle Heights.

13

Bill Kimple's mind was on his work as he drove through downtown Los Angeles on that late December day in 1938. He hardly noticed the incongruity of the scene: the burlesque of the holiday season which southern California has a talent for producing. Fake snow glistened on sun-baked palm trees. Storefront Santa Clauses perspired under their red flannel uniforms and caps. The streets bustled with frantic pre-holiday activity.

Bill Kimple turned the car at last into the Boyle Heights area and proceeded to Soto Street. Peering out, he finally spotted number 829. He pulled the car to a stop and eased his lanky frame out of it, slamming the door behind him. He took a quick look around the neighborhood, walked up to the house and rapped on the door.

A matronly lady, heavy with child, answered his knock. She listened impassively to his identification of himself — Bill Ward, from the party's Los Angeles headquarters, assistant membership director. He had come for the registrations.

Sarah Reznick scarcely glanced at him as she admitted the tall man with the sloping shoulders. She noted only that he probably was asthmatic. Dr. Samuel Reznick hardly glanced at the visitor either. The man was there on a routine errand. It didn't seem important. The Reznicks were rather new party members — and would not remain party members for long. They remembered that the man who had brought the forms to their house in the first place had been asthmatic, and assumed this was the same man.

Kimple quickly picked up his bundle of registration cards, bade the couple good-night, and climbed back into his car. But he did not go to party headquarters to deliver the forms. He made a long detour into the Eagle Rock section of comfortable middle class homes, and drew up at the neat, one-story stucco home occupied by Captain William F. Hynes, late of the Red Squad, now head of a small Los Angeles police intelligence detail.

The Red Squad as such had been abolished. Mayor Fletcher Bowron of Los Angeles decided that Hynes's unit was primarily an anti-strike squad to stifle labor union activities and that it was often "engaged in extra-legal activities." Hynes retained his rank but he had been downgraded. Nevertheless, he lost none of his enthusiasm for rooting out Communists. Evidently he felt he could count on influence in high places. And whenever J. Edgar Hoover of the FBI came to town, Hynes would make every effort to see him. Hynes eagerly welcomed his right-hand man, Bill Kimple when Bill came to the door bearing some of "the goods." Hynes and Kimple seated themselves at the dining room table and began to pore over the records of Communist party registrations. Methodically, and with grunts of satisfaction, Hynes made copies of the cards, to be tucked away in his files for future reference.

It was a big job to keep up with the party. By this time the party's membership in Los Angeles county had risen to about twenty-eight hundred and it was always encouraging likely prospects to fill out the application blanks. The party was even a bit careless about it. In some cases a party member would take it upon himself to make out an application for a prospect without the prospect's knowledge. Thereafter the party would send another member to talk with the prospect and determine whether the process of enrolling him should be completed.

In the Pasadena branch, a registration card was used in lieu of an application. Each of these registration forms carried the telltale "bug," the printer's mark which identified Communist party documents. The registration form then went to the membership director and on up through the apparatus until finally it would reach the San Francisco membership director, the only party functionary empowered to issue the "books" which indicated full membership in the party. The book was issued in a fictitious party name and a party stamp affixed. Thereafter, every year, the comrade had to turn in his old book and be issued a new one. It was a sort of party security check.

It was not the first time, by any means, that Hynes and Kimple had hunched over that dining room table to examine registration forms. As a courier Kimple had moved about in various party branches to transport records to party headquarters and thus had access to membership information. Kimple, Hynes and Clara Osvald would swiftly transcribe the copies of party forms onto prepared mimeographed sheets which Hynes always had on hand and Kimple would show up at party headquarters in plenty of time.

This night Hynes came upon one form which stopped him.

"What's this — a Chinese?"

Kimple examined it and nodded. Who was this man? Kimple didn't know.

"He uses the party name 'Decker.' I wonder why he took the

name 'Decker' for a party name? I wonder if he knows Comrade Decker?"

There was a female comrade in Los Angeles known to the police as Comrade Decker, and Hynes wondered aloud whether the Chinese whose name was on the form before him knew her and took the name for that reason. It would not have occurred to Bill Hynes to wonder whether the registration was genuine. And he didn't know Hsue Shen Tsien from Confucius.

But it had been the first Chinese name he had come across in his years of ferreting out secret Communist party members, and that was something worthy of notice. Hynes and Kimple pondered the registration for a few moments. Hynes shrugged, transscribed the data from the unsigned registration card, and went on to the rest. The lot was tucked away in the files to yellow, forgotten.

Another segment of the net had been fashioned. Without knowing it, Kimple and Hynes that night planted a time bomb with a long fuse.

14

The careful police work of Hynes and Kimple might have gone completely to waste, for all either of them knew, once the war erupted.

The war changed the lives of all of those who had been attending the cell meetings, and especially it changed the lives of members of the Suicide Squad.

By the time the nations of Europe were mobilizing, Tsien had his Ph.D., *magna cum laude*, in aeronautics and mathematics, and with Malina was well advanced in rocketry research.

Then Adolf Hitler and the man whom the Nazi Fuehrer had pictured as his worst enemy, Josef Stalin, signed a mutual non-aggression pact, and the gates of war were ready to be opened. The event rocked the world and hit the Communist party in the United States with the force of a hurricane. The incomparable cynicism of the man who was supposed to lead the workers of the world to "peace and socialism" spread disillusion among the comrades. They deserted the party in droves.

For Unit 122 in Pasadena, it was a death blow. The Unit just withered and died for lack of interest or support.

Hitler sent his Nazi legions into Poland to bathe that helpless nation in blood. Stalin took his share of the booty, a big slice of eastern Poland, and moved his troops into it. Britain and France declared war on Germany; in the United States the cries were for neutrality. For a while the world watched what it called a phony war, a sitzkrieg, on the Western Front. Nothing was happening. France felt safe behind her Maginot Line. Then Hitler's armies suddenly gobbled up the low countries — and France.

The events quickened the pace of preparations in the United States. The experimenters at Caltech were making strides and they had come to the point where they were going to try a jet-assisted takeoff. A daredevil pilot climbed into a light plane, to which the experimenters had strapped a rack of rockets. The project sprayed the airstrip with fireworks and the plane never got off the ground.[1] But Frank Malina and his crew persisted.

Then, in the most daring project of all, the Suicide Squad stripped a plane of its propeller and towed the craft down the runway with an automobile. On the plane's nose, the pilot had pasted a safety campign poster reading: "What about tomorrow if I meet with an accident today?"

The idea of the automobile was to give the little craft speed for takeoff. As the car released it, the craft shot into the air, climbed and then glided back safely to the runway. Well before

Pearl Harbor, the Suicide Squad had achieved America's first manned flight by rocket power alone. JATO — jet-assisted takeoff — was about to become a reality.[2]

The changes in the lives of the Pasadena scientists were coming swiftly now. What had been called the Aerojet Engineering Corporation adopted a new name: Aerojet-General Corporation, destined to play a part one day in virtually every U.S. space program. It was formally incorporated in March 1942 with Dr. von Kármán as president, Dr. Malina as treasurer, and Parsons, Forman and Martin Summerfield as vice-presidents. The latter three devoted themselves almost exclusively to problems of liquid and solid propellants for rocket engines. Tsien drifted away from the group, engaged in classified work in aeronautical research. Tsien's friend, Dr. Sidney Weinbaum, disappeared from his life. He had gone east into war industry.

The work of von Kármán and Malina on GALCIT Project No. 1 took an added urgency with reports of British Intelligence that the Germans were developing missiles at Peenemuende. Dr. Tsien was called for consultation with von Kármán and Malina to examine these reports and report back to the Air Corps on the outlook for long-range, rocket-driven projectiles. Their report to Washington in November, 1943, was to bear the name Jet Propulsion Laboratory.

Thereafter, Tsien and Malina saw one another less and less frequently. Tsien was preoccupied with his own secret work, Malina with Aerojet, the brainchild of his Suicide Squad.

Bill Hynes, who had probably forgotten completely the name H. S. Tsien, retired in 1943 and a year later, William Kimple, after twenty years of devoted service underground, an incredible dedication which robbed him of a normal life, also retired. The war had changed matters with regard to Communists. Hitler was fighting both the United States and the Soviet Union. That made the two allies.

Once again, Washington called upon von Kármán. General Arnold asked him to set up a Scientific Advisory Board to the

Chief of Staff of the U.S. Army Air Force. This board would be charged with probing all possibilities of conflict in the air in any future war. Von Kármán left Aerojet in the hands of Malina and went to Washington.

"Of all the experts whom I suggested for the Air Force Scientific Advisory Group in 1945," von Kármán would write in his memoirs, "my friend, H. S. Tsien . . . at the age of thirty-six . . . was an undisputed genius whose work was providing enormous impetus to advances in high-speed aerodynamics and jet propulsion. For these reasons I nominated him for membership on the Scientific Advisory Group." [3]

Tsien accepted the invitation. The Army Air Force conferred the rank of colonel upon him. When Germany eventually surrendered, von Kármán and Tsien flew to the Black Forest to probe the secrets of the men who had produced the frightening "buzz-bombs" which struck England late in the war — the V–1 and V–2 rockets. Tsien inspected the German scientists' wind tunnels and was among those who recommended a similar program in the United States.

Unfortunately the Americans found little that was of concrete value because the Russians had cleaned out everything which could be carted away. The U.S. did get the benefit of some German scientists who preferred to take their chances with the United States rather than with Russia, and fled westward, and enough remained of the installations to tell a revealing story to experts such as Tsien and von Kármán.

Back at Caltech, the Jet Propulsion Laboratory — swollen to a staff of two hundred and sixty-four during the war — began to develop advanced ideas from studies made by Tsien, von Kármán, Summerfield and Malina working in collaboration. The project dealt with jet propulsion for missiles and high-speed aircraft. The laboratory now was on the verge of success with a high-altitude rocket.

Out of all this labor, the WAC Corporal missile was born and fired at the new White Sands Proving Grounds in New Mexico in the fall of 1945. It soared to two hundred and thirty-five thousand feet, a new altitude record. The faint outlines of the space age were discernible.

The United States was grateful to Tsien, particularly for what he had done during the war. The War Department and Army Air Force awarded him a commendation for "Meritorious Civil Service" and praise for "outstanding performance of duty." There was also a commendation from the Ordnance Department of the Army Air Force for Dr. Tsien "For outstanding performance of duty during the period September 1939 to September 1945 while serving as Group Supervisor, Jet Propulsion Laboratory, Caltech."

From James B. Conant and Vannevar Bush of the Office of Scientific Research and Development, came a special certificate for Dr. Tsien who "participated in work organized under the Office of Scientific Research and Development through the National Defense Research Committee, contributing to the successful prosecution of the Second World War."

"On behalf of the Government of the United States of America," it continued, "this certificate is awarded in appreciation of effective service."

In addition to all this, there was more official praise for Tsien for his study of the possibilities of applying nuclear energy to propulsion.

Dr. Malina and Dr. Summerfield, now armed with the results of the WAC Corporal tests and the detailed information Tsien and von Kármán had brought back on Germany's V–2 rockets, began seriously to study the prospects of flight into space, their concern being how a rocket might escape the pull of the earth's gravity.

Caltech promoted Tsien to assistant professor and then associate professor of aeronautics, but he left in 1946 to accept a full professorship at the Massachusetts Institute of Technology. As Tsien moved east to M.I.T., two other scientists — Wang Kan-chang and Hua Lo-keng — moved westward, and yet another named

Chien Wei-chang moved out of California and back to Chiang Kai-shek's China. The names of all three would figure importantly in Dr. Tsien's future.

Wang Kan-chang left the University of Berlin, where he had been working on beta rays, and turned up at the University of California in Berkeley. Then thirty-nine, Wang was already recognized as a nuclear physicist and had been appointed a research associate at Berkeley. Hua Lo-keng had made a name for himself by the time he was twenty-four, writing learned articles for American, British, Soviet and Japanese scientific journals. Like Tsien a man of Shanghai, Hua arrived at the University of Illinois from England in 1946 to continue a distinguished career in mathematics. Chien — his American friends called him W. Z. and Jimmy — was an amiable Chinese scientist who made no bones about his sympathies for the Chinese Communist cause at the time. He had worked at Caltech on problems of high-speed flight, dreaming of rockets which would penetrate outer space. His fellow-feeling for the Communists dated to the mid-1930s when he participated as a youngster in Mao Tse-tung's "Long March." It failed to bother his American colleagues in science.

Tsien, at M.I.T., was out of sensitive government work for the time being. But his colleague and compatriot, physicist Chao Chung-yao, was more deeply involved with American nuclear experimentation than ever. As a respected and admired nuclear man who had been in the United States for twenty years, Chao had reached something of inner circle status among U.S. and allied scientists. He mixed with the Americans well, and amiably. Chao was accepted — and trusted.

15

Dr. Chao's slender figure — tall for a Chinese — weaved in and out among the array of American scientists almost unnoticed. Like all the others, the round-faced Chao wore goggles so dark that no natural light could seep through. The physicist listened tensely.

"Tick . . . tick . . . tick . . . tick . . ."

The metronome was lashed to an open microphone aboard the battleship *Pennsylvania*, once a gallant lord of the seas but now — in July of 1946 — a desolate target awaiting destruction in the waters of the Pacific off Bikini Atoll. With each tick of the metronome the tension mounted.

Operation Crossroads, they called it. The tests enlisted the services of an Army-Navy task force of 42,000 men, 200 ships and 150 aircraft near the coral ring in the Marshall Islands. The mighty armada would preside over the first atomic bomb explosions in peacetime. The U.S. Government invited observers from many friendly lands. The Republic of China dispatched Dr. Chao from his U.S. campus to be an official observer for Generalissimo Chiang Kai-shek, America's wartime ally.

The official observers waited aboard ships anchored ten miles from the target area. They listened through earphones to the ominous-sounding ticking as dawn tinged the waters with a reddish gold. Hours later a B–29 Superfortress bomber called Dave's Dream approached the target area, a serene lagoon where seventy-three doomed vessels, including the *Pennsylvania*, were clustered. Doomed along with the ships was an assorted menagerie of goats, pigs and rats, strapped to the ships.

"Bomb away — bomb away and falling."

Forty more almost unbearable seconds ticked away. Then the

metronome went silent. An enormous fiery ball scorched the sky. The observers, watching through protective goggles, felt a shock wave beat against their eardrums and a rush of heat.

On the horizon, the fireball spread its fury in all directions. Then the ball itself collapsed. The finger of a cloud clawed upward, its whiteness streaked with shades of rose. A nuclear mushroom, terrifyingly beautiful, billowed out from the top of the cloud.

Three weeks later, the observers, Chao among them, watched as a second Bikini bomb was exploded. They were to return home convinced that the tests were appropriately named Operation Crossroads. The world, indeed, was now at a crossroads. One road could lead to international control of the frightening force the scientists had seen unfolding and to the use of atomic power for peace, progress and prosperity. The other road could lead to cataclysm for the entire world.

Chao Chung-yao removed his goggles and pondered the implications of what he had witnessed. For Chao, too, at forty-four, a crossroads had been reached. He was at Bikini representing a China in chaos, reeling from the agonies of civil war in the wake of global conflict. It seemed to him that Chiang Kai-shek could not win.

For Chao, Bikini summed up just what his twenty years of labor in the United States might mean to him in the future. Some day his China, under one leader or another, would regain her balance. China was a huge nation, populated by hundreds of millions, among whom there would be a vast amount of untapped scientific talent.

Chao came from the thin layer of privileged Chinese. He had not seen his native land since 1926. He had enrolled at Caltech at the age of 24 and plunged into his work with a deadly earnestness which brought him a Ph.D., *magna cum laude*, within four years.

Along the way, Chao mingled with other Chinese students and with a select group of Americans. He was popular. His mind was constantly alert, his wit unfailingly quick. At work he was invariably serious and conscientious. At play, he was an amiable companion who liked tennis or an occasional outing. He loved music with a passion rivaling that of his compatriot from Shanghai and fellow-scientist at Caltech, Dr. H. S. Tsien. Like Tsien, he neither drank nor smoked, and like Tsien he was the classical figure of Chinese scholar, but unlike his colleague, he could enjoy small talk.

Tsien didn't. With Tsien, those who could not speak the language of science were aliens in his world. Because of his absorption with his work and with matters of science, some of his acquaintances — notably the ladies in their circle — often regarded him as rude. To his students, Tsien was a martinet, an exacting taskmaster who dragged the best out of them in spite of themselves.

Chao was different. He liked an occasional party, even though he would do no more than touch a ceremonial sip of wine. He liked to venture into Chinatown for Chinese meals, and take American acquaintances along with him. He enjoyed what social life he had, but there had not been much of it, because Chao, too, was utterly absorbed in his work, and for many years had been considered a top-notch physicist whose studies were fundamental to nuclear research. He was not the sort of man who ever would have to steal secrets. The secrets were in his head. As a senior research fellow at Caltech, Chao had a wide reputation for his work on the scattering of gamma rays by atomic nuclei, a study basic to probing the mysteries of nuclear power.

Those who knew Chao well on the campus never entertained the slightest doubt about his loyalty to the U.S. But they were aware, too, of the strong family ties in China. Chao one day would have to make a difficult decision: to return to China, even though it might be under an unwelcome regime, or to be a wanderer for the rest of his life.

Like Chao, Tsien also felt the strong pull of family ties. And it caused him mental anguish. Soon after he settled down in his full professorship at M.I.T, Tsien received word from Chiang Kai-shek's China that his mother had died. Tsien now worried about his father, then sixty-seven, and his adopted sister in Shanghai. It had been twelve years since he had seen either. He decided to go to China for a visit to comfort the old man.

16

At number 111 Lane 1032 on the Yu-yuan Road in Shanghai, things were little different from what he remembered of a dozen years before, and Shanghai itself had changed little.

Tsien spent much of his time searching out some former students of Dr. von Kármán who had since returned to China, so that he could report on them to his colleague. And then he saw Yin Tsiang whom he had not seen for many, many years — since both were youngsters. Yin's father now was an important general in Chiang Kai-shek's army, and Yin had been given the best of everything, including a European education, where she concentrated on studying music and voice culture. She had become a beautiful woman of cosmopolitan charm. The mutual interest in music provided a new bond between the two, and Tsien, after a whirlwind courtship, persuaded her to marry him.

They were married in the summer of 1947, and, for a time, Tsien considered settling down again in China. He had been recommended for the presidency of his alma mater, Chiaotung University. But Chiang Kai-shek's Minister of Education judged Tsien, then thirty-seven, too young for so exalted a position, and the recommendation was rejected.

Tsien was depressed by his homeland. In letters to von Kármán and others he spelled out in gloomy detail all the misery and suffering he encountered in Chiang's domain. And after three months, he had had enough. He decided to bring his bride back with him to the United States. On September 26 they boarded a plane for the United States by way of Honolulu.

In Hawaii, Tsien, like all returning aliens, was met by customs officials. It was routine. Tsien had gone through it before. There were the usual questions, including the question whether he had ever belonged to the Communist party or any organization advocating the overthrow of the government of the United States by force and violence. Far from wanting to overthrow the United States, Tsien already had contributed liberally to supporting it in the great war. Casually he scribbled a "no" in answer to the question, and just as casually forgot all about it.

Back in the United States, Tsien confided to friends that he believed Chiang Kai-shek was on the way out in China. It was, he predicted, only a matter of time before Mao Tse-tung and the Communists would overwhelm the mainland in the civil war.

Tsien went back to M.I.T and teaching as other Chinese scientists in the United States — men like Wang Kan-chang — were packing up to return to China. Tsien seemed to have decided the United States would be his home. His first child, a son Yung-kang, whom he called Yucon, had been born an American, and Tsien filed a Declaration of Intention to become a citizen of the United States. He could see exciting vistas ahead.

Caltech and Princeton were vying for his services. Both universities now had jet propulsion centers set up by the Daniel and Florence Guggenheim Foundation. Tsien did not have to debate long over which bid he would accept. He wanted to work with von Kármán. He saw his life's career carrying on what von Kármán had begun in the exploration of wind and space. To Tsien, the old Hungarian-born scientist, known only to a select few in the United States, was the epitome of genius in his field.

Tsien returned to California as Goddard Professor of Jet Propulsion. He was keenly interested in the possibilities of nuclear engines and was looking forward to research on the subject at the Jet Propulsion Center.

At thirty-nine, Tsien was at the pinnacle of his career, and the prospects seemed limitless as he prepared to take up the study of jet propulsion for commercial aviation and scientific purposes. The foundation had appropriated five hundred thousand dollars to support seven years of study in the field by the Caltech and Princeton centers, and this meant Tsien would have a thirty-thousand-dollar annual budget to work with, along with whatever equipment he might need. He was prepared to push into the region of the unknown, the field of supersonic speed.

Tsien prepared to settle down in California in that summer of 1949, but, as he knew, it would not be easy. The war had not diminished the antipathy toward Orientals and in Pasadena, especially, there was firm resentment. Tsien finally found a place in Altadena, another Los Angeles suburb. It was a neat house of redwood clapboard, its spacious lawn ringed by a rail fence. Eucalyptus trees lined the road on Buena Loma Drive. From his new house Tsien could look above the treetops and see the slopes stretching eastward to the dome of Mount Wilson Observatory, the sun glittering on its silver shell.

It was the fall of 1949, and Tsien seemed as content as any Chinese could be in Southern California. Momentous events were taking place in the world, but then, momentous events were taking place in Tsien's laboratory too.

At about the time Mao Tse-tung, now established as the red emperor of China, was traveling to Moscow to knock on Joseph Stalin's door in quest of military and economic help, Tsien was headed eastward from California to New York. His mission was to address the annual convention of the American Rocket Society.

Tsien strode across the red-carpeted splendor of the Statler Hilton Hotel in New York City and took his place at the lectern, trim and professorial looking in his conservatively-cut dark business suit. He looked out over a distinguished audience. Among those eager to hear him was his friend, Dan A. Kimball, by then

President Truman's Undersecretary of the Navy, whom Tsien had known in Aerojet-General. Kimball was to be the dinner speaker, and had prepared an address calling upon scientists to produce a "stockpile of proven research" which would be as necessary to Americans' future as any stockpiles of weapons or strategic materials. Tsien was one of the men who could contribute to the stockpile of research.

Tsien held the audience of scientific men spellbound, as he described a new age now within the grasp of scientists and engineers. For his colleagues at the convention, Tsien outlined a vision of a future in which Americans would travel in outer space. People then living could hope to ride a rocket from New York to Los Angeles in less than sixty minutes. Businessmen would become transcontinental commuters.

The transcontinental rocket liner, Tsien predicted, would be shaped like a fat, sharpened pencil almost eighty feet long and nine feet in diameter. Set midway between nose and tail would be a pair of small wings. On the tail would be two small fins and one slightly larger vertical fin. The vehicle would be powered by a ramjet engine as well as a rocket motor.[1]

The rocket ship would vanish from sight seconds after takeoff. It would not be seen again until just before landing. For the first 1,200 miles, the ship would reach almost 10,000 miles an hour as it carved an elliptical path across the atmosphere, reaching a height of 300 miles. At that point, the rocket liner would curve downward, toward earth. It would strike into the earth's atmosphere once again and, like a non-powered glider, it would coast the remaining 1,800 miles to its destination, and would land at only 150 miles an hour. With obvious satisfaction, Dr. Tsien held up an outline sketch of this future ship for an enthralled audience to see. And the ship was no mere dream. It was in blueprint design already, and both the United States Army and Navy were experimenting with designs for such vehicles. This was Tsien's finest hour in the United States.

"His conclusion was clear and startling," reported *Time* magazine.[2] "Present day technology is capable of building a transcontinental rocket ship."

Tsien now was giving his scientific imagination full play. He was deeply interested in the possibilities of a future nuclear engine, and hoping to carry on research at Caltech toward developing one. He turned out an essay on the subject which for years was regarded in scientific circles as a classic work.

But, absorbed though he was in his work, Tsien had his worries, too. He was disturbed by the word from China. He had heard of letters coming from the mainland, now under communism, to other Chinese scientists, and now he had received a letter.

It was in his father's hand — or was it? It was a letter full of news, but between the lines it seemed ominous, threatening.

17

H. S. Tsien read and reread the letter. The shaky hand seemed genuine enough, and yet he could not escape the impression that there was something wrong about it. They were not the words he would have expected his scholarly old father to use — and yet . . .

Mother China wanted him to come back, the letter told him. China was now "people's China." All the people were as one under the great Mao Tse-tung, all determined to engage in "heroic construction." "Our five-million-strong city," Shanghai, had become the great, teeming seaport of "people's China." Cotton mills were humming. Markets were alive with farmers. The broad streets and the boulevards where the foreigners so long had humiliated the people now belonged to the people themselves. No longer would the imperialists exploit the people of Shanghai . . .

His father, the letter said, was ill, badly in need of a second stomach operation, yearning to see his son before death came at last. Tsien's mind drifted back. His father, Chia-chih, now would be sixty-nine and alone. Tsien had the respect and reverence for his father typical of so many Chinese. What would happen to the old man in his last years if his son did not go back?

He knew of letters to other Chinese in America since the Communists had come to power in China. They were full of a combination of persuasion and implied threats. If a letter said a father was suffering from a disease, it could mean that he had been arrested. If it said the father's health was in worse condition than the mother's, it could mean that the father was in political danger.

He had known cases of other Chinese being lured back against their will — scientists who had American-born wives or children. A man would be told a good position would be waiting for him in the motherland. Then he would receive the offer of plane tickets, to be delivered by a neutral embassy. He could fly, for example, to Geneva where contacts would be waiting for him, or perhaps from the west coast to Hong Kong. Arrangements would be made then to get him back into mainland China to see his parents. He would be promised a red carpet reception. And, whether he was aware of it or not, the chances of his ever leaving China again would be just about nonexistent.

Tsien was familiar with the case of one of his colleagues who had refused to believe the letters about his parents at first, and had refused consistently to go back. The letters kept coming, each one more nagging than the last, each one more threatening to the welfare of his relatives. The scientist finally went to an institution, with a nervous breakdown. And he was only one of many cases of Chinese in the United States who were considered useful to the new China.

Tsien gazed out the window of his neat Buena Loma Court home into the pale December sunlight which bathed Altadena in a hazy glow. He reflected on his dilemma. Yin was pregnant. They were expecting their second child in the spring. He had prospered and had decided to become a citizen of the United States. His children would be native-born American citizens and he could look forward to a prosperous future for them.

China — the China he had loved — was undergoing stormy, revolutionary change. He reflected on how Peking would look now — lovely and serene under its white mantle of snow, but deceptively peaceful. Underneath, it would be boiling with turmoil. Surely, he would be useful to Mother China, and surely he would be permitted to use his talents to the utmost, without interference. Or would he?

On the other hand, the climate in the United States had become colder for Chinese. One was hardly aware of it in the sheltered academic atmosphere of the Caltech campus, but on the outside, things were different. Hardly a day went by but that the radio shrilled with demands of politicians seeking to determine "who lost China."

"Who lost China?" When had it ever belonged to the United States in the first place, that it could be "lost"? The newspapers were filled with stormy fulminations of Senator Joseph R. McCarthy, insisting that the U.S. State Department was infested with subversives. American policy, McCarthy was sure, had betrayed Chiang Kai-shek to the Communists.

To Tsien, the Communist conquest of China had come as no surprise, but it brought problems for him. He was far from alone in his troubles. Thousands of Chinese — students and graduate students — all over the United States shared the problems with him. Their difficulties multiplied as the months sped by into the tense spring of 1950, with America in near hysteria about the Communist threat in Asia. There was an almost psychotic fear of the very word "Communist," a passion for total security and a search for scapegoats. A witch-hunt for subversives and spies shattered the boundaries of rational pursuit of national safety.

Some of the Chinese scientists and students in the United States

77

were particularly aggrieved by the activities of the Immigration and Naturalization Service. One such was Hua Lo-keng, the University of Illinois mathematician. Hua had begun his career as a scientist at the University of Berlin in Germany as a Boxer fellow, then shifted to the University of Cambridge in England. From there he moved to the United States and spent four years at Illinois. Hua had been receiving letters from the mainland, filled with promises, yet laced with veiled threats against his family. He slipped out of the United States in February, 1950. Tsien had known Hua from the early Shanghai days and had known of his wide reputation as a scientist. He noted with concern Hua's sudden flight with thirty other Chinese students in tow.

When he arrived in Hong Kong, Hua was met by Chinese Communists who were prepared to make the most of his arrival. How much of what Hua said and did in Hong Kong was voluntary is problematical. It appeared that the Communists there had thrust his statements upon him. In any event he signed a letter "To the [Chinese] Students in the United States."

There were three main reasons why he left America, the letter said. First and foremost were the immigration regulations; second, the color conflict in the United States, and third, a lack of freedom for Chinese there. He urged all Chinese students to leave America.

Hua crossed over into China, drilled en route by an emissary from Peking named Tsao Pai-chang. Tsao instructed the students and Hua on just what would be expected of them in the way of propaganda and in the way of work assignments. Immediately, Hua was assigned to the Academy of Sciences as chief of scientific calculation research, his work essential in the nuclear field. He would go on to become director of the Mathematical Institute of the Academy, and one day would be given a large share of the credit for the speed of China's nuclear weapons program.[1]

Tsien worried about the changing climate in America and its effect on him and other Chinese, but he was able to put his personal worries aside and plunge into new work on the possibilities ahead for the conquest of outer space. By now he enjoyed a reputation as the most brilliant authority in his field, mathematical analysis of the basic problems of high velocity phenomena. Under Dr. Tsien, the work of the Jet Propulsion Laboratory was concerned primarily with research in the development of jet power for civilian and commercial use.

Tsien's contributions "were essential to the development of high-speed aerodynamics and jet propulsion in the United States," wrote his old friend and mentor, Dr. von Kármán, in 1950. By that time, Tsien's work was removed from that area of the laboratory whose research was being supported by armed services funds, but he did have clearance. He had applied routinely for security clearance in October, 1949, just as he had in the past when he was working on secret defense programs. As in the past, the security clearance had been granted as a matter of routine. Tsien considered the application merely a formality, since he had been cleared long before as a consultant to the Government and to Aerojet-General. By this time he was considered the company's most important consultant after von Kármán.

By the spring of 1950, Tsien probably had made up his mind about his future: it was in America. Those who knew him well were sure that he had finally decided to remain in the United States and go ahead with his plans to become a citizen.

But events were conspiring against Tsien.

The McCarthy hearings were now in full bloom. The heat spanned the continent. At the University of California, the Board of Regents voted unanimously to discharge a hundred and fifty-seven members of the university staffs for failing to make formal declarations that they were not members of organizations aimed at overthrowing the U.S. Government by force. On the other side of the continent, the Government asked an appeals court in New York to uphold the conviction of eleven leaders of a rag-tag U.S. Communist party, charging they were engaged in espionage and conspiracy to seize power by force, strangle the American economic system, destroy American freedom and establish a Soviet America.

The CHINA CLOUD

The McCarthy hearings and the general atmosphere of hysteria sent government agencies scurrying through the records to turn up prospective subversives. No department wanted to be caught in the McCarthy storm. Agencies in the more sensitive fields began reviewing those who had clearance for secret work. One of the early victims of this diligent hindsight was an old friend of Tsien.

In April, 1949, Dr. Sidney Weinbaum had applied routinely to the army for security clearance. It was granted, just as routinely. But three months later, Dr. Weinbaum was rocked by the news from Caltech that the army had lifted his clearance. Two months later he was appearing before an army industrial employment review board to be closely questioned on his activities of the late 1930s. Had he ever been a member of the Communist party? Had he ever advocated the overthrow of the U.S. Government by force and violence? Had he ever used an alias, a party name? The scientist denied it all.

Resting in the records of defunct Unit 122 was a slip of paper which said that Sidney Weinbaum, of 325½ South Wilson Avenue, Pasadena, was the holder of 1939 Communist party Membership Book No. 1021, with the party name of "Sidney Empson." The chemist persistently denied that he ever signed any such registration.

The interrogation of Weinbaum was just an omen of things to come. The heat of the Communist-hunt would become even more intense in the wake of the Chiang Kai-shek debacle in China and the growing tension in Asia. Washington kept a wary eye on South Korea, jutting like a dagger pointed in the direction of American-occupied Japan. High U.S. military men journeyed to Seoul to confer with the craggy old iron man of South Korea, Syngman Rhee, about guerrilla clashes between his troops and those of the Soviet-backed North Koreans entrenched beyond the 38th Parallel. Suddenly, on a Sunday morning, Korea echoed to the thunder of guns.

Korea would mean the end of the line for many a talented Chinese in the United States. Those studying on American campuses would come under strict observation of the Immigration and Naturalization Service. Tension and confusion would mount among the Chinese whose visas were about to expire. They would be subject to deportation, and probably arrested if they tried to go.

For Chao Chung-yao, the physicist once welcomed by the inner circle of America's nuclear weapons experts, the dreary saga would end with his flight from U.S. authorities and his return to China on the eve of his country's entry into the Korean war with "volunteers." Able scientists armed with the latest and best in American education would flee along with him. Others just disappeared. Many stayed on in the United States, afraid to go home to a Communist regime and determined to make the best of an adopted land.

For H. S. Tsien, who had commanded the respect and applause of fellow scientists across the American continent, the hot and violent summer of 1950 was the beginning of a long agony which started when the FBI appeared at his door.

18

The late spring day had started without any hint of disaster. In the early morning, before the prevailing west winds rolled in with the smog, brilliant rays of sunshine played across the slopes of the Sierra Madre. Shadows edged their way bit by bit across the wiry, arid chaparral and into the canyons carved out by centuries of earthquakes and erosion. Thousands of feet up, Jeffrey pines glistened in the sun, a dark green band for the white crown of snow.

Dr. Tsien gave a tender parting salute to his young wife, his two-year-old son and newborn daughter before his usual quick drive to the campus and absorption, as ever, in his work. It was such a day that the two agents of the Federal Bureau of Investigation chose to pay their visit.

The FBI men were politely efficient. They possessed information that Dr. Tsien had at one time been a member of the Communist party. Tsien stared at them. The agent in charge read from his notes. Specifically, the information was that Dr. Tsien had been a member of Professional Unit 122, Pasadena Branch, as of 1939. Was he still a member of the Communist party?

Of course, Tsien told them, he never had been a member of the Communist party, much less used a party alias, as the agents had suggested.

"You were not John M. Decker?"

He was not, he said, ever John M. Decker.

Did he know Dr. Sidney Weinbaum? Yes. Did he know Frank J. Malina? Yes. Did he know Frank Oppenheimer? Yes. Jackie Oppenheimer, Frank Oppenheimer's wife? No. Jon Dubnoff? Yes, he had known him.

"In the period we are speaking of, Dr. Tsien, that is, from 1938 to 1941, did you sometimes visit these people in their homes?"

"Yes. I got to know them, especially for their interest in music and their interest in Oriental things."

"They were sympathetic to China?"

"Yes, and that is one thing that attracted me to them. I am a man of China. I was glad to hear when somebody had sympathy for China."

"Did you go to these homes by invitation?"

"Sometimes I just dropped in without first calling them."

Sometimes, there would be other people on hand when he arrived, Tsien explained.

Now the questions seemed to become sharper, more hostile. Did he ever pay dues to the Communist party? No, of course not. Did he attend meetings of the Communist party? Not to his knowledge. Tsien answered with his customary scientific directness. He told them what he knew, avoided commenting on what he did not know.

On and on the questions droned, now from one agent, now from the other. Finally they exhausted their line of investigation and prepared politely to take their leave. What would happen now? The agents couldn't tell the scientist for certain, but it appeared likely, they told him, that his security clearance would be removed. Suddenly Tsien was aware that his American world was about to collapse.

For Tsien, the blow had fallen at a critical moment. He had been worrying about the condition of his father who perhaps was desperately in need of another stomach operation.

Tsien's security clearance was, indeed, promptly lifted. Numbed by this development — it meant he could no longer work on Air Force projects — Tsien debated his next move. He did not take long in making up his mind. He went directly to his superiors to lay the matter before them.

Tsien went first to his immediate boss at Caltech, the tall, slow-speaking and easy-going Dr. Frederick Lindvall, then chief of the Division of Engineering. His long, six-foot-four frame sprawled in his desk chair, Dr. Lindvall puffed reflectively on his pipe as Tsien poured out his story.

"Well," the Chinese said in conclusion, with a slight shrug of resignation, "I guess I'm an unwelcome guest in this country."

Dr. Lindvall was shocked, as were most members of the faculty. He was even more shaken by the idea that Tsien was considering now leaving the United States.

"Naturally," Dr. Lindvall remembered, "he was upset. There was some embarrassment associated with it. He had been an individual scholar — somewhat withdrawn — and he continued in that pattern. He made no nasty remarks."

Tsien then went to see Dr. E. C. Watson, who was dean of the faculty at the time. Tsien stood facing the dean, his full underlip set in a hard line.

"I'm returning home," he announced. Dr. Watson was startled. "For heaven's sake, why? You're happy here."

Tsien drew himself up to his full five-feet-seven, chin raised, dark eyes flashing through the steel-rimmed spectacles. He spoke slowly, deliberately.

"I was brought up to believe that when you're a guest, you do nothing to offend your host. I'm a guest in your country. I'm an unwelcome guest, and I'm going home."

This was in character for Tsien, Dr. Watson reflected. He had come from a well-to-do, proud and aristocratic Chinese family and his upbringing would have taught him a code like that. There was no way to talk him out of it. Tsien felt he was being hounded. Somebody evidently had decided that Tsien was in reality a hidden Communist, a former member of Unit 122.

"There was no proof, but they kept hounding him," Dr. Watson recalled. "From then on, he began to suffer because of his friends. But everybody went to bat for him."

Nobody on the campus, Dr. Watson insisted, ever thought of Tsien as a member of the Communist party. And Tsien, he felt certain, would not have contemplated going back to China at all had not his world at Caltech been suddenly exploded.

"Tsien gave no indication of any disloyalty to the United States," recalled Professor Horace N. Gilbert, then chairman of the faculty committee for foreign students.

"He had loyalty to his family in China, perhaps more so than Americans would have. The family system is quite close in China. Then we jumped on him with police-state methods. This hurt him in a personal way. He felt he wasn't welcome in the United States, which was pretty logical."

In mid-June, soon after he learned that his security clearance was gone, Tsien made inquiries for a reservation on the S.S. *President Wilson* of the American President Lines. He went to the line's office with the idea of purchasing tickets for himself and his family for Hong Kong, Britain's outpost at the door of mainland China. He was told it would be necessary to get a transit visa for Hong Kong, intending to go on to China.

Tsien informed Dr. Watson at Caltech that he wanted eventually to return to the United States and resume his career, although he could not be expected to say exactly when he would be back. With the blind spot for politics so often a characteristic of the scientific mind, it evidently had not occurred to Dr. Tsien that he would be unable to go in and out of his native China at will. He seemed at that moment to feel that when the ugly mess about his past acquaintances was cleared up, he would probably be able to continue where he had left off. Perhaps, too — as some of his friends believed — he thought he could get his father out of Shanghai to Hong Kong and one day bring the old man to the United States with him.

Then came another blow. On June 22, 1950, newspaper headlines blared the story that Tsien's close friend, Dr. Sidney Weinbaum, had been arrested at his Pasadena home and indicted for perjury, for telling the Army industrial employment review board, a year before, that he never had been a Communist. Weinbaum would face trial in late August. The development may have strengthened Tsien's resolve to get out of the United States. The net seemed to be closing in on him. Tsien wrote a letter in July to an organization called the International Trade Service Association in Seattle, Washington, which, he had been told, could help clear up complications concerning his application for a Hong Kong visa. It was difficult to get the visa from the British Consulate in Los Angeles. Tsien's Chinese friends at Caltech who had tried to do so ran into the same obstacle. Some of the students intending to leave informed him of the existence of the Seattle organization.

Then he wrote another letter, this one to the Department of State in Washington. It was a straightforward announcement of his intention to leave the United States. He wanted to know what steps were necessary. The replies were discouraging. The complications were entirely too much to cope with so far as passage on the American President Lines was concerned. But Tsien learned from Seattle that if he would decide instead to go by air, using Canadian Pacific Airlines, the Seattle organization could arrange the Hong Kong transit visa for him. Accordingly, he purchased tickets on that line in mid-August.

Tsien told his superiors once again that he intended to leave toward the end of August. Once again the faculty, dismayed at the prospect of losing him, begged him to reconsider.

"The authorities of Caltech wished very much that I would remain and their idea would be that if I appealed and if I finally obtained (security) clearance, then I possibly would remain here, for one thing, and, secondly, I think it is also quite important to Caltech that they do not want to have such a thing hung in the air," Tsien recounted a few weeks later.

"For that appeal I was recommended to Colonel Francis M. Wray, asking for a hearing, and in that letter I mentioned that I wished to have this hearing arranged as early as possible, because I was planning to get out of the country toward the end of August."

Clearly, Tsien was not thinking of sneaking away. He was listening to his Caltech superiors, weighing their position, their side of the question. Because of them and his consideration for them, he would go through the motions of appealing the order which had lifted his security clearance.

Accordingly, Tsien flew to Washington on August 21, on the advice of Lee A. DuBridge, president of Caltech. The first man he went to see was Dan Kimball, the Navy Undersecretary. He laid the whole situation before Kimball. The tall, blue-eyed undersecretary drew on a long cigar and listened intently.

"They claim I'm a Communist," Tsien said.

"Tsien, I don't think you're a Communist," Kimball shot back. "I've never seen anything to make me think you had any interest in politics at all."

Tsien persisted. "They've picked up my clearance. I couldn't do many of the things I was going to do at the university. I've decided to go back to China because I'm Chinese, of course. And I don't want to build weapons to kill my countrymen. It's that simple."

The statement rocked Kimball.

"You can't leave. You're too valuable."

Tsien stood his ground. But he told Kimball the university did not want him to go.

"I agree with them that they shouldn't let you go back," Kimball told Tsien. "I think you ought to stay at Caltech."

Hadn't Caltech, Kimball wanted to know, offered him a mathematics professorship, which wouldn't require any security clearance? Tsien nodded. And then he surprised Kimball. The Chinese abruptly agreed to stay on. He agreed it would be satisfactory to remain as a mathematics professor at least while his status was being cleared up. He would not leave the country without the written permission of both Kimball and President DuBridge of Caltech.

Kimball sent Tsien to see a lawyer, Paul Porter, to whom Tsien once again outlined the story. A hearing on Tsien's clearance appeal had been scheduled for the next day, August 23, but that would be too short notice for Porter to complete necessary preliminary work. Porter sent Tsien back to Kimball on the morning of August 23 with the suggestion that the hearing be postponed. It was put off indefinitely.

Tsien had promised to stay on — but not forever. It depended upon what happened to his appeal. Perhaps he would ask Kimball and President DuBridge after that to release him from his promise, perhaps not.

"Now that I have this hearing postponed indefinitely, I can go back to California and think about the matter," Tsien told Kimball. "I will let you know about my decision."

That afternoon, Tsien boarded the plane for Los Angeles.

19

The moment Tsien left Kimball's office, the Navy Undersecretary picked up the telephone and called the Justice Department. Under no circumstances, he told the department, was Tsien to leave the United States.

"I'd rather see him shot than let him go," Kimball was known to have told friends. "He's worth three to five divisions anyplace."

Kimball, on leave to Washington from Aerojet-General, of which he had become president, knew Tsien's worth to the United States and his potential worth to a hostile power. Tsien had been probably the most important of Aerojet-General's consultants, now that the company, a brainchild of the original Suicide Squad members, had blossomed into a sprawling corporation which would have a role in virtually every U.S. rocket and space program from then on.

Alarmed at the prospects of Tsien's genius and know-how being placed at the disposal of Communist China, Kimball also worried that the Chinese might be driven by fright to slip out of the country. He appealed to the Justice Department to leave Tsien alone, to await the legal and orderly unfolding of developments.

The opposite happened. The Department of Justice put out word to the Immigration and Naturalization Service that Tsien should be watched constantly, to guard against his sudden flight from the United States. The Immigration Service arranged to have Tsien followed, which turned out to be an entirely unnecessary exercise.

Although Tsien had made inquiries about leaving, and had made preparations to send some of his property, including his papers, to China, he evidently had no intention at that moment of going back personally until given permission by Kimball. Tsien had given his word. Those who knew him well were confident that he would keep his word.

By chance, Tsien's seatmate on the way back to Los Angeles was a fellow scientist, and their conversation made the time pass swiftly. Almost before he realized it, the plane was circling over the midnight mugginess of Los Angeles. When it had taxied to a stop, Tsien rose and stretched, weary from the long flight. He bade his seat companion a pleasant good-night. The door opened and admitted a blast of steamy August night air. It also admitted Allan G. Juhl, general investigator of the U.S. Immigration and Naturalization Service.

The six-foot agent towered over the slightly built Chinese as he read in a matter of fact tone an order to Tsien not to leave the United States. The order was signed by H. R. Landon, district director of the U.S. Department of Justice, Immigration and Naturalization Service. The Justice Department had moved swiftly after hearing from Kimball. Perhaps its speed had been dictated by the word from Los Angeles on seizure of Dr. Tsien's documents.

Tsien had not known, but on the day he left for Washington, Customs had pounced on eight cases of books and documents he had intended to send to his father's Shanghai address, by way of Hong Kong. Judge Ben Harrison ordered the documents — the crates weighed eighteen hundred pounds — seized, and a swarm of federal agents, possibly a dozen or more, descended on the Los Angeles Harbor warehouse and combed through the papers.

Tsien gave up the idea of leaving the United States. The development at the Los Angeles docks, the new order not to go and his promise to Kimball made it useless even to think about going. Tsien cancelled his plane reservations.

The day after his return from Washington, he went to an Altadena bank with his wife. From Yin's account and her safety deposit box they withdrew two hundred dollars, about four thousand dollars' worth of war bonds and Yin's jewelry. As Tsien explained:

"On the twenty-fourth I was still thinking — in fact, we were thinking — that possibly my wife and the children would travel to China. So on the twenty-fourth, the decision in the family was that I certainly would remain in this country because I have this order, but Mrs. Tsien and the children would go to Hong Kong."

The Tsiens' second child, Jung-jen — they nicknamed her Mamie — was only a month old at the time. The boy, Yucon, like Mamie a native-born American, was just past two. Once again, the political naïveté of Dr. Tsien was evident. Should the Communists have gotten hold of his family, they would have had him, too.

Dr. DuBridge called Tsien to his office to inquire about the results of the expedition to Washington. Tsien reported to him not only what had happened in Washington, but the midnight incident of the no-can-go order on the plane at Los Angeles Airport. He told Dr. DuBridge he would stay in the United States, but that Mrs. Tsien and the children might still go to China without him. Dr. DuBridge expressed regret that the Tsien family might be thus separated. And a few days later, Tsien changed his mind. The family would stay together.

The cases of documents, meanwhile, had caused a sensation, and nourished the growing American anti-Communist hysteria which had grown swiftly since the outbreak of the war in Korea. "Secret Data Seized in China Shipment," cried one headline. The Government, declared its inspectors, found code and signal books, photographs and sketches, negatives and blueprints, notes and writings and a wealth of technical data on rocketry and allied research. It turned out later that some of the codebooks were logarithm tables.

Before he had given his word to Kimball to stay in the United States, a disillusioned Tsien had been making preparations to leave. He had prepared this shipment of his papers — notes from lectures, books, various other documents, some still bearing the stamps of "confidential" and "secret." He called in the Bekins Van and Storage Company of Pasadena to do the packing. By chance, this was the same firm which had been called for a similar assignment by Dr. Chao Chung-yao, the nuclear physicist at Caltech, who also had decided that America of the McCarthy era was no place for a talented Chinese.

The firm's agent had told Tsien these was nothing to worry about so far as Customs was concerned. The agency would handle everything. It would take care of placing the shipment aboard the S.S. *President Wilson* and send him the bill. Tsien at that time was still hoping to sail on the *Wilson*. Tsien signed copies of declarations for the agency to process.

The agency's man mentioned nothing about the possibility that Tsien would need clearance from the Commerce or State Departments where technical data was involved, but the scientist insisted.

"I also knew," said Tsien, "that Dr. Chao, who was at Caltech then, wanted to take out something at that time, mainly some instruments for experiments in physics, and that he evidently had some difficulty."

Tsien reminded the agency of this, but the agency man responded, "You don't have to worry about it at all, because this is of an entirely different character." Tsien said he was under the impression it was all just a routine matter. The agency man had not seen the material in advance, but the books and documents still were uncrated and open to his inspection. Tsien said he had extracted any material he thought might still be classified and not yet outdated, and had locked it in a cabinet, thereafter turning over the key to Dr. Clark Millikan of Caltech. The materials he intended to send out of the country were "related to the field of my profession, and it was natural that if I was going to carry on in my profession, I needed these materials." He had in mind that once back in China, he would become a teacher.

Tsien insisted all along that the papers were declassified, in effect, and outdated. Time would prove him right. Most of the documents were destined to be returned to him except for a few judged to be the property of the U.S. Navy and the National Advisory Committee for Aeronautics.

Questioned about the documents, Tsien averred that any information possibly of any significance to the defense or military posture of the United States, "by honor I would not give to a second employer."

But from the time he returned from Washington, from the time his documents were seized, Tsien became a marked man.

20

If Tsien's shadows did not want him to know he was under constant surveillance, they did a poor job of it. The scientist was fully aware of their presence. From the window of his Altadena home he could look down the walk, past his spacious lawn and beyond the rail fence, and see a figure seated in a dark sedan, watching the house on Buena Loma Court. The man in the car, half hidden behind the limp eucalyptus trees, seldom moved, his eyes fastened on the house. Slowly and inexorably Tsien's world was falling to pieces around him. He read daily in the newspapers the progress of the trial of his friend, Dr. Weinbaum. They had asked him to testify against his friend. He had refused.

Other friends of Dr. Weinbaum on the Caltech campus had begun a campaign to collect funds for his defense. Heading the drive, complained U.S. Attorney Ernest Tolin, was Dr. Linus Pauling, chairman of the school's chemistry department. The Government charged that Weinbaum, who had been employed on secret atomic research at Caltech, had perjured himself by swearing to the army review board that he was not and had not been a Communist.

Dr. Weinbaum insisted over and over that he had not been a member of the party and had signed no document linking him to it. Before Federal Judge Ben Harrison, the same judge who ordered the seizure of Tsien's documents, the prosecution charged that Weinbaum, using the party name of Sidney Empson, was in fact a recruiter for the Communists, especially among Caltech students. Caltech was as shocked by the charges against Weinbaum as it had been in the case of the charges against Tsien.

"We (at Caltech) had no information casting doubt on the loyalty of Dr. Weinbaum," the newspapers quoted President Du-Bridge. "We always try to assure ourselves of the loyalty of all faculty members."

Tsien read the testimony of others. There was Dr. Frank Oppenheimer, now admitting under questioning that he had been a Communist party member from 1937 to 1939 and that gatherings at his home in that period had in reality been meetings of Unit 122. Dr. Oppenheimer could not, however, recall whether Weinbaum had been at any sessions which had been party meetings. Nor could Dr. Oppenheimer testify, to his knowledge, that Weinbaum was, in fact, a Communist.

Tsien read about the trial and was all the more certain his own turn would be coming soon. He began to take for granted the surveillance at his home, knowing that at some hour, someday soon, a figure would emerge from the car in front of his house, come up the walk and take him away from his wife and his two small children.

As the Weinbaum trial dragged on, Tsien kept more and more to himself. Over a period of several days he failed to show up at all at the Jet Propulsion Laboratory. The agents assigned to tail him failed to catch even a glimpse of the scientist. Perhaps they got panicky, wondering whether Tsien had disappeared and was on his way, somehow, back to China.

The agents wired Washington for advice and standby orders to arrest Tsien. They had, in reality, no cause for fright. Tsien was not intending to slip away. He simply had decided to work at home, as he often did, with the complete absorption of which he was capable, even though he was aware that a new blow might fall at any moment.

On September 6, the suspense ended. A late afternoon sun tinged with gold the dark redwood clapboards of the Tsien home as a new sedan pulled up. Two figures emerged. Tsien, looking out his window, recognized one of the men immediately. It was the man who had met him on the plane that midnight two weeks before and served him with an order not to leave the country. The big man now rapped on the door. Tsien's wife, her delicate round face taut with anxiety, went to the door, carrying her infant daughter Mamie in her arms.

Agent Allan G. Juhl, a snub-nosed revolver cradled in a holster hidden under his business suit, a pair of handcuffs dangling from his belt, politely introduced himself and his companion, Bill Kaiser, a fellow investigator for the Immigration and Naturalization Service.

"I remember that day vividly," Juhl would recall years later. "Mrs. Tsien had the baby girl in her arms when she came to the door. I asked for her husband, and he soon appeared. It was curious. There was no sign of emotion. But there was a hint of recognition on his face. It was almost as if he were saying to himself, 'Well, it's finally over.'"

Juhl, in his deliberate style, read the warrant of arrest. The Department of Justice had decided that Tsien Hsue-shen was "an alien who was a member of an organization, association, society or group that advises, advocates or teaches the overthrow by force or violence of the Government of the United States."

Dr. Tsien listened in silence, his face a mask. Then he excused himself, disappeared beyond the foyer and then reappeared with a shaving kit, three books and a portfolio of papers. He kissed his wife and children good-bye and stepped out into the sunlight, dwarfed between the two six-foot Americans. The agents waited until they reached the car to search their prisoner, out of a compassionate feeling for Mrs. Tsien. Finding him unarmed and harmless, they put him into the back seat of their sedan for the long drive southward through Los Angeles.

"Tsien was exceedingly docile," Juhl has recalled of that day.

"But he never volunteered any information. A very reticent person. He didn't speak unless he was spoken to. He answered all the questions in just as few words as he could, extremely politely."

It had been close to five in the afternoon when the two agents took Tsien from his home into custody. The last rays of sunlight were bouncing off the fish canneries and across the sails of fishing fleets as the sedan cruised across the bridge to San Pedro, past weather-beaten shacks and oil storage tanks, then along the waterfront where cranes swung cargo aboard seagoing vessels.

Tsien remained stoically silent for the better part of the ride. The sedan glided past the guards standing watch by wire gates. The black car came to a halt behind the buff-colored Immigration and Naturalization Service headquarters. The party disembarked, entered the building and went up to the third floor, the detention headquarters.

They locked Tsien in a cell. As the doors closed behind him, the scientist could look past the bars southward toward the Federal Prison. Beyond it, the sunset reddened Long Beach Harbor. Tsien wondered about his old friends. His mind dwelt on the past, on the old days on Caltech's campus, on the gatherings, then so innocent-appearing and now haunting him. He wondered what had become of Weinbaum in his ordeal in Federal Court. He could not have known it at the time, but the day after Tsien was arrested, his friend Weinbaum was convicted on perjury charges by a jury in Judge Harrison's court. Tsien's detention was a week old when Judge Harrison sentenced Weinbaum to four years in prison. The court refused bail for Weinbaum because the scientist once had access to secret information in the Jet Propulsion Laboratory, and "might know things that would be of benefit to those who seek to destroy us."

Dr. Weinbaum's wife, Lena, and his twenty-year-old daughter, Selina, rushed through the crowd about him and kissed him before deputy marshals led him away to the county jail to await transfer to a penal institution to be selected by the U.S. Attorney General. Weinbaum's attorney, Ben Margolis, seeking bail pending an appeal to the Circuit Court of Appeals, had argued that his client was a victim of the current anti-Communist hysteria and an atmosphere of witch-hunting. Time after time, Weinbaum had denied with an emphatic "No" that he ever had been a party member or that he ever had used any party name. Margolis, in his final appeal to the jury, contended that the government's case should have been labeled "Operation Get Weinbaum." The prosecution, he insisted, had threatened to "get the jobs" of innocent persons who might refuse to testify against Weinbaum.

Only once in the long and dreary proceedings had Weinbaum lost his calm. In final arguments, U.S. Attorney Ernest A. Tolin recalled a letter telling of Dr. Weinbaum's claim that his father in Russia was a counterrevolutionary who had been slain by the Communists. Tolin told the jury it would have been better to have had the writer of that letter take the stand and testify on the subject. Weinbaum leaped to his feet, his fists clenched.

"I don't lie about my father," he shouted.

Judge Harrison pounded his gavel and glared at the defendant. Weinbaum sank back momentarily into his seat but then was on his feet once again protesting. The bailiff ordered him to remain silent.

But now, at last, Weinbaum's public agony was over. And over, too, was another brilliant scientific career. Now it would be the turn of Weinbaum's close friend, the Chinese who had been so lavishly praised and decorated for his wartime service to the United States, who had astonished and fascinated erudite audiences of scientists with his visions of the future.

For Tsien, the days in detention were misery. Most of his cellmates were Mexican wetbacks, swarthy, nameless transgressors caught in the U.S. Immigration Service dragnet, now chattering together in unintelligible Mexican-Spanish. He lived in virtual isolation at the San Pedro Detention Center. Never before had he felt such loneliness, such confusion, such frustration. He scarcely touched the meals served from the Detention Center mess, scorning the food as inedible. Tsien always had liked good food. He liked planned and varied meals, and he often had said he had found too much sameness in American food. He even liked at times to fuss about the kitchen, experimenting in the Chinese way, varying ingredients to change the character or flavor of a dish. Now he found the sameness of the meals appalling. He preferred often to remain hungry, waiting to eat well only on the days that Yin could come with Chinese dishes she had prepared at home.

The monotony was broken only by visits from his wife, his acquaintances from Caltech, his attorney and his interrogators. On Saturday afternoon, nine days after his arrest, he received a visit from his attorney, the square-jawed, tough-talking Grant Cooper; his friend and administrative superior Dr. Frederick Lindvall; and Dr. DuBridge, Caltech's president. They all tried to explore, as Dr. DuBridge put it in a letter to Navy Undersecretary Kimball, "some of the puzzling elements of this case, which seems to have given rise to some suspicion of his (Tsien's) integrity, at least in the minds of the Department of Justice." DuBridge wrote Kimball:

I can dismiss their inquiries about his Communist associations, for I think that there is very little evidence, if any, which has been brought to our attention indicating his membership in the party. His friendship with those who are known to be members of the party is well known and easily explainable, but I am convinced that his associations with these people were not on political grounds, and that he never knowingly participated in any Communist gatherings.

The arrangements which he made in regard to going to China involve, of course, a long and complex history which we reviewed in detail with him. It appears to us that the steps he took were perfectly logical, understandable and open. He attempted to make reservations on the boat, leaving Los Angeles at the end of August, though he was later told that these reservations could not be confirmed. He wrote the

State Department asking advice as to how he might get clearance to leave, and the State Department office which has to do with personnel exchange advised him on the possibility of being included with a student quota returning to China.

He explained in this letter to the State Department his intentions and desire to leave, requesting help in securing necessary assistance. Later, when the possibility of his going under a student quota on the boat appeared small, he arranged through the Canadian Pacific Airways to secure air transportation via Vancouver, British Columbia, to Hong Kong. A travel agency, subsidiary to the Canadian Pacific Airways, assisted him in getting all the clearance for transportation via this route and necessary visas for transit through British territory in Canada and Hong Kong. To the best of my knowledge he never denied making these arrangements. On the contrary, he made them openly and informed us here at the Institute of his plans. I understand he also informed you and Mr. Porter of them at the time he was in Washington in late August.

Finally and most important, Dr. Tsien assured us that he no longer had any intention whatsoever of trying to leave the United States, and I have in my possession now, from him, a letter in his own handwriting which he willingly wrote and signed on last Saturday morning, dated September 16, 1950, which reads as follows:

"I, Hsue Shen Tsien, hereby promise and swear to you, Dr. Lee A. DuBridge, and to you, Mr. Dan Kimball, that I will not leave nor attempt to leave the United States without first obtaining permission in writing from you and each of you.

"Signed,
"Hsue Shen Tsien
"Witnessed the date above written:
"Grant B. Cooper
"Frederick C. Lindvall."

I am personally confident that he means this pledge sincerely and I am confident that he would, under no circumstances, break it or attempt to break it. If you have equal confidence in him, possibly a call from you to . . . the Department of Justice . . . might result in an order for Dr. Tsien's release. We would all certainly appreciate anything you feel you can do.

Kimball would have his hands full to do anything at all. Disaster was raining on the scientists in California. The security clearances of Dr. Frank J. Malina, Dr. Martin Summerfield, and a number of others of Tsien's student-day contemporaries already had been picked up.

"Because they were young and liberals, it was assumed they were Communists," Kimball said later, recalling the times. "Well, I didn't believe they were, and still don't. Martin Summerfield had his clearance lifted for a couple of years and he got it reinstated. Frank Malina — the same thing with him."

Malina and others had been special targets of the House Un-American Activities Committee, but Tsien had lost touch with his old friend and had not heard from him for two years. In the interim, Malina had gone to Paris and forsaken his pursuit of aeronautical science. The man who, perhaps as much as any other had helped prepare America for its assault on outer space, lived as an expatriate and worked for UNESCO — the United Nations Economic, Social and Cultural Organization — in France. There he indulged his passion for art. He originated a mobile art form, with sound, which reflected his awe of the interplay of light, shadow and motion. He kept a link with his past only as an officer of an international association of aeronautical scientists.

Kimball took an active interest in Tsien's trouble. He went to Los Angeles to confer with Grant Cooper, who had been brought into the case as Tsien's defense attorney by Caltech's legal advisers. Kimball proposed that Tsien be released from custody, but evidently the Justice Department was determined to brand Tsien, once and for all, as a deportable Communist.

Cooper called on Tsien at the Detention Center, and was blunt with his client. He told Tsien right off that if he ever had been a Communist to say so. It would make a difference in how the case was handled. Tsien replied calmly: he had never, to his knowledge, been a member of the Communist party. He agreed to make such a statement under oath, knowing full well the penalty for perjury.

At Cooper's suggestion, an unofficial preliminary interview with Tsien was arranged with an array of military and government representatives on hand, "for the purpose," as he put it, "of ascertaining the truth."

Two high officers from the Army Materiel Corps, an officer of the U.S. Navy's zonal intelligence office in Los Angeles, an assistant U.S. attorney, two U.S. Customs officials, and two representatives of the U.S. Immigration and Naturalization Service were all on hand to question and listen. Among them was Albert Del Guercio, of the Immigration and Naturalization Service, who was the prospective examining officer in the proceedings against Tsien.

Cooper had been seeking Tsien's release on bail. The decision rested with the U.S. Attorney's office, and thus Cooper hoped to enlighten that office with the unofficial interview. Max F. Deutz, the easygoing, unflappable assistant U.S. attorney, was prepared not only to listen but to have a stenographic record made of the interview. Dr. Tsien had volunteered to answer questions put to him by any of the party. It was understood that the talk was informal and would have no official weight.

Attorney Cooper began the questioning, taking Tsien back through the years to the time when he first landed in the United States on a scholarship to the Massachusetts Institute of Technology. Tsien recalled his trip back to China in 1947, his marriage with Yin Tsiang, his return by way of Honolulu, his Declaration of Intention to become a U.S. citizen.

"Were you a member of Professional Unit 122 at Caltech, of the Communist party or any organization having for its object the overthrow of the United States Government?" Cooper asked.

"I was not a member of any of the organizations mentioned," Tsien replied evenly.

"Did you know Dr. Weinbaum during the years from 1937 on?"

"Yes. I know Malina. And Dr. Dubnoff. I know many people. But I am only going to mention the names which possibly have meaning."

"Did you visit frequently at the home of Dr. Weinbaum?"

"I ought to say this: that I know Dr. Malina very much better. In fact, that was because of our common interest in the fields of study and research. And it is through Dr. Malina that I was introduced. He was in my own department while the other men were not in my department. Dr. Weinbaum is in the Department of Chemistry and Dr. Dubnoff is in the Department of Biology, and Dr. Malina introduced me to these men and their families."

"Did you from time to time visit in their respective homes?"

"Yes. I got to know them — not immediately — I do not recall exactly what ones in what year, but I got to know them very well for their interest in music and their general interest in anything Oriental and Chinese."

"At that time, in conversation which you had with these people, did they speak with feeling and sympathy about the plight of China at that time?"

"Yes, they were quite so, and that is one aspect which attracted me to them. You will recall that is when the time of the Sino-Japanese war started, and certainly as a man of China I am very glad to hear any sympathy people have for China."

Tsien explained how he often dropped in uninvited on the Weinbaums, because he had gotten to know them so well. Sometimes, he said, they would be alone, sometimes others would be there. Sometimes Malina and Dubnoff would be there, he went on. Tsien would drop in about once a week, usually on Wednesday because his schedule then gave him more leisure that night. Never, he said, had he suspected he might be attending Communist meetings.

"As you look back," Cooper asked, "now with your present suspicions, would you say they might have been Communists?"

"The answer is yes," Tsien replied. "I certainly would suspect that they would be because of certain knowledge I have now from the newspapers."

"That is particularly, I take it, you have reference to the Weinbaum trial?"

"Yes."

But Tsien continued to insist he never intentionally took part in a Communist meeting.

"Did you ever have any knowledge, directly or indirectly, that your name was on their membership roll as a member?" Cooper demanded.

"I did not."

"Did you ever have a membership card in any Communist unit or organization?"

"Not to my knowledge."

"Did you ever sign one?"

"No."

"Did you ever have one in your possession?"

"No."

"Did you ever see one with your name on it?"

"No."

"Did you ever join a Communist organization or did you have a card under a fictitious name?"

"No."

Cooper brought Tsien back to the day the FBI called on him.

Tsien said, "During these talks with the agents of the FBI, they told me of the situation, that they know of me at that time, that it was very likely I would not be cleared for classified work."

What was the effect of that?

Tsien began to talk now in great mouthfuls of sentences. The words poured out in a torrent, and sounded as if he were translating in his mind, although under normal circumstances his English would sound perfect.

"It had a rather drastic effect," he replied, "because of this, that I have been receiving letters from my father and because an elderly gentleman like him has always wished that I go back to China and his poor health was known to me for some time, but I just went along on my work, because I was so busy, and when you are always plugging along in your work you seldom give your personal situation much of a review or think of it, but it was quite a shock to me that I might not be cleared for the classified work and to my mind that brought me to think of my personal problems, and at that time I thought about whether to stay in this country or plan a trip back to China. I was further disturbed when looking at this situation about the possibility that there would be an open hostility between the United States and whatever government is in the mainland of China. In other words, the mainland was practically controlled by the Communist regime."

Tsien returned to the theme again, as if it was much on his mind.

"The coming operation of my father and also the possibility of this hostility between the United States and the Communist China, and since my father is in China under Communist China, then if such a hostility took place, then I would have no means of sending money over to my father, who is completely dependent upon me and supported by me, and I was very much disturbed about this possibility, so my wish would be this, that some settlement could be made so that these difficulties of supporting my father would be removed or at least made fairly secure and if something very serious would happen, these questions would be settled, and I actually informed Professor Watson that it is my wish that finally I would be able to come back to this country and continue my work here, but of course I made very clear to him that Caltech would not expect of me a definite date when I would be back."

Tsien told of his trip to Washington to see the Navy Undersecretary.

Cooper then put in:

"Mr. Dan Kimball, the Undersecretary of the Navy, was in my office on Friday of last week. He had come to my office at the suggestion of the authorities at Caltech. He made this statement to me: 'Hell, Tsien is no Communist. He is not going to leave this country.' In brief, he telephoned the United States Attorney and informed him of that fact. He informed the United States Attorney that if Tsien gave him his word that he would stay here, that would suffice for him."

Cooper relayed Kimball's suspicion that Tsien had been put under pressure, through his father, by the Chinese Communists.

When Kimball told the Department of Justice Tsien should not under any circumstances leave the United States, he had not meant that Tsien should be locked up, Cooper related. He wanted Tsien released from custody.

Tsien was released on fifteen thousand dollars bail and allowed to return to his wife and children. But his ordeal was just beginning.

21

Dr. Tsien went home to wait, and to wonder what was happening to him. He was bitter. Two weeks looking out of his cell at fish canneries and oil storage tanks had strengthened his feeling that the United States no longer was any place for him or his wife and children. He was confused. He wanted to talk to somebody — and

Tsien was not by nature a talker — somebody among his colleagues who might understand and sympathize with his position.

William Zisch, then vice-president of Aerojet-General, had a personal affection for Tsien, regarding him, as Zisch put it, as "by far the most effective and valued consultant in the whole stable of consultants" the company had.

Zisch knew Tsien as a sensitive man, a quiet man and much a loner — a man nobody really knew. Many who had met him on social occasions, particularly the ladies, were puzzled by him. He tended to be blunt when he disagreed, and he was uncommunicative about his private affairs.

It was Tsien's sudden change of character which made one night memorable for Zisch. The Aerojet official, learning of the scientist's release, telephoned his home in Altadena. Tsien's normal schedule would have brought him to the Aerojet plant in a few days, and the company still had no official notification that he would not have the privilege of access to classified material.

Zisch intended, to save Tsien embarrassment, to go and talk with him briefly about that problem, and perhaps to suggest diplomatically that there was no need for him to appear at the plant. Tsien invited Zisch to his house, and the company official drove to Altadena, expecting to stay perhaps only a matter of minutes.

He was struck by the pathos of the scene as he entered the ordinarily neat and tidy home. Furniture was pushed aside, rugs were rolled up against the wall, and the floors echoed hollowly to the sound of footsteps. It was the home of a family which was about to move out. Perhaps the Tsiens had expected the word soon.

Tsien appeared calm, but it was obvious to anyone who knew him that he had been badly hurt and was still stunned by what had happened. Tsien conducted his visitor to the breakfast room, and then decided to move into the sitting room, despite its rolled rugs and disarray of furniture. It was close to six o'clock when the two men began talking.

The words came in a torrent from the Chinese scientist. It was as if, suddenly, in spite of himself, he wanted to pour out the whole story to somebody — anybody. He wanted, he told Zisch, to go back to the Orient, but he did not want to go to Red China.

"Tsien gave me the impression," Zisch remembered, "that he was going to cause his father to join him in Hong Kong, and he would then spend the remaining years with his father there."

Tsien talked on and on, and the two men were so absorbed that they failed to notice that darkness had fallen. He talked with passionate earnestness about Dr. Theodore von Kármán, as if he truly loved the old scientist and all that his genius represented. He had wanted to stay on and continue working with his beloved mentor. His real wish, he said, had been to remain close to the old man in his waning years and to carry on the things that von Kármán was interested in. Tsien recalled that he had made a decision long before to devote both himself and his career to the old scientist. He looked upon von Kármán as his intellectual father.

He went on and on about von Kármán. With the first visit from the FBI, Tsien had suddenly realized that he might be forced to give up his life's work. It was then, he said, that he felt he ought to go home.

He talked about the agents who had knocked on his door and who had told him they knew he was a Communist because they had a copy of a card.

"This was not true," Tsien insisted. Zisch had not asked him if it had been true. Tsien volunteered the denial.

One thing which bothered the Chinese deeply had been the agents' questions about his friendship with Frank Malina. Tsien counted Malina as one of his warmest and closest friends. And they were trying to condemn Tsien because of his friendship with his fellow scientist because they suspected Malina was a Communist. To Tsien, it didn't seem to make much sense.

Then he talked of China. "China will always be China," he was sure. "I don't care what happens — communism or call it what you will. China will always be Chinese. There is no way that a country such as Russia or any other system would overtake the Chinese." His words were prophetic, at a time when Americans were, for the most part, certain that China could be nothing, under communism, but another satellite of Moscow.

The minutes sped by into hours — one, two, three and four of them — as Tsien talked on and on. It was a long while before Zisch remembered to snap on the light and expose once again the scattered furniture, the rolled up rugs, the lamps pushed aside into corners.

"I left that evening," said Zisch, looking back on the time, "with the feeling of being distressed because I felt he wasn't adequately communicating with appropriate individuals and that the situation had developed in such a fashion that he felt put upon.

"There was no way, really, to persuade him that fair play would prevail in the end. . . . for some period of time after this, I proclaimed to my associates that there was nothing about the question of communism that was attractive to Tsien on the basis of his own volunteered statements to me, and I believed him.

"From his aspect, it looked like very heavy-handed treatment that he was receiving, because here was a fellow who was proceeding as a highly respected technical man in aerospace sciences, doing a constructive job for our country — as best as my friends and I could observe — making an original contribution."

The contribution, indeed, had been substantial. For example, said Zisch, "the whole concept of Dynasoar is a concept of his. . . ." The Dynasoar concept involved plans for a spacecraft, a manned orbiting device which would move in and out of the atmosphere, skipping around the world almost like an aerial porpoise. The idea combined aerodynamics and space research.

What about those books and papers Tsien had crated to send to Red China via Hong Kong? Evidently, that had been the result of Tsien's first shock at being accused and having his security clearance lifted.

"At the time," Zisch recalled, "Clark Millikan, who was the director of the Guggenheim Aeronautics Laboratory at Caltech, had come out publicly, was quoted in the press, as saying that these documents that Tsien was taking were not of a classified nature at this time, and he was very strong in his support of Tsien in the press.

"It later turned out that these books were his own and he did not violate any security regulations, but of course that expression was printed in the back pages of the newspapers, and my mother-in-law to this day still believes he was escaping with the crown jewels."

22

"What is your name?"

"Hsue Shen Tsien."

"Do you speak and understand the English language?"

"Yes, I do."

"Will you please stand and raise your right hand. Do you solemnly swear that the testimony which you are about to give in this proceeding will be the truth, the whole truth and nothing but the truth, so help you God?"

"I do."

The power and majesty of the United States confronted Dr. Tsien in a grubby little room ten by twenty feet, in a downtown Los Angeles building. The aseptic pale green walls seemed to close in on the occupants. Although it was November 15, they perspired in the heat. There was no air conditioning. Raising the windows would only admit the discordant clamor of truck traffic and clatter of street cars rolling by along the boulevard just one floor below. Venetian blinds were lowered to shade the sunlight's assault on the chocolate brown linoleum floor.

The men arrayed against Tsien were led by Albert Del Guercio, examining officer for the Immigration and Naturalization Service of the Department of Justice, a vigorous and relentless prosecuting attorney who had been one of the original anti-subversive investigators for the service in the 1920s. Presiding was Roy Waddell, the hearing officer. Stenographer Mary Clinton was poised and ready for a long and arduous job. A scattering of spectators and newspaper reporters waited, bored, for the rituals to be finished.

Appearing for Tsien in his defense was Grant B. Cooper, who had won esteem in numberless trials, including several sensational murder cases.

Hearing Officer Waddell continued with the rites:

"You are charged in this proceeding with being in the United States in violation of immigration law, in that you entered this country at Honolulu, Territory of Hawaii, on September 27, 1947, and that you appear to be subject to the Act of October 16, 1918, as amended, in that you are found to have been, prior to entry, a member of the following class set forth in Section I of the Act of October 16, 1918, an alien who is a member of an organization, association, society or group that advises, advocates or teaches the overthrow by force or violence of the Government of the United States. Do you fully understand the nature of that charge?"

"I do." Tsien blinked as he remembered, entering the United States that September three years before, newly married to Yin, reading the routine questionnaire of the Immigration Service and automatically answering "no" to a question whether he was ever a member of the Communist party.

The hearing officer turned the proceeding over to Examining Officer Del Guercio, who promptly lodged an additional charge against Tsien based on the Subversive Activities Control Act of

1950. It made Tsien subject to being taken into custody and deported.

Once again, Tsien was asked his name, and he spelled it out. He testified to his birth in Shanghai on September 2, 1909. He testified to his original arrival in the United States fifteen years before on a scholarship of fifteen hundred dollars a year, furnished by the United States from the Boxer Rebellion Indemnity Fund. He testified to his transfer to Caltech and to the presence there at the time of about fifteen other Chinese students. He assured the examining officer there was no other H. S. Tsien. Then Del Guercio got down to the business at hand.

"While you were at the California Institute of Technology and particularly during the years 1938 and 1939, did you ever use the name of John M. Deckard?"

"I did not," Tsien answered.

"E-r-d?"

"I did not."

"Decker?"

"I did not."

"While you were attending the university — the California Institute of Technology — in 1938 and 1939, did you join the Communist party of the United States?"

"I did not."

"While you were attending that institute, did you attend any meetings of the Communist party?"

Cooper objected. He would not object, he said, if it was phrased "knowingly attend." He was overruled, for the first time. He would in the course of the hearings object two hundred times, and almost every time be overruled by Hearing Officer Roy Waddell. Tsien was directed to answer.

"I did not attend meetings of the Communist party to my knowledge."

Now came the questions about Tsien's friends.

"Do you know a Sidney Weinbaum?"

"I do."

"You knew him in 1938?"

"Yes, I did."

"And you knew him in 1939?"

"Yes."

"Is he the Sidney Weinbaum who was recently convicted in the United States District Court for perjury?"

"Yes."

"Do you know Jon Dubnoff and his wife, Belle Dubnoff?"

"Yes, I do."

"Do you know a Frank Oppenheimer?"

"There I have to be specific. When I say 'no,' I mean not as friends. Frank Oppenheimer — I don't know him as a friend. . . . I only saw Frank Oppenheimer on the campus of California Institute."

Del Guercio went down a list of names. Some Tsien knew, some he did not. He identified Frank Malina as a particular friend, "very much so."

"Would you say that Frank J. Malina was one of your best friends in this country?"

"That is correct."

Tsien had not, by that time, heard from Malina for two years. His old friend was an expatriate in Paris.

"Do you know Frank J. Malina as an admitted member of the Communist party of the United States?"

"I do not know."

"Did he ever tell you he was a member of the Communist party?"

"He did not."

"You remember, did he testify before the Un-American Activities Committee . . . ?"

Cooper interrupted. He would have an objection when the question was completed. But Del Guercio did not complete the question. Instead, he went back to ask again if Malina had ever told Tsien about being a member of the party.

"He had not admitted it or told me so," Tsien replied.

Then more names from the past . . . "Mr. Tsien," Del Guercio shot out, bearing down now, "during the latter part of 1938 and 1939, did you or did you not attend meetings with all or some of the persons that I have mentioned?"

Cooper objected that Del Guercio had not specified what kind of meetings. The examining officer withdrew and rephrased the question.

"In answer to my question if you had ever attended meetings of the Communist party in 1938 and 1939, you replied that you had not. Is that correct?"

That was not Tsien's answer, Cooper protested. "He said he never attended them to his knowledge."

"Now," said Del Guercio to Tsien, "will you explain that answer?"

"Yes, I will." And Tsien explained once again how he went to "gatherings" but did not know they were Communist party-organized.

Del Guercio pounded away some more at the theme of "meetings." Then he wanted to know if communism was discussed.

"I do not recall that communism as a principle or philosophy was discussed as such in the meetings. The inferences of communism I am quite sure were discussed — mentioned . . . as a force in the political scene of the world."

"Were they favorable to communism . . . these discussions?"

Tsien replied, "Nobody would agree; the young students — they always argued. I don't believe in any of these discussions there was a uniform, unanimous opinion. There was always somebody against something, and that's my recollection. . . ."

Tsien could recall only three homes at which he attended gatherings — those of Malina, Weinbaum and Dubnoff. It was possible there were others. "When I took Sidney Weinbaum to a certain place, naturally — if the host saw me there and asked me in for to stay for a while, sometimes I was busy, I refused — sometimes I did, but these homes I do not know — I could not recall the names."

Del Guercio sparred with Tsien and his counsel for a while, recalling the "don't leave" order at Los Angeles Airport, questioning Tsien about his top secret work at the Jet Propulsion Laboratory, and getting on to the books and papers Tsien had crated to send out of the country and the seizure of the crates by the United States.

"What was your purpose in going to China?"

"My purpose in going to China was to straighten out family affairs, mainly in connection with my father and my adopted sister."

"And you intended to remain there, did you not?"

"That is not my intention, but practically I may have to be there for quite some time."

Now came the crux of Del Guercio's case.

"To whom do you owe allegiance?"

"I owe allegiance to the people of China."

"And who are the people of China?"

"Four hundred fifty millions of them."

"Four hundred fifty millions living there under Communist China?"

"Some of them are."

"Do you feel that you owe allegiance to the Nationalist Government of China?"

"If they are the controlling — if they are doing work for the good of the people — then I owe allegiance to them."

"Are they?"

"That is — we have yet to see."

"You are not certain in your mind that they are?"

"They have previously not been doing very good work."

"Well, is the present government of Communist China doing good work for the people of China?"

"I have no information."

"You have no information, but you were going there?"

"Well, if I stay there I am going to find out."

"What did you intend to do with all that material that you

were taking out with you — the literature on aeronautics and jet propulsion?"

"That is part of my knowledge and it belongs to me."

"What were you going to do with it?"

"That is going to remain in my mind."

"Were you going to make it available to China — to Communist China?"

"That is my property. I have the right whether I going to give it to somebody else, like selling my ability to anybody."

More sparring, and Cooper reminded Del Guercio that Tsien had filed a U.S. citizenship application, indicating that if it had gone through he would owe allegiance to the United States. Del Guercio once again dipped back into the past, to Tsien's trip back to China in 1947, to his marriage to Yin and the birth of his two children in the United States. Then he came back to the key matter of allegiance.

"Let me ask this question. You are a permanent resident of this country, are you not?"

"Yes."

"And as such, you are subject to the provisions of the Selective Service Act?"

"Yes."

"In the event of a conflict between this country and Red China, would you fight against Red China for the United States?"

Cooper objected and was overruled.

Calmly now, Tsien said, "I am not able to answer this question because the situation has not arisen as described by the charge."

"The situation has not what?" snapped Del Guercio.

"The situation has not realized. In other words, the United States now is not declaring a war against Communist China, and that would require a lot of thinking about the problem."

"But you are not in a position at this time to state whether or not you would fight for the United States against Red China in the event of war?"

"I have not considered that question."

114

Cooper rose to protest, but the examining officer said he would give Tsien every opportunity — "all the time you want to answer it."

Protested Cooper, "You can't make up your mind in five minutes. If you want to let him think about it some more, give him time. If you want to let him think about it, we can wait here six months."

"We will wait here six months," Del Guercio retorted.

Cooper asked Tsien if he could make up his mind in the next fifteen minutes. Tsien thought he could. Cooper told him to think about it.

Five minutes ticked by slowly. Tsien sat and reflected. Then Tsien looked at his interrogator with a wispy smile and said, "I can't answer the question now."

"You can't or won't answer the question now," Del Guercio demanded.

Tsien was stung. His face clouded with anger.

"I can — c-a-n — answer the question now," he snapped, "and the answer is as follows: I have already said that my essential allegiance is to the people of China, and if the war between the United States and Communist China is for the good of the people of China, which I think is very likely to be, so then I will fight on the side of the United States — no question about that."

"But you will make the decision first? You will determine whether it is for the good of the Chinese people?"

"That decision, yes, I would make."

"You will not permit the Government of the United States to make that decision for you?"

"No, certainly not."

Del Guercio veered to Korea. He asked Tsien if he would be willing to fight there for the United States. Cooper objected that it was beside the point at issue, and was overruled. But Tsien seemed eager to answer.

"Well," the Chinese responded, "in fact, I have already given the answer some time ago in answer to the question — regarding a question I think often asked about whether I am willing to bear arms for the United States. The answer is 'yes' as blanket answer, and my answer about the Chinese question, since it is a very specific one I only consider it in all its aspects and details, and answer so, but if the answer you wish to have in general, then the answer is 'yes.' "

"Let me ask this question. Would you make available to the United States the knowledge that you acquired in this country?"

"I have already made available to the United States."

"Let me ask the question . . . further make available your knowledge on aeronautics and on jet propulsion for the use of the United States against China?"

"The answer to that question is the same as the answer to the question about bearing arms against Red China."

23

William F. Hynes — the "Red" Hynes of the Red Squad — stepped out of the past and into the limelight. The situation had all the elements of drama necessary for lurid headlines: a foreign scientist, national of a country now under communism, top secrets, defense work, undercover espionage by the police, secret papers.

Hynes, his sandy hair now darkened and streaked with gray, still very much the professional policeman though now retired for seven years, was gazing for the first time upon the man whose life he had so profoundly affected. Now he was appearing as a Government witness against Dr. Tsien. Del Guercio questioned him.

"Have you ever been a member of the Communist party of the United States or any of its predecessors?"

"Yes, sir, I have," Hynes answered evenly.

"During what years?"

"During the year 1922 and for a period of about eight months in 1922 when it was known as the Workers party of America."

"You state that you had — particularly in the year 1938 — an operative or operatives who were members of — undercover members of the Communist party reporting to you?"

"Yes. They were undercover operatives of the Los Angeles Police Department engaged in covering the activities of the Communist party and its members."

"Was one William Ward Kimple such an operative . . . ?"

"Yes, and for a number of years prior thereto, also."

Del Guercio brought him back to the latter part of 1938. Had Kimple presented him with certain Communist party registration cards? Yes, Kimple had — forms sent out by the party in New York dealing with 1939 registration of members. Cooper objected that Hynes could have no knowledge of what the Communist party in New York had been doing, and Del Guercio withdrew the question.

Hynes claimed familiarity with the workings of the party, and with its practice of registering members. Cooper objected to his testimony as hearsay. The hearing officer permitted the line of questioning to continue.

Bill Kimple, alias Ward, had brought party forms to Hynes's home, the former Red Squad chief went on — over the protests of the defense attorney — registration certificates and Communist party membership books for 1938 and 1939.

"What did you do with those records?"

"I copied — myself and Mr. Kimple copied — onto prepared mimeographed sheets containing practically the same information as on the registration card, copied the information off the 1939 registration records onto the mimeographed sheets, in my own handwriting . . ."

"Did you make such a copy of one H. S. Tsien's . . . ?"

Cooper objected. It would be hearsay. He was overruled again.

Del Guercio showed Hynes a copy of a registration form listing the name of H. S. Tsien.

"Yes," said Hynes, "I recognize it. This is my own handwriting . . . and everything there."

The mimeographed forms were in a strong, penciled hand, and bore a date in December, 1938.

The copy, said Hynes, was prepared "from a 1939 Communist party membership registration form bearing the printer's number from the printing house of the Communist party. The form contained the information that I had transcribed onto this sheet.

"I had occasion throughout the period of my investigation of Communist activities to learn that this bug number appearing on there is also the same bug number printed on most all of the Communist party literature published officially by the Communist party out of the city of New York."

Cooper protested that this was the rankest sort of hearsay. He pointed out that the registration form was in Hynes's handwriting, that there was no original to show that Dr. Tsien ever signed or executed any such registration.

The form contained the notation "1938 Book # NM," and immediately below that "N.B." Hynes explained: "NM" would mean "New Member" in 1938, "N.B." meant the member had "no book."

Del Guercio had the mimeographed form marked "Exhibit 6." It was Exhibit 6 which condemned Dr. Tsien.

In later years, Allan Juhl, the investigating agent of the Immigration and Naturalization Service, would remember Exhibit 6 vividly.

"This piece of paper," he would say, holding up a copy of it, "blew the lid."

It bore in one corner, in Hynes's handwriting, the notation H. S. Tsien, and on the other, the party name "John M. Decker."

A photostatic copy of the document was marked and entered as evidence. Hynes insisted that to his knowledge of the way the Communist party worked, it was a copy of an original.

Hynes said, "Basing my testimony on the transcript and on the instructions issued by the party for the taking of this registration, this record and transcript of the information from the 1939 record would indicate that H. S. Tsien was a member at the time this registration was taken and a member of the professional section of the Pasadena — the professional group of the Pasadena section in 1938."

Del Guercio entered as Exhibits 8 through 25 Hynes's copies of forms purporting to be registrations of other members of Unit 122, including forms made out in the names of Malina, Weinbaum, Dubnoff and Frank Oppenheimer, copied, Hynes testified, in the presence of Kimple and Clara Osvald, at Hynes's dining room table that night in December, 1938.

Hynes testified that a 1939 party membership book was made out in the name of "John M. Decker." Books, he insisted, were issued only in party names in the cases of individuals of importance, where disclosure of true identity would be a disadvantage to the party.

Hynes was excused, and now yet another figure stepped out of the past. William Ward Kimple — party name Bill Ward — was called to the stand. He, like Hynes, also was looking for the first time upon Tsien, whose life Kimple had drastically altered. Hynes remained in the hearing room to listen.

Kimple recalled joining the Communist party in Hollywood in 1928, assisted in his infiltration by Clara Osvald. In 1938, he said, "I was functioning as a member of the membership commission of the Los Angeles Communist party," his party duties to keep records of members, where they were, what they were doing, how they lived up to regulations.

"I was an assistant to the head director," he went on, after futile objections from Cooper. "My duties consisted of keeping a check on the various transfers that came into the party from other sections, transfers out, keeping check on the units to see to it that they did not lose their members, did not permit floaters in and out. And once a year we would register the members, issue new books, check on dues payments to see to it that there were dues paid for each member in the party."

Did Kimple, as a member of the party commission in 1938, come into possession of a "Communist party registration card in the name of H. S. Tsien?"

"My answer is I did," Kimple replied after Cooper's objections had been gaveled down. ". . . I was transporting it from the home of the Communist party member who had been designated by the county committee to fill out the 1939 books and I was transporting that group of cards from his house in Boyle Heights over to Los Angeles. . . . I took that particular group to Captain William F. Hynes's home, where we made copies of them."

The Government produced a copy of Exhibit 6, the purported Tsien registration.

"This is the copy that was made at Captain Hynes's home," Kimple replied.

"Made from what?"

"Made from the original 1939 registration of this comrade, Tsien."

Cooper was on his feet, his face flushed with anger.

"Now, your honor, please, I move to strike the answer — the appellation of 'comrade' on the ground that it is certainly a conclusion of the witness. There is nothing in the record thus far to indicate that he has signed or joined any organization of this type."

"Overruled," snapped Hearing Officer Waddell.

"Can't we even strike the 'comrade'?" Cooper demanded.

Waddell ignored the plea. Del Guercio asked Kimple, "Did members of the Communist party refer to themselves as 'comrades' among themselves?"

"Yes, sir," said Kimple.

"That is common practice among members of the Communist party?"

"That is a common practice, yes, sir."

"And that is the salutation — ordinary salutation — between one member of the Communist party and another?"

"Yes, sir."

Cooper snorted, "I'd hate to tell you what I call them."

But the "comrade" remained in the record. It was difficult to escape the impression that the Government had made up its mind in advance and that the hearing on Tsien's deportability was little more than legal window-dressing.

For the record, Grant Cooper challenged the Government to produce "any document signed by Dr. Tsien indicating that he was a member of the Communist party." If it did, said Cooper, he would with Tsien's permission withdraw from the case. The Government never met that challenge.

Cooper cross-examined Kimple, to demonstrate that it was not even necessary for a person judged by the Communist party as a desirable member to know he was being registered.

"Mr. Kimple," Cooper began, "if I were seeking to join the Communist party of the United States in 1938 or 1939, was it necessary for me to fill out an application blank — for an individual to fill out an application blank?"

Kimple answered, "An application blank had to be filled out, but it did not have to be done in the handwriting of the applicant."

"Now, with whom — let's assume that there was a unit at Caltech — if I sought to join the unit at Caltech, what individual in that unit would I have to make arrangements with to join the Communist party?"

"Any member of the Communist party."

"All right. I would just tell some member of the Communist party that I wanted to join. That would be my first step, or I would be asked to join, is that correct? That would be my first step?"

"That would be the first step, yes, sir."

"Now, after I made my intention known to some member, what would be the next step?"

"When a person indicated that they wished or were willing to become a member of the Communist party, a second party member was supposed to also interview the applicant."

"In other words, two members would be assigned as a more or less investigating committee?"

"Yes."

"And it might be any two members of the group?"

"That is correct."

"I take it then that it would be the duty of those two members to more or less talk to him and determine whether or not he was sincere. I suppose that would be among the things that they would seek to learn?"

"Now, it could be, or it could be two members who knew the applicant and had been — "

"And would vouch for him?"

"And had been around him long enough to know him."

"And if they knew him, would say he was all right, and if not they would more or less check and find out if he was sincere in becoming a member of the party, and would adhere to its teachings, is that correct?"

"Yes."

"What would the third step be?"

"The application card would be turned in."

"The application card that you are talking about is the application card — Government's exhibit — "

Del Guercio interrupted. "We don't have an application card. We have a registration card."

"There is no application card appearing in evidence at this time?" Cooper asked Del Guercio. The examining officer said there was not.

Cooper turned his attention back to Kimple.

"Have you ever seen such an application card?"

"Many times."

"Was the application card uniform? By that, I mean in a unit — we will say assuming there was a unit at Caltech, a unit at San

Pedro, a unit in Hollywood, or a unit in some city in Ohio or some city in New York — was there a uniform application card?"

"There was."

"And, I take it, it contained the name and address, and what else would it contain?"

"The occupation, the nationality. It contained the names of the two sponsors."

"Was that sometimes signed by the applicant? The application card or the application blank?"

"Sign it?"

"Yes," Cooper said, encouragingly.

"Well," said Kimple, "they didn't have to be signed. They were filled in. Sometimes they were filled in by the applicant. Sometimes the party member who had filled them in, signed them."

"Was there a space provided for the signature of the applicant?"

"I don't believe so. I don't want to state definitely until I check. It has been a long time since I have seen one."

"Was there a space provided in the application blank denoting the fact that he had submitted his dues with the application blank or that he had agreed to pay the dues?"

"I believe it stated in the application blank that he agreed to the principles of the party and there was no dues paid at the time of the — "

"That isn't my question, though," Cooper interrupted. "Was there a space provided in the application blank — this being the third step, now — that indicated he had paid or had agreed to pay the dues other than his — other than a statement that he agreed to abide by the tenets of the organization?"

"I would not like to answer that unless I had an opportunity to review all that, because I haven't seen one of those for a good many years."

"In other words, it may have been there and it may not have been there?"

"That's right."

"And there may have been a bug on it and there may not have been a bug on it."

"No. There was a bug on it."

"What other information was subscribed on this application other than his name and his address, his occupation and the country of his birth?"

"I believe they wanted to know if they were a member of any union."

"Generally speaking, was it the same general information that is in the Government's Exhibit 6?"

"The information on this card is much more complete than what was on the application blank."

"In other words, the information on Government's Exhibit 6 is much more in detail than on the application blank?"

"That is correct."

"All right. Now, an application blank having been filled out, either in the handwriting of the applicant or someone else, what was the fourth step?"

"The comrade who recruited the new member would turn the application blank in to the membership director of the unit."

"That would be — assuming it was Caltech — to the membership director at Caltech?"

"The Caltech unit, yes."

"Who had the power, if you know, of determining whether the individual should or should not be made a member?"

"May I answer that by giving you the further steps of the application card? . . . After the application went into the hands of the membership director, it then went into the hands of the section membership director who, in turn, put it into the hands of the county membership director. It was then sent to the San Francisco — to the district membership committee and there the book was issued."

"All right. I take it, then, that the unit director, which would be the director of the local unit, would make a recommendation that he be accepted."

"No, sir."

"In other words, the mere forwarding of the application blank signified that they were willing to accept him, I presume?"

"The fact that the two members of the party vouched for him signified that it was all right for him to be let in."

"Now then, when the registration book was issued by the — "

Kimple stopped him. "Pardon me, sir — registration book?"

"Whatever you call it — membership book — was issued in San Francisco, that did not mean he had yet paid dues, did it?"

"No, sir."

"Now may I have the registration book, please?" Cooper corrected himself. "I mean the membership book?"

The Hearing Officer handed a sample over to him. Cooper went on.

"Now, when the membership book was received by the member, on the very first page there is a blue page with perforations indicating that it is to be torn off and returned to the membership director with the signature of the applicant, indicating that he had received his membership book, isn't that true?"

Kimple examined the book. "That is correct, sir."

"Now, would that signature be either his own, shall I say, legitimate name or the party name, either one?"

"Well, it should be in the name that the book is issued under, which would be the party name."

"Then with the one — now the one who receives this book, of course, is the member?"

"That is correct."

"Now the member having received this book and having filled out — signed his name, being the party name, and the state, district, county, city, section and branch, and a date therein — there is a space provided for an initiation stamp. Where did the applicant receive his initiation stamp?"

"The initiation stamp would be in the book when it comes to him."

"I see, and then it would be the duty of the applicant to mail that to someone or give it to someone?"

"No. He would return it to the membership director who issued him the book."

"That would be in his unit?"

"In his unit, yes, sir."

"He would hand that to him?"

"It would not necessarily have to be handed to him in the unit."

"I understand. It could be handed to him in the street, if he wanted to?"

"Yes."

"Now, this particular blue page that is torn out — it is torn out, obviously?"

"Yes, sir."

"Given to the membership director in the unit. What would be the duty of the membership director in the unit with respect to this blue page that is torn off and handed to him?"

"That goes back right up through the same steps as the application card."

"That goes through the chain back to San Francisco, is that right?"

"Yes."

"Now I notice on the second page hereof, there is a space provided for the information which is contained in the blue front page which is torn off. I take it, with respect to that page, the party member may or may not fill it out, as he chooses?"

"No. I wouldn't say that, because that was filled out by the party who issued the book."

"Presumably typed in?"

"No, it was written in."

"And also a party stamp placed on there, is that correct? There is a space provided for a party stamp or a signature?"

"I don't know — "

"Didn't you have one when you were a member of it?"

"I certainly did."

"And you are deserving of credit for a lot of good work done. Now, with respect to this registration card, being Government Exhibit 6, who filled in that registration card?"

"That registration card was filled in at the unit meeting, in all probability — there were a few exceptions — by the comrade designated by the Los Angeles County Membership Commission to perform that function."

"In other words, that Government Exhibit 7 (a sample registration form) was not filled out by the member himself?"

"No."

"Was there also a membership card that was also given to party members?"

Kimple was puzzled. "A membership card other than the membership book?" Cooper said, "Yes." Kimple replied negatively.

"What, then, other than the first page of the membership book was required to be signed by the applicant or member?"

"I do not recall anything other than that."

"All right. Now, what do you mean by registration of a member or comrade?"

"Each year the party, can I say, took stock of its members to see to it that they had not lost members during the year, to see to it that each member was paid up in dues, and to see to it that the county membership director knew just where each comrade was — where he was functioning."

"All right. Before a man could be registered, he had to have paid his dues, number one. Is that correct?"

"Yes."

"Or he might make satisfactory arrangements with the unit to pay up at a later date and have a note to that effect from the dues secretary. Is that correct?"

"That is correct."

"And each comrade must turn in his 1938 — turn in his old book and pay five cents for a new book. Is that correct? . . . And if that wasn't done, he couldn't be registered, isn't that true?"

"If he had not paid his dues."

Cooper turned to the subject of recruitment of party members. "That," volunteered Kimple, "is a very big subject, depending largely upon the individual. I wouldn't go down here to an unemployed group . . . and people in those categories and talk to them the same as you would talk to college students and professors. Various techniques . . . were used. Sometimes open meetings were held."

"How do you describe an open meeting, please?"

"An open meeting for recruiting members as a rule was a meeting held at usually the meeting place of the unit and a portion of the business of the meeting was turned over to a capable comrade who could explain the activities of the party to prospective members who had previously been invited to attend this meeting with the purpose of — "

Cooper stopped him. "Let me ask you this: Did you ever personally attend a meeting of Professional Unit 122? . . . Did you ever attend a meeting of that unit?"

"I would not know, sir," Kimple replied.

They discussed various methods of recruitment — personal contacts, social gatherings and the like — and then Cooper shot out:

"When was the first time, Mr. Kimple, that you saw Dr. Tsien?"

"I have never seen Dr. Tsien before just now — that is to the best of my knowledge."

"Now let me ask you this, with respect to Government Exhibit 6: Do you know who prepared that form? Was that a form prepared by the so-called Communist party, or was that prepared by the police department for its convenience?"

"That form I made," Kimple replied.

"Government's Exhibit 6 (purportedly Tsien's party registration) was a form that you yourself made in your work in the police department?"

"Yes, sir."

"And it wasn't an official form of any organization except the police department in its work?"

"Yes, sir."

"In other words, you, in the work that you did in a conscientious endeavor to learn about persons who were members, or that you believed to be members of the Communist party, from the records you had made — you or Captain Hynes copied these in either his handwriting or your handwriting, as the case might be?"

"That is correct."

"You copied them from these registration certificates, is that correct?"

"That is correct, yes, sir."

"That were not in the handwriting of the member?"

"No, sir."

"They were in the handwriting of some alleged member of the Communist party?"

"Who was designated — "

Now it was Del Guercio's turn to object, to the use of the word "alleged." He claimed the evidence showed the material was an official record of the Communist party. Cooper and the examining officer wrangled over the point, and finally Del Guercio withdrew his objection. And the Kimple answer was that, yes, the registration certificates from which he had copies were in the handwriting of alleged Communist party members.

On redirect, Del Guercio asked Kimple whether the registration which came into his possession indicated that Tsien was a new member of the party in 1939. Kimple answered simply that "Government's Exhibit 6, as I recall it, was a new member in 1938." But Del Guercio persisted, and Kimple testified that Communist party Membership Book 1004 was assigned to Tsien for 1939.

Cooper was at Kimple again.

"Mr. Kimple, you don't honestly mean to suggest that you remember the number of that registration card — 1004 — from 1939 to the present time, do you?"

"I do not remember the number that I saw but I do know that I checked the book against the registration card before the book was issued to the membership director to return to the unit, to be sure that there was no slip in the mechanics of registration we had."

"Did you ever see a membership book issued in the name of H. S. Tsien?"

"No, sir."

"And did you assume at this time such member must have been 1004 because you see it on this Government Exhibit 6?"

"That is right."

"But you have no recollection of it? Obviously, seeing it now does not refresh your memory as to the number that was on it at the time."

"No."

"That is all."

The testimony would appear to have damaged the Government's case against the Chinese scientist. It had brought out clearly that there had been no proof of Tsien having either signed anything or even having personally made application for party membership. It could have been done by somebody else, entirely without his knowledge.

Tsien had won a skirmish, but the outcome of the battle continued to seem foreordained.

24

After two long days the hearing was suspended. Tsien was at liberty to go home, still under fifteen thousand dollars' bail. But he was virtually a prisoner under house arrest. He was forbidden to leave the area of Los Angeles County without official permission.

"That was the hardest part for Tsien, those first months after the hearings," Dr. Frank Marble reminisced later. Dr. Marble was a fellow professor in the jet propulsion field who had tried to console Tsien in his trouble.

"After a day or two of the hearings, it didn't matter what anybody said," Marble recalled. "It was like a case of an appendix; diseased or not, you just go in and cut it out. Tsien never lost control. But that was the time he came nearest to being shaken. It took him a while to get over it all."

Tsien looked to his profession as the answer to his problems. "I might as well go back to work," he told Dr. Marble, and he did, with a vengeance. He began working furiously, at a clip which permitted him to turn out a technical paper every month for four consecutive months, a rare achievement in his field. For a while, the outpouring of work seemed the only way he could suppress the worry, the resentment, the frustration.

He plunged wholeheartedly into the teaching of mathematics, and was a tough taskmaster. He was always coldly formal, always scholarly, and he pushed his students hard. What they turned out under his direction was almost invariably first rate.

He was a glutton for work. On top of all his other interests, he began working on a book on engineering and cybernetics, the latter a subject which had fascinated him ever since his days at the Massachusetts Institute of Technology. He was sure that high-speed computers would be of enormous help to the management decision process in American industry. His friends judged he had hit upon the field which would become the next phase of his brilliant career.

But the hearings reopened in February and the Government called Richard Rosanoff, who had testified against Weinbaum. He described himself as a Communist party member while he had been a Caltech student in the spring of 1938. He had, he said, boarded at the Weinbaum home.

"Who recruited you?" Del Guercio asked.

"Dr. Weinbaum."

"Into the Communist party?"

"That's right, Dr. Weinbaum."

"You have identified the unit as a professional unit, number 122?"

"Yes, sir."

"And who was the — if any — leader of the unit?"

"There comes a question — when you say 'leader,' do you mean held official position as a leader? If so, I don't know the answer. As to the actual leader, the man who was the driving force, the man was Dr. Weinbaum."

Rosanoff knew Frank Malina, but "I can't recall that I definitely knew of Malina's membership, although I did know that he was interested in those things and that he was close to it."

Del Guercio asked, "Do you know the respondent here, Dr. H. S. Tsien?"

"I believe we were slightly acquainted at that time," Rosanoff replied. "This is an awful long time ago — I am terribly sorry — I can't recall any time definitely having met Dr. Tsien. I knew who he was. I was able to pick him out of a photograph, but I was a little surprised that I was able to do it, frankly." He turned to Dr. Tsien, in an aside. "No offense, Dr. Tsien. It has been a good many years."

"Did you ever have any conversation with Sidney Weinbaum about Dr. Tsien?"

"Yes."

Cooper objected and was overruled again.

Rosanoff went on, "It was at some time in the period of my own Red activity. Dr. Weinbaum and I — and, as a matter of fact, occasionally others — discussed — oh, I suppose we discussed almost everybody, as I testified in the Weinbaum case. . . . However, we discussed Dr. Tsien as a prospective Communist."

He could not be definite, he said, on what Weinbaum had said about Tsien, or whether anybody else was present at the time. He indicated there had been only one such occasion when Tsien was discussed. His testimony would seem to have been more harmful than beneficial to the Government's case.

Nor was the Government much more successful with its next witness, Sylvan Rubin, a physicist from New York who had attended Caltech from 1936 to 1939 and had been, by his own admission, a Communist party member in that period.

He was, Rubin said, a member of Professional Unit 122. He knew Weinbaum, identified him as a unit member, but could not say for sure whether party meetings were held in Weinbaum's home.

"Do you know the respondent, Dr. Hsue Shen Tsien?" Del Guercio asked.

"I do. . . . Yes, I am acquainted with him."

"Do you recall how you first met Dr. Tsien?"

"No, I can't recall how I met him. I know that I was somewhat acquainted with him, probably slightly acquainted at the time I was an undergraduate at the Institute."

Rubin could not recall where he had met Tsien.

"Do you recall now if you attended any meetings of the Communist party with Dr. Tsien?" Del Guercio continued.

"No. I can't recall that specifically."

Was it possible he met Tsien at a Communist meeting? Cooper exploded in protest at the examining officer's question, and again was overruled. And Rubin replied, "It seems fairly probable to me." The motion to strike the reply was denied. Del Guercio pressed the opening.

"Is it more probable that you met Dr. Tsien at those Communist party meetings that you described than it was that you had met him otherwise?"

Another Cooper protest, another protest overruled.

"Do you," Del Guercio asked Rubin, "have any particular reason for remembering Dr. Tsien in 1938 and 1939?"

"From that time until I was questioned on this matter by FBI agents, possibly a year or two ago, I had no reason at all to attempt to recall that," said Rubin.

That, Del Guercio implied, was the only reason Rubin could not place Tsien definitely at a Communist meeting. Again a Cooper protest proved futile.

Now Tsien was back on the stand again, once again denying affiliation with the Communist party.

"I did not join the party," he said. ". . . . To my own knowledge, I am not a member of the Communist party. I was not a member of the Communist party."

Then the Government questioned him about Chao Chung-yao.

25

U.S. officialdom in Southern California sensed a plot and eyed Tsien and Chao Chung-yao as its chief architects.

Given the temper of the time, it should have been no surprise to anyone that Chinese scientists in the United States, and particularly in California, should decide the time had come to get out.

The events from June to September of 1950, beginning with the intrusion of the FBI on the Caltech campus, had rocked the academic community, and had struck the Chinese in that community with explosive force. Tension was rising daily between Peking and Washington as the Korean war rose in ferocity. Chinese who had spent the World War II days in America could remember what happened to Japanese in those days. They were well aware of the distrust of Orientals in Southern California. The outlook for the Chinese and their families was far from a pleasant one, and they made plans to get out. Perhaps some were sympathetic to the Communist cause in China, perhaps some were drawn by strong family ties to the mainland. Perhaps some felt they had no choice, that they were being driven out.

Chao Chung-yao laid his departure plans carefully. He had gone to the Bekins company to have his belongings crated. Among the things he packed up were instruments purchased in Boston for use in his experiments. He had been at Caltech since 1926, and was by now a physicist of renown in the scientific community.

By coincidence, Chao chose to book passage on the *President Wilson*. With everything in readiness, Chao even had a farewell party, a dinner among Chinese friends in Los Angeles' Chinatown.

Agent Allan Juhl, the man who had arrested Tsien, tried to keep Chao from leaving, and failed. "I was given this case as a matter of rush investigation — hot priority," he would remember later. "I was told to drop everything and move it."

"We tried to get something on both men (Tsien and Chao) to hold them. That piece of paper, the Communist party registration, blew the lid for Tsien. But we couldn't find anything derogatory on Chao in that short space of time.

"Chao also had boxes of stuff with him, and we put some kind of no-can-go order on him. But Chao's was lifted in a matter of days, and he went out on the *President Wilson*, leaving Tsien behind. Honolulu is the first stop on the way to the Orient, and our agents physically verified his presence on that, rather than wait for the papers to come in later on."

The U.S. Army was waiting for Chao and three other Chinese students when the *President Wilson* docked at Yokohama. Military police marched aboard the liner, arrested the four men and took them ashore. They were held for "complicity" with Dr. Tsien in a plot to turn over nuclear secrets to Red China. The U.S. Army claimed that Chao and his friends were carrying restricted documents taken from Caltech. At this incarceration Radio Peking bombarded the world's airwaves with protests, appealed to the Communist-operated World Congress of Peace to denounce the arrests.

The U.S. Army of Occupation did not reveal what, if anything, it had learned from Chao and the three students in his retinue. But, in any event, the four were released a few weeks later and sailed on to Hong Kong, where they were detained only overnight. Next morning they were escorted across the frontier into Red China. On reaching Canton, Chao let his bitterness burst out. He accused the United States of oppressing Chinese, and he seemed to look forward to a time of revenge.

"The United States," he proclaimed, "is a country where the A-bomb will cause the gravest disaster. America's well-developed and centralized industry will make her a prime target. Americans fear the A-bomb more than any other people."

When Chao slipped away, Tsien still was under FBI surveillance. By the time Chao reached Japan, Tsien was behind bars, and by the time Chao reached Canton, Tsien was free on bail, waiting for the long ordeal of the hearing to determine his deportability. Now, as the pale February sun filtered through the blinds of the dismal hearing room, Examining Officer Del Guercio probed the connections between Tsien and Chao. He had some difficulty with pronunciation, and Tsien asked for a full spelling of the name. Del Guercio showed him a memorandum containing four Chinese names.

"Yes," said Tsien. "The first one I know. His last name is Chao, Chung-yao."

He did not recognize two of the other names, but did a third, Lo Shih-chun, who was a student at Caltech's Aeronautics Department.

"You have read newspaper articles saying that the two you mentioned — that you stated you knew — and the other two — "

"Yes," Tsien put in.

" — have departed from the United States and arrived in China and have set up a jet propulsion school in China — Communist China?"

"I do not know."

"You have read newspaper articles about that?"

"I did not ever read a newspaper article to that effect."

"Or to any effect?"

"I have no news — no information — about them after they have arrived in China."

"Did you give any of those people any literature or information on jet propulsion or on guided missiles to take to China?"

"I did not."

"Did you know that they had in their possession literature and articles written by you?"

"Not to my knowledge," Tsien responded after his lawyer's objection to the question was overruled.

"Literature and pamphlets written by you?"

"Not to my knowledge."

"You lived with Mr. Chao, didn't you?"

"No. Never."

"Did he live at your home?"

"Never."

"Did you know him intimately?"

"No."

"As a matter of fact, he had made arrangements to leave on the same ship that you had arranged to depart on, did he not?"

"That was only known to me after he left. I didn't leave on that ship."

There had been newspaper reports quoting intelligence sources that Chao, on his return to China, had begun setting up some sort of laboratory, probably in connection with nuclear research, which was his specialty. But by this time, China was deeply involved in the Korean war with her "volunteers," and there would be little resources or opportunity for Chao to get very far.

Del Guercio now dropped the matter of Chao, and once again returned to Exhibit 6, the registration form with Tsien's name on it.

"I could not explain things I have absolutely no knowledge of," Tsien replied.

"Well, did you have any enemies who would, for the purpose of deceiving, register you as a Communist party member?"

"Since I am under oath I can only answer the truth, and I do not know the matter connected with your question."

"In other words, you can offer no explanation for this registration, assuming it is a correct one?"

"No, I cannot offer explanation of things which I have absolutely no knowledge of."

"Are you willing to state under oath now that you have no sympathy for Communist China?"

"I do not know the conditions in Communist China, and —"

"Well, that is equivocating. You know about the conditions in China as much as anybody else does."

This brought on yet another wrangle with the defense attorney. Then Del Guercio asked Tsien, "Do you believe in a dictatorship of the proletariat in any country?"

"I do not believe that."

"Is not the present government in China a dictatorship?"

"I have no information about that, and my answer to that question is conditioned by my experience that things in China, especially government politics, was never quite the same as they say they are."

The hearing adjourned again, and there were no more until April, when the Government called Richard N. Lewis, an assistant professor of chemistry at the University of Delaware. Lewis had been a Caltech student in the 1930s.

At first, Lewis had declined to testify on grounds of self-incrimination. But now he waived that constitutional privilege. He testified he, too, had been a member of Professional Unit 122 during his Caltech student days, using the party name of Richard LaSalle. He testified he had seen Tsien at "the majority" of closed unit meetings between the latter part of 1938 and sometime in 1942.

"Were Communist party dues paid at any of those meetings?" Del Guercio asked him.

"Yes," Dr. Lewis replied.

"By yourself?"

"Yes."

"By anyone else?"

"Yes."

"Did you ever see the respondent, H. S. Tsien, pay dues at any of these meetings — pay Communist party dues?"

"I don't remember."

Del Guercio asked him if Frank Malina was a member of the unit.

"As far as I know, he was a member," Lewis replied.

"Did you know whether Jon Dubnoff was a member of that unit?"

"Yes, he was a member."

"Did you know Frank Oppenheimer?"

"Yes."

"Was he a member of that unit?"

"Yes."

Name by name, Del Guercio went down the list of those associated with Unit 122. Lewis remembered all the rest as members.

"Did these persons that you have just identified attend closed Communist party meetings in which the respondent, H. S. Tsien, was present?"

"Some of these people I have only a faint recollection of, and I can't remember whether any one of them was there at any given meeting when Dr. Tsien was there."

Lewis was "fairly certain" he had seen Tsien at meetings from 1938 to 1941.

"I can remember that he attended, but I can't remember any particular meeting. I can't give you the date or even the subject matter that was under discussion."

"What is a closed Communist party meeting, Mr. Lewis?"

"The term, as I understand you, it refers to one of our regular meetings to which non-members were not usually admitted. Occasionally prospective members would be admitted."

"You knew Dr. Tsien as a member of the Communist party?"

"All I can say is that I believe he was a member."

Throughout all this line of questioning, Cooper objected repeatedly; as was the custom he was overruled each time.

Cooper called as a defense witness Jon Dubnoff, who identified himself as organizer and "the first member" of Unit 122 at Caltech.

"We came together primarily, I feel, as a study group," Dubnoff said in response to Cooper's questioning, "and . . . there wasn't a marked line between what one might call an open meeting and a closed, except if outsiders were there it would automatically be open, without materially altering the type of discussion that took place. . . . They were primarily study groups on international affairs and political theory, reviews of books and articles."

"Now," asked Cooper, "based upon your present recollection, was Dr. Tsien ever a member of the Communist party, Professional Unit, at Caltech?"

"To the best of my knowledge, he was not a member."

"To the best of your present recollection, did you ever collect dues from him?"

"I don't recall collecting dues."

Del Guercio cross-examined. Could Tsien have been a member of Unit 122 without Dubnoff's knowledge?

"I don't think so," Dubnoff replied.

"What do you think?"

"It is my impression that he was not a member."

Del Guercio put the witness through an intensive grilling, but failed to shake him on the point.

And now the proceeding at last was drawing to a close. Once more Tsien was obliged to take the witness stand. Under questioning by his own counsel, he recalled his early days at Caltech and the love of music he shared with Malina and Weinbaum, the days of the Suicide Squad and its early experiments with rockets. And then, finally, Cooper's question: "I will again ask you, did you ever knowingly or willingly join the Communist party at Caltech?"

"I did not," said Tsien.

Once again, for the last time, Del Guercio cross-examined him. To him, Tsien's final answer was: "I never joined the Communist party."

At five o'clock on a hot afternoon in April, the ordeal at last came to an end. And on April 26, the decision came down from the hearing officer. Tsien was "subject to deportation on the grounds that he has been found to have been . . . an alien who was a member of the Communist party of the United States."

Tsien had fully expected it.

"I sensed a feeling of frustration in Tsien," said one official who had sat in on the proceedings. "Not belligerent — very composed and quiet, friendly. I had the feeling he understood the problem, he understood why it had happened, but he was frustrated."

"At times I actually feared for his mind," a grieving Dr. von Kármán said of his Chinese friend.[1] Understandably, Tsien had lapsed into a fit of deep despondency. His colleagues tried to snap him out of it, to talk to him, to console him. Von Kármán even telephoned him from Europe, where the old scientist had been setting up an aeronautical research organization for the North Atlantic Treaty Organization.

Tsien should try to take it all philosophically, his friends pleaded. They reasoned with him. It was not unusual in America for scientists to be suspect. Americans tended to mistrust intellectuals. He should not take it all so seriously. It would blow over someday and he would be vindicated.

But Tsien began to avoid people, to bury himself in his books. He lived in his private limbo, a man without a country, declared undesirable by the United States and subject to deportation and yet forbidden to go — indeed, forbidden to leave the precincts of Los Angeles County.

"I was convinced, as were virtually all my associates, including Clark Millikan, the excellent Dean Ernest C. Watson, William Zisch, George S. Schairer and President Lee DuBridge that Tsien was not a member of the Communist party or had anything more than social associations with some individuals who were later identified as Communists or Communist sympathizers," von Kármán would write later.[2]

Von Kármán was convinced the Immigration Service had acted entirely on hearsay, and many an American colleague of Tsien regarded the Immigration and Naturalization Service as singularly stupid and hopelessly ensnared by its own bureaucracy.

26

Because of Red China's entry into the Korean war, a wave of fear swept the community of Chinese students in the United States. Most were cut off from the financial assistance their parents had been sending from China. Universities and foundations tried to help, but some students inevitably got into difficulties with the Department of Justice.

Repeatedly, the State Department urged the Justice Department to put into effect a law permitting selected Chinese to remain in the United States and to work and study. The Justice Department authorities permitted almost none of them to work after school hours or during the summers. Chinese students were not allowed to leave school to earn their livings nor could they take on full-time jobs. A student who accepted a job was likely to be served with a warrant of arrest, forced to return to his campus under the custody of an official, and then served with a warrant of deportation.

At the time of the Korean War, there were more Chinese students enrolled in U.S. colleges and universities than at any time since the first one had arrived a century before. About 3,600 were enrolled in 454 colleges and universities in forty-seven states and the District of Columbia, plus another thousand not enrolled, but working on theses or undergoing special technical or professional training.[1]

During World War II at one time or another there had been about ten thousand Chinese students in the United States, and in the dawn of the nuclear age they had placed heavy emphasis on technological training. Chinese students born in China of Chinese parentage made up the largest single group of foreign students, with the exception of the Canadians. Almost half the Chinese were in studies which could relate to nuclear development.

The irony of it all was overpowering. The United States had on its soil the cream of China's scientific brainpower. Some of the scientists trained in sensitive fields were told officially they could not leave the United States under any circumstances, but official bureaucracy, ineptitude in Washington and callousness on the part of the general public all combined to force enormously gifted men to abandon their adopted homes and return to an uncharted and even ominous future in their homeland. One panel of U.S. experts which later on went through mountains of documents about Chinese who had been scientist-students in the United States found out that it was the Immigration Service which had been the prime motivating factor in their return. So it was that they were ordered to remain, yet forced to leave.[2] They took back with them heavy cargoes of bitterness.

Many Chinese were reluctant, however, to return to the mainland. They feared the new Red regime. The students for the most part had come from families with bourgeois backgrounds who now would be regarded as "enemies of the people." Some probably were eager to go back and take part in building a new future promised by Mao Tse-tung, but even then they would be suspect, having so long been exposed to Western and American ideas. Perhaps this ideological divide could have been used as the instrument to persuade the hesitant among the most talented Chinese to remain in the United States. But the opportunity was lost in a Washington fog.

"The Chinese Communist war in Korea has produced a whole series of small interdepartmental wars in Washington, the latest between the State and Justice Departments over the future of Chinese university students in this country," wrote James Reston in the *New York Times*. He quoted one professor, decrying the black atmosphere of suspicion, the Washington hysteria about "softness" on communism, the harsh official attitude toward Chinese students.

"It is criminal," said the professor, "to send back our friends, and idiotic to send back our enemies — since all of them are highly trained. No sensible government would let any of them go near Peking, whether they wished to go or not — and ninety per cent of them wish not to go!" [3]

There were demands from university officials for help for Chinese students, but Washington dragged its feet. When some federal aid finally was available, it was too late for most and too little for all. Some of the top Chinese talent, graduates holding Master's and Doctor's degrees, found themselves washing dishes in restaurants or working in Chinese laundries, laboring as janitors or peddling chop suey, to eke out a living. Even when they gained limited permission to work, the Chinese still were at a disadvantage without American citizenship, and citizenship was hard to come by. Even if a Chinese succeeded in changing his non-immigrant alien status to that of immigrant with permanent residence, five years had to elapse before citizenship could be conferred. Without citizenship, the Chinese could not hold civil service positions or posts in any public schools or state universities, nor could they work for many private corporations which handled government contracts. Lawyers, doctors and dentists could not practice because they could not get licenses. [4]

Peking knew well what was going on in the United States with regard to the Chinese students, and tried to make the most of it. While Americans turned deaf ears to pleas to help the Chinese students in their confusing situation, Peking's propaganda played heavily on the theme of persecution of the students. Dr. Chih Meng, director of the China Institute of America, issued a plea and a warning. He urged at least five million dollars in aid to the Chinese students. He warned that many of his country's most talented young men would become discouraged and go to Communist China with all they had learned in the United States. Dr. Meng, who had once roomed as a student with China's Chou En-lai and who had known Mao Tse-tung before the Chinese leader's rise to power, issued a warning to America:

"If we fail [the Chinese students in the United States], you cannot convince the millions of Chinese people that we really are their friends. But if we help them now, it would have a more lasting effect than any number of military volunteers." [5]

The advice went unheeded. And many a brilliant Chinese student, harassed also by propaganda letters and threats from Peking, fearful of what might happen to his family, came to the conclusion he had no choice. Many stayed on, in spite of it all. But too many left, and among them were the most talented.

Many were in the same position as Dr. Tsien Hsue-shen: declared deportable and yet detained because they were too valuable to let go.

27

And there was Jimmy Chien, Dr. Tsien's student and protégé.

"Jimmy Chien was different from all the rest who came out here to Caltech. He liked to take a drink, along with the Westerners."

Homer Joe Stewart, one of the most brilliant men in U.S. rock-etry, worked closely with Chien Wei-chang — they all called him Jimmy — on the Pasadena campus in those early days of missile re-search.

"Jimmy was a wonderful fellow," Stewart told the authors. "He was a Communist and said so openly. He was here in the 1930s and left in 1947. Membership in the Communist party was no bar to security clearance in those days.

"Chien was a hard worker, but a real mixer. He was the only Chinese in the whole group who would drink an American cock-tail. He liked martinis. I once asked him why, since all the other Chinese didn't drink anything except maybe to sip a little wine at dinner to be polite to a hostess. Jimmy told me, 'If you're out on a Manchurian plain in the wintertime, you've got to keep the fire going.' "

There had been times when Jimmy really had to keep the fire going. He liked to tell his colleagues at Caltech about the days when he went on the Long March, the incredible trek by Mao Tse-tung and his followers in the mid-1930s, across mountains and valleys, rivers and swamps, through all manner of hardships, to escape the pursuing forces of Chiang Kai-shek's Kuomintang Army.

"Jimmy talked of that march with affection, as any soldier does of his war experiences. It was a period of high adventure for him."

Stewart went on: "I remember one time Chien and I climbed a mountain out in Death Valley — one of the lower ridges. It was a field test, and we took along a fellow from New York who had never been out of the city. We thought he ought to see some of the countryside. We chose a small peak. It was a steep walk, and the New Yorker barely made it. Chien was in good physical shape. We talked about other things rather than politics. He told us about a strange custom in northern China, where they cook pota-toes in oil so they can get them above the boiling point."

Chien Wei-chang — sometimes he was called Chien Wei-zang or W. Z. Chien — became just Jimmy Chien on the Caltech campus. He was a rare, offbeat sort of Communist who probably would be as much at home at a Rotary Club luncheon as at a cell meeting. A gregarious bachelor, he cut a social figure unlike any other of his countrymen on the campus. He left behind sharp memories among his colleagues, probably more than had any other Chinese student save the remarkable Tsien.

One of the Chinese who knew Jimmy well was C. C. Lin, who cast his lot with the United States and became a professor at M.I.T. Lin worked with Chien in the mid-1940s. Both men were earning their doctorates at the time.

"Every once in a while," remembered Stewart, "I would see them at luncheon. They would get into wild arguments, with their hands flying, full of fire and fury, going at it in Chinese. I used to ask them what all the fuss was about. Sometimes it was politics, but other times they were just arguing over the luncheon menu. I remember one fine dinner party they organized for us at a local restaurant. They both were bachelors and they decided to throw a party for eight or ten people. They worked out a very elaborate menu for us, complete with shark's fin soup . . . the works."

Chien, Lin and Tsien Hsue-shen all were involved in the early stages of rocket and guided missile research at Caltech. Tsien directed a research group; Stewart succeeded him. Later, Lin moved eastward. Chien went back to China in early 1947, two years before the Communist takeover.

Despite Tsien's fame both on campus and throughout the world of rocketry, Stewart ranks Chien tops in some respects. "Jimmy did some very good things for us. He helped set up some of the jet trajectory work . . . the voyage to the planets."

With cheerful aplomb, Jimmy Chien made friends. Sipping his Martinis, Chien attracted company and reveled in the social whirl shunned by others of his countrymen.

Professor Lin recalled Chien and their years together, first in China and then in America.

"Jimmy was more interested in politics than I was," Lin related. "He was an activist. When we were in school together in China, Jimmy was very dissatisfied with the Kuomintang government. We went to the same school, Tsinghua University in Peking. That was back in 1933 to 1935. I don't think he was a member of the Communist party, but he was active in the student movements.

"There was a lot of student activity then. I would compare it to the present day in the United States. The Japanese were making inroads on the Chinese mainland. And the student movements were in a fervor.

"Chien was actively anti-Japanese. He was always trying to urge the Nationalist government to do more against the Japanese. That was before 1937 when the war broke out. The Communists were making a strong bid to fight the Japanese. The central government was not.

"In those wild days, Chien belonged in the activist clubs. The student movement was divided into two groups. One was slightly off center to the right, the other to the left. Chien belonged to the group that was slightly left of center.

"I don't know," said Lin, "if Chien had strong connections with the Communists. He probably was not an agent. The agents were the quiet ones. One of those we least suspected turned out to be an agent and became president of the university after the Communists came to power."

Chien played a role in one of the most colorful episodes of student demonstrations in China of the mid-1930s. The students had staged a strike as part of their political upheaval. They organized a group to ride bicycles along the railroad tracks to their homes, some journeying all the way from Peking to Nanking. They were determined to present a petition to Chiang Kai-shek demanding that his regime be more aggressive in fighting the Japanese.

Both Chien and Lin were awarded Sino-British scholarships in 1940 and went to Toronto University. Lin remained a year. Chien stayed on for twelve more months, joining Lin in 1942 at Caltech. In Pasadena, Chien worked as a research engineer and took part in many of the experiments that led to U.S. space achievements under such innovators as Stewart and Jimmy's countryman, Tsien Hsue-shen.

Jimmy Chien vanished from Caltech in 1947, and his American friends lost all touch with him after the Mao regime took control in 1949.[1]

28

Calamity dogged the footsteps of Tsien and his brilliant friends. While Tsien brooded over his lost career and what he could only regard as the blind injustice of his adopted land, his friend, the chemist-physicist Sidney Weinbaum, sweated out his term for perjury at McNeil Island. Dr. Frank Malina, the moving spirit of the Suicide Squad which helped launch America into space, was in Paris, working with UNESCO. Now wearing a Vandyke beard, Malina had virtually abandoned science and turned to the life of an expatriate artist. Frank Oppenheimer was on a Colorado ranch.

And the strange young chemist, John W. Parsons, with whom Tsien, Malina and the others were associated in the daring Suicide Squad experiments fifteen years before, now made the headlines. This time he made the headlines because he was suddenly dead at thirty-seven, under mysterious circumstances.

Parsons, self-taught and possessing a vaulting imagination, had with nothing more than a high school diploma made himself one of the nation's leading authorities on explosives and jet propulsion. He was one of the five founders of Aerojet Engineering Corporation, brainchild of the Suicide Squad, but sold out his interests immediately after the war, when the company, by then Aerojet-General, was on its way to becoming involved in virtually every U.S. rocket and space program.

Aerojet mourned his loss. "He was a loner," one company official said sadly. "He liked to wander. But he was one of the top men in his field." Many of the basic patents for JATO (jet-assisted takeoff) were obtained under Parsons's name, and as a vice-president of Aerojet he had headed the solid propellant development project.

That June, Parsons was hot on the trail of a completely new explosive substance which would be far superior to any commercial blasting material then in existence. The experimental explosive with which he was working was considered far safer than other detonants. Parsons was a careful, systematic scientist. That made his death a baffling mystery.

One hot afternoon, Parsons was packing for a trip to Mexico, where he planned to carry out further research. As Parsons stepped into the makeshift laboratory in his garage, a deafening roar shattered the sunny calm of Pasadena. Parsons took the full, dreadful force of the blast against his body. The explosion blew a hole in the floor directly under the section where the chemist had been standing. Then a second explosion rocked the area. The force was so great that it shattered windows of a building in an adjoining estate. Doors, walls, partitions, the floor and the ceiling of the garage laboratory were demolished. A bathtub was toppled on its side. Near the tub lay the crumpled body of John W. Parsons.

The young chemist had been packing bottled explosives into a box to take with him on his trip. But the scene the police found in the garage was, said a friend of the chemist, "completely out of character" with Parsons's scientific methods. The friend, a Los Angeles chemical engineer named George W. Santmyers, concluded from the evidence that "somebody else" had put quantities of explosive refuse into the exposed trash and garbage containers at the rear of the laboratory. Parsons never would have been that careless.

"For Parsons to have disposed of such materials in that manner would be in the same category as for a highly trained surgeon to operate with dirty hands," Santmyers told the police.

In another Pasadena home, Parsons's 58-year-old mother, Ruth Virginia, was with an elderly crippled friend when word came of her son's death.

"I can't stand it any more," Mrs. Parsons cried. Her friend looked on in stupefied shock as she reached for a bottle of sleeping pills and gulped down forty-five capsules. While her friend sat helpless in a wheelchair, unable to move, Mrs. Parsons slumped over in a chair in the living room, never to awake. Four hours after the explosion which killed her son, Mrs. Parsons was dead.

With grief Tsien read of the sudden end to a career which had helped make science fiction become established fact. Once again, brooding, Tsien turned to work for consolation, and despite the stigma which had been placed upon him, Tsien was regarded highly by his fellow scientists. In July, 1953, he once again addressed the Rocket Society, this time on the theme of reaching for the moon. It might be done, Tsien theorized, from a man-made platform suspended in space thousands of miles above the earth. He presented page after page of equations describing just how a space station might solve the problem.

"It is hoped," he concluded, "that the present investigation will give future generations of astronautical engineers a rational basis for designing space ships."

For another two years, Tsien plugged away at his studies — cybernetics, space problems. He was not working on anything classified any more, but his studies were still of profound interest to the scientific community. He saw nothing of his friends of the Suicide Squad days. Sidney Weinbaum, after serving three years of a four-year sentence, emerged from prison on McNeil Island and inquired of Caltech's Dean Watson about the status of Tsien. Dean Watson advised the physicist not to visit Tsien, since such a contact could only make the rocket expert's life even more complicated. Probably the FBI or some agent of it still was watching both Tsien and Weinbaum, and the latter avoided looking up his old friend. He never saw him again.

29

The letter arrived at Tsien's home in Altadena on August 5, 1955. Tsien took in its contents at a glance.

"You are advised," it said, "that the order of this Service, dated August 23, 1950, has been revoked and you may depart from the United States.

"So that no difficulty will be encountered in leaving the United States, please keep this office advised of all plans and arrangements made for your departure."

That was a polite way of telling Tsien he was being deported. The order of the Immigration Service, to which the letter referred, had been the ban on his departure imposed five years before on Tsien's arrival at Los Angeles Airport after a futile trip to Washington to appeal the lifting of his security clearance. It meant that the deportation order, issued as a result of the 1950–1951 hearings, now was in effect.

Tsien and his wife quietly packed their belongings and booked passage on the S.S. *President Cleveland* for Hong Kong. The Justice Department did not bother to inform Tsien's attorney, Grant B. Cooper, that the ban had been lifted and the deportation order was in effect. Cooper, attending a bar convention in San Francisco, learned of the order from his secretary, who spotted the news of Tsien's departure in the newspapers.

Angrily, Cooper protested to the Justice Department. In turn, it sent an apologetic letter to him, noting that, "inadvertently," a copy of the letter to Tsien had not been sent to the attorney.

"Shortly thereafter," said the letter to Cooper dated September 28, "Doctor Tsien contacted this office advising that he had made arrangements to effect his departure from the United States. His departure on September 17, 1955, has been verified by this service."

Cooper retorted:

"To say that I was shocked at the inadvertence of your department in not notifying me, as Dr. Tsien's attorney of record, is to put it mildly. It had always been my intention, when your department evidenced its intention to deport Dr. Tsien and take him into custody for such a purpose, to file a petition for a writ of habeas corpus so that the proceedings could be challenged in the courts. . . . This letter is written for the purpose of protecting Dr. Tsien's rights in the event he should at some future time determine to return to the United States. . . ."

But Tsien had not informed his attorney, either. He wanted no more of writs of habeas corpus, no more court challenges, no goodbyes — and no return to the United States.

A few of Tsien's old friends and colleagues from Caltech boarded the S.S. *Cleveland* for a last farewell. Dr. Frank Marble and Dr. Duncan Rannie, who had shared with Tsien the satisfaction of exploring the future, chatted with him about his plans.

An ocean voyage would be good, Tsien felt. It would be restful. There would be many things to do, many things to talk about. He and Yin would have to instruct the children, two little American Chinese, in new and strange ways, even in new and strange names. In America their names were Yucon and Mamie. Now they would have to learn the Mandarin names, Yung-kang and Jung-jen. For them not to know those names would be an offense to their old grandfather in Shanghai. "The children have forgotten their Mandarin names," Tsien told his visitors with a smile.

There were newspapermen at the dock. Tsien still was hot

copy. And to them, Tsien said: "I have been artificially delayed in this country from returning to my country. I suggest you ask your State Department why. Of your State Department and myself, I am the least embarrassed in this situation. I have no bitterness against the American people. My main objective is the pursuit of peace and happiness."

But he did have bitterness against the U.S. Government, its bureaucrats, its officials. As the S.S. *President Cleveland* sailed out of the harbor, two FBI agents watched, silent and unsmiling. The liner slowly disappeared from view in the Los Angeles mist.

That day, headlines proclaimed rumors: that Dr. Tsien and thirty-nine Chinese students who sailed with him were being allowed to go home in a swap deal by the State Department for eleven American airmen, released at about that time by Communist China. The fliers had been imprisoned in Red China after their planes had strayed or were chased north of the Yalu River, during the Korean war.

"SWAP FOR U.S. FLIERS RUMORED AS SCIENTIST SAILS FOR RED CHINA," cried a headline in the Los Angeles *Times*.[1]

Indeed, four days before Tsien sailed, U.S. and Red Chinese ambassadors in Geneva had concluded repatriation negotiations and pledged their governments, unilaterally but publicly, to recognize the right of other countries' nationals to return to their homelands if they so desired.

Piously, the State Department denied any trade.

"I note the newspaper suggestion that Dr. Tsien was 'swapped' as part of a deal for the release of the eleven U.S. airmen," said a spokesman. "It would be totally contrary to our principles to be swapping or exchanging individuals or groups of individuals. The United States has not been engaged and is not now engaged in swapping human beings."[2]

Said Professor Marble, later, "We chatted about all those rumors of a trade. But Tsien snickered about it. I don't imagine we will ever know the truth. But if that is what happened, it was a poor trade."

Said Professor Rannie, "I think the Government just decided that after five years of being cut off from classified information, anyone is decontaminated."

The man who had been Tsien's administrative superior in Aerojet, one-time Navy Undersecretary Dan Kimball, no longer was in government.

"Tsien did get word to me that he wasn't leaving on his own accord," Kimball recalled of that time. "He was being sent out. And I called up the State Department. I called up the Navy Department and told them I thought they should protest, because I thought Tsien was entirely too valuable to *let* leave the country. Matter of fact, if I had anything to do with it, I wouldn't have let him leave the country under *any* circumstance. He knew too much. He had too much brains."

Was there a trade?

"Well, I'm sure the State Department's got some records of it, and possibly the CIA may also have. There may have been a trade with the Chinese for some other people, which is perfectly understandable. I'm sure there must have been *some* kind of trade because the Chinese must have known what they wanted to get."

Would Tsien have stayed in the United States for good if the FBI hadn't been after him in the first place?

"I think he really was rather sad," recalled Dean Watson of Caltech. "He was certainly resentful over the treatment he received in this country. I always felt he would have stayed. Some felt he might not have."

And his old friend Sidney Weinbaum, who knew from his own experience what Tsien had gone through, thought likewise.

"I'm pretty sure at that time when these things happened, he wanted to stay," Weinbaum remembered. "But he is a proud person. Disrespect was shown to him. They don't trust him, so that was enough for him to feel — well, there is something between the United States and China that they don't trust him. At that time he was close to Chiang Kai-shek. There was no question about his desire to come back."

And William Zisch of Aerojet-General thought Tsien would have made America his adopted home if America had not turned on him.

"I have no question about it at all," he said. "He expressed this. His real desire was to continue on, to be close and to study with von Kármán in von Kármán's waning years. . . . He'd really made a decision to devote himself and his career to Theodore von Kármán and that association, and looked upon him really as a father."

In any case, it was all over now. The S.S. *President Cleveland* steamed into Hong Kong Harbor the evening of October 8, 1955. The lights of the storied British Crown Colony flickered across its towering hillsides and down to the water's edge, where Chinese junks maneuvered past the dark hulls of ocean liners.

A patrol boat roared out from the wharf, across the choppy waters. It docked alongside the *President Cleveland*. With crisp salutes, Hong Kong police climbed aboard. They escorted Tsien, his family and the thirty-nine Chinese students down the gangplank to a waiting launch and sped them across the harbor to police headquarters. A phalanx of guards barred eager newspaper correspondents from approaching Tsien, but after two hours gave in to their importuning. The interview was brief and unproductive.[3]

REPORTER: What about the confiscation of your papers?

TSIEN: At the moment, I cannot talk about this.

REPORTER: Are all the Chinese students in the United States willing to return to China?

TSIEN: I cannot talk about this.

REPORTER: Before you went to the U.S.A. where were you educated? Can you tell us about this?

TSIEN: That is not important at all. I don't think I have to answer you.

REPORTER: Can you tell us of any of your friends who have not been released?

TSIEN: We Chinese students do not have the freedom of speaking in the United States, and I have no intention of answering for them.

REPORTER: Did the American Consulate send someone to question you?

TSIEN: Why don't you go and ask the American Consulate yourself?

REPORTER: After returning to China, where would be your destination? Shanghai, Peking or Tientsin?

(*No answer.*)

REPORTER: Was your daughter born in the States?

TSIEN (*after a moment of reflection*): Yes.

REPORTER: If your daughter was born in the States, is she still a U.S. citizen?

TSIEN: You can check that yourself.

REPORTER: Does your daughter speak Chinese?

TSIEN: This is my private affair. I refuse to answer the question.

REPORTER: What was the reason the U.S. Government approved your leaving?

TSIEN: No reason given.

REPORTER: When did you marry your wife?

TSIEN: It is beside the point.

REPORTER: Were you under observation?

TSIEN: I don't know.

REPORTER: Do you have all your books and luggage?

TSIEN: Majority of them.

REPORTER: Was part of it confiscated?

TSIEN: Yes.

REPORTER: What was confiscated?

TSIEN: According to American export rules, you are not allowed to bring out anything which you cannot get from a shop.

REPORTER: Do you mean that your aeronautical engineering notes were confiscated?

TSIEN: All the notes, such as a diary.

(*A Chinese reporter put in a question in English.*)

TSIEN (*smiling*): I think every Chinese should speak the Chinese language.

SAME REPORTER: I speak only Cantonese and English.

TSIEN: I think Mandarin is widely used in China, and you are a Chinese. You should learn Mandarin.

(*General laughter.*)

That was it. Tiny Jung-jen lisped a Mandarin "thank you," and the Tsiens turned their backs on the Hong Kong press.

It was almost midnight when Tsien and his family boarded the train from Hong Kong to Shengshui, the last British checkpoint before reaching the frontier of Communist China. British guards boarded the train and checked the passes of all the passengers.

The train chugged on to the last stop at Lo Wu, at the edge of British territory. There, the railroad tracks led across a fifty-yard bridge over a narrow stream. On one side of the iron rail British guards stood stiffly erect in their starched khaki uniforms with short pants and knee socks, armed only with their billy sticks. On the other side stood Chinese border guards in their drab gray uniforms. They carried rifles, and had pistols strapped to their belts. Across the barbed wire, the travelers could catch a glimpse of a brilliant red star and a white "dove of peace" adorning a sentry post.

The train came to a halt. Tsien, in a well-cut dark suit and white panama hat, stepped down to the wooden planks of the bridge. He took one lingering look behind, the last he would see of the non-Communist world.

"I have come to serve my fatherland," he said, softly.

With those words, Tsien picked up his belongings and walked across the bridge into Red China and into a new life.

Early the next morning, the Tsiens arrived in Kwantung and were welcomed at the railway station by a delegation of scientists. That night he attended a dinner in his honor at the Student Union of the Natural Science Institution.

Four days later, Tsien's father met his two grandchildren for the first time. The family stayed at Shanghai two weeks and then boarded a train for Peking.

As Tsien stepped from the train, a delegation waited to greet him — the sort of delegation which would be sent to attend the arrival of an important personage.

Two stepped forward to greet him. One was scholarly looking, a bit younger than Tsien. At the sight of the other, Tsien gave a quick start of recognition and then broke into a broad smile.

He knew the younger man well. It was "Jimmy" Chien — Chien Wei-chang. He had been a rocketry specialist in his student days at Caltech. He had been Tsien's student and protégé. And he, too, had left the United States for good.

The man who headed the welcoming delegation also had left the United States forever. He was none other than the noted University of Illinois mathematician — Hua Lo-keng.[4]

Seldom thereafter did any of their American friends hear from Tsien, Chao or the others.

Peking's Communist party was careful of its most important scientists, and that meant the scientists who were able to advance China's military potential. Promises which were made in the letters to the United States to lure scientific talent back home were scrupulously kept. The returnees were given good apartments, honored treatment, the best of whatever poverty-stricken China had to offer, and were put immediately to work, isolated from the tumult of Communist politics.[5]

Quickly, Tsien became director of the Institute of Mechanics in the Academy of Sciences. He was appointed to the board of the Department of Physics, Mathematics and Chemistry. He was named to the National Committee of the Chinese Scientific and Technological Association. He became chairman of the China Aerodynamics Society and chairman of the China Astronautical Society. He became head of the Department of Modern Mechanics in the Institute of Sciences and Technology.[6] But the party did not induct him as a member — evidently it took time to decontaminate him after his long stay in the United States — until three years after he returned.

By the time Tsien returned to China, Chao Chung-yao, Hua Lo-keng, Wang Kan-chang and other alumni of illustrious American educational institutions were already hard at work on China's nuclear program. Caltech's Chao was deputy director of the Institute of Atomic Energy. It was he who established it. He, too, was named to a variety of scientific boards and commissions. So was Hua Lo-keng, who, by the time of Tsien's repatriation, was deputy director of the Department of Physics, Chemistry and Mathematics of the Academy, director of its special Institute of Mathematics and director of its Institute of Computer Techniques, in which Tsien soon would collaborate with him.

Chien San-chiang, the alumnus of the University of Paris and student of Frédéric Joliot-Curie, became overall director of China's nuclear program, with Wang Kan-chang of the University of California as his deputy director. Nieh Jung-chien, then an army marshal and a physicist with European training, would be the military-political chief of the program.

China, emerging from the wreckage of long years of war and revolution and the shock of the Korean War, was grievously short of senior scientists in the early 1950s. Until 1955 there was little surface evidence that Red China was doing any more than laying a hopeful groundwork. But under Chao, Caltech's gift to Peking, and Chien San-chang, with his University of Paris experience, Peking was mobilizing the great potential it had in the influx of returned scientists from America and Europe — particularly from America.

Of the top two hundred Chinese scientists ready to go to work in earnest on a nuclear program for newly Communist China, more than three quarters had received their training abroad, and of those the top eighty were men educated in the United States. The quality of the scientists produced by American education was the best. Those who studied in Russia were not up to the same standards. Many of them had been selected for training in the Soviet Union on the basis of political reliability as well as scientific capability.[7] The men who had been in the United States had come from old Chinese families — the bourgeoisie — with a tradition of scholarship. Most had been sons of privileged families and had been given the advantage of solid basic education. The families of the proletariat and the peasantry, whence more politically reliable students were chosen, had not been able to afford education for their children.

Once communism came to power in China, the new regime was desperate to get top-grade students back from the United States. Peking immediately undertook an intensive campaign to persuade the students in America to leave. The Communist party, in possession of complete lists of all Chinese who had been sent to the United States to study under the Chiang Kai-shek regime, sent abroad the word that special honors and special treatment awaited those who would come home.

Apart from rocketman Tsien and nuclear physicist Chao, there were a number of others at Caltech whose contributions to the Peking program must have been invaluable.[8] Hsiao Chien had just turned thirty in the summer of 1950, and at the same time achieved his Ph.D. at Caltech. He was an expert in high energy physics, especially cosmic rays. Nobody at Caltech could remember just how he dropped out of sight.

"Hsiao had to leave suddenly," remembered Dr. Carl Anderson, a Nobel Prize winner who had been a student contemporary of both Chao and Hsiao. "People around here believed he was a Communist. It sticks in my memory that he wrote a letter to someone here when he got home and extolled the virtues of communism.

"He was an able student, though nothing like Chao. I never asked him or inquired about political things, but just from what people said, I know he had an interest in political things. I remember something about his family came up — he had to get back. It was nip and tuck on his getting away."

Perhaps Hsiao, too, had received an implied threat from Peking.

Kuo Yung-huai won his Ph.D. in aeronautics at Caltech and became a protégé of Dr. Tsien, serving as his assistant in rocketry. He developed into an able scientist. Kuo had little interest in politics. He was a polite, good-looking young man who had become a close friend of his teacher. Kuo was brilliant in his own right. He had been a professor of aerodynamics at Cornell before arriving at Caltech. He had met a Chinese graduate student at Cornell and married her, but she left him to go back to China, and after the roof fell in on Dr. Tsien, Kuo slipped away.

Hu Ning, during World War II, also worked with Dr. Tsien on the Caltech rocket project. He slipped out of the country years later, vanishing without a trace.

Meng Chao-ying earned his Ph.D. at Caltech in physics. He was destined eventually to become a physicist at Tsinghua University in Kunming.

Chiang Chia-hua, a physicist, took his Ph.D. at Washington University in St. Louis. He went back to China in the mid-1950s.

Shi Ju-wei studied at Yale University. He became one of China's able nuclear physicists.

The list is long and impressive — men like:

Tang Ting-yuan, University of Chicago, 1950, became a research fellow of the Institute of Physics of the Chinese Academy of Sciences.

Li Cheng-wu, Ph.D., Caltech, 1951, in nuclear physics, became a research fellow of the Institute of Physics, Chinese Academy.

Hsiang Jen-sheng, physicist, alumnus of Rutgers.

Ko Ting-sui, expert on metal research, universities of California and Chicago.

Hou Yu-chun, Ph.D., University of Michigan, spectrochemical work.

Chu Kuang-ya, nuclear physics, Caltech and University of Michigan.

Chang Wen-yu, Princeton, 1945–1949, specialist in cosmic ray research and observations of the fine structure of alpha particles and gamma rays emitted in mu-mesonic atom transitions.

Hung Chao-sheng, Massachusetts Institute of Technology, 1948, became associate research fellow, Institute of Applied Physics, Chinese Academy of Sciences.

Ko Ting-sui, University of California, 1944, physicist who worked on secret U.S. projects, became a board member of the Department of Physics, Mathematics and Chemistry, Chinese Academy.

Chu Kuang-ya, Ph.D., University of Michigan, 1950, nuclear physicist who became a professor at Peking University.

Ma Ta-yi, studied at Harvard University, became deputy director of Peking's Institute of Electronics.

Ying Cheng-fu, Brown University, 1952, returned to China to work on ultrasonics, especially in application to solid state physics.

The list could go on and on (see the Appendix, pages 299–309).

Europe's help to China's army of science was substantial, though not nearly as great as that of the United States.

Europe provided Chien San-chiang, who eventually would be director of the Red Chinese nuclear program, and was the early training ground of a number of those, including Chien's deputy, Wang Kan-chang, and the mathematician, Hua Lo-keng, before they finished their studies and training in the United States.

Chien San-chiang and his wife, Ho Che-hui, both studied as physicists at the University of Paris under the Joliot-Curies, Frédéric and Irène, who were known for their ultra-leftist leanings. Those who knew Chien in Paris felt he was far from a Communist at that time. But once communism took over in China, the new regime conferred upon him considerable political prominence, in all probability because he was one of the few men in China at the time capable of planning for a nuclear program. Chien, born in Chekiang Province in 1910, had been a graduate in physics of Tsinhua National University in 1936 and went on from there on a scholarship from the Chiang Kai-shek government to study in France. He won the French Academy of Sciences physics award in 1946 for research on gamma and alpha rays and the tripartition in nuclear fission of uranium. He had a reputation for brilliance.

China still was under Chiang Kai-shek when Chien returned in 1948 to become professor of nuclear physics at his alma mater, Tsinghua. As soon as the Communists took over, he was given an honorary political position as deputy chairman of the All-China Democratic Youth Federation. This was a favorite device for placing scientists in political jobs. Many a scientist — including Rocketman Tsien — would become deputy chairman of the Youth Federation.

Chien melted in with the Communist way. He was a delegate to the various propaganda meetings of the Communist-inspired World Peace Congresses in Europe, and he also became an executive secretary of the Sino-Soviet Friendship Society at a time when the friendship was just about beginning to sour.

Wang Kan-chang, the University of California alumnus, was born a native of Kiangsu Province in 1907, the son of a provincial doctor of medicine. He was graduated at the top of his class from Tsinghua University in 1934, and from there went to the University of Berlin on a scholarship granted by the Chiang Kai-shek government. There he studied under the renowned nuclear physicist, Dr. Lise Meitner. Wang went back to China during World War II, but immediately after the war left for the University of California as a research associate in physics. He returned again to China while it still was under Chiang, in 1948. A year later, when the Communists took over, Wang became a top researcher in nuclear physics. Eventually he studied in collaboration with Bruno Pontecorvo, the Italian-born British physicist who fled with Britain's nuclear secrets to the Soviet Union, and became a Soviet citizen. Wang was a cosmopolite, western in his ways, a natty dresser and an amiable mixer.

Nieh Jung-chen studied engineering in France, natural sciences in Belgium, and military sciences in the Soviet Union. He was as much politician-soldier as he was scientist, however. He was an ideal man for political-military charge of China's March on Science. Nieh was an army marshal before all ranks were abolished in later years, and was destined to become a member of the inner circle of party rulers.

Those were only a few of the scientists whom Europe had contributed to a China which, as communism took over, had been poor in senior talent. All the senior men had bourgeois backgrounds. All ordinarily would have been suspect once back in China. Their good fortune was that they could be helpful in the nuclear program, and thus their reeducation would be far less painful than the process inflicted upon intellectuals in other fields.

The physicists concentrated on their science and forgot about politics, although with their backgrounds of long years of study abroad, they remained cultural aliens in their own homeland.

III

NUCLEAR BOOMERANG

30

What happened to Tsien Hsue-shen, Chao Chung-yao, Wang Kan-chang, "Jimmy" Chien and all the other American-educated scientists from the time they left the United States was part of the incredible history of a decade which saw a determined Red China push into the nuclear age in the midst of violent internal Chinese political explosions.

Not long after he returned from California, Missileman Tsien bade farewell to his pretty wife and his two children and headed for a long stay in Russia, one of a select group of senior Chinese scientists — all educated in Europe or America — who would participate in joint nuclear research with the Russians. Chao, Wang and many another who had studied in the United States were Tsien's fellow members in the group. So was Chien San-chiang, the Joliot-Curies' protégé from the University of Paris.

Chien San-chiang by now was the chief of China's new Physics Research Institute in Peking, with Chao as his first deputy. He was no stranger to Moscow, nor was Chao by this time. Both had been there in the chill days of February and March, 1953, for a stay of five weeks with a delegation headed by the dread Lo Jui-ching, then Red China's Minister of Public Security.

While Chien's delegation of scientists was in Moscow that first time, Josef Stalin died. Chien, Chao and the rest of the scientists filed past the bier to pay their solemn respects, but they were in Russia not to mourn, but to bargain. They stayed on long after the Stalin funeral, questing for technological help, and by that, the Chinese meant help on the path to nuclear weapons capability.

Publicly, Chinese Communists spurned nuclear weapons. Mao Tse-tung had called the atom bomb a "paper tiger" useful only for scaring people. Privately, they craved nuclear power, and the presence of the Chinese scientific delegation in Moscow was clear evidence of this hunger.

The mission of Chien San-chiang and his delegation could well have been the beginning of the process which profoundly shook the whole Communist world. It led first to Soviet help, then to nervous Soviet second thoughts and finally to the noisy row in which Peking's eagerness for the bomb played a dominating role. It led eventually to a series of agreements on technology, collaboration in the search inside China for the raw materials of atomic power and to participation by Chinese scientists in research at the Joint Institute of Nuclear Research at Dubna, near Moscow.

And it was to Dubna that Tsien, Wang, Chao and Chien, along with many other senior scientists and many a lower-echelon one from China headed in 1956, when Peking's Great Nuclear Leap Forward was about to begin.

From the beginning, 1956 was a year of furious activity. Displaying eagerness for speed, the Chinese Communist party Central Committee had met in January and produced a call for a March on Science. Chairman Mao himself announced a "long-range plan for the elimination of backwardness in the economic, scientific and cultural fields." It had to be launched at once. Immediately, a planning committee was set up under the leadership of Marshal Nieh Jung-chen, the vice-premier who had been European-trained in nuclear physics. To the Committee for Scientific Development were named six hundred scientists who were to be helped by seventeen Russian advisers.

They were charged with drafting a twelve-year program to be presented in September to the party's Eighth Congress which, of course, would automatically approve it. The plan then would go to the Soviet Union for help from China's Russian comrades. The stated objective: "to bring our country up to the present-day world level."

Premier Chou En-lai transmitted the program to Soviet Premier Bulganin with a request that Soviet scientists look it over. That was a tall order. The documents totaled five million words, and to look them over the Russians had to set up twenty-six consultation groups with 640 Soviet scientists taking part. China then sent a 120-man delegation to Moscow to confer. One form of help would be Chinese participation in the joint research at Dubna, to which China was contributing twenty per cent of the cost.

The extent of this assistance would prove fairly astonishing, given the normal Russian aversion to power in a nearby nation. Scientists and engineers by the thousands traveled from China to the institute, set up at the junction of the Volga River and the Moscow Canal. Several villages had been cleared away so that a system could be created to provide hydroelectric power in abundance. A huge artificial lake adorned the area, just east of the main highway to Moscow. The complex included two- and three-story buildings erected with the usual Soviet attention to drabness: all of dull, yellowish-brown concrete. Near the main buildings were the apartments for participating scientists.

By the time the Chinese scientists reached Dubna, the two Caltech men, Tsien and Chao, were securely established as heads of the nuclear bomb-missile program. Chao was one of five deputy directors of the Institute of Atomic Energy which he had founded, and rocketman Tsien's importance had been underscored by a picture of him which had been seen by foreign scientists. It showed him seated at a wooden table, dressed in a military uniform without insignia. Seated next to him, smiling, was Mao Tse-tung.

While Nieh Jung-chen and Chien San-chiang were in overall military and administrative charge, respectively, of the atomic program, Chao and Tsien were of at least equal stature. The evidence suggests that Tsien became a commuter between Dubna and Peking.[1]

The CHINA CLOUD

Back in China in August, 1957, at a time when a group of American students was traveling there against the wishes of the U.S. State Department, Tsien was trotted out for their benefit as a sort of exhibit. His bitterness at America had not lessened. Tsien told the forty-one young Americans that the Soviet Union would soon overtake the United States in all phases of aircraft development. He had seen the extent of Soviet rocket development while in Moscow and had evidently been impressed.

A short time later, the Russians shocked the United States, and precipitated a high-level panic which generated a heated controversy over a "missile gap." Sputnik I, the world's first artificial earth satellite, was sent into orbit, demonstrating the heavy rocket thrust at the command of the Soviet military. It suggested that the U.S.S.R. soon would be capable of deploying intercontinental ballistic missiles. When, finally, the Americans put their own first satellite into orbit, seeming small by comparison with the heavy Sputnik, Tsien wrote an article for a Soviet scientific journal about it. He concluded that "the mighty United States has given birth to a mouse." [2]

Perhaps it was Tsien's anger over the treatment he had received in the United States which sustained him in the late 1950s. It would seem unlikely that a man of his intellectual capacity and devotion to pure science could be undismayed by what was going on in his motherland at the time. Those years were unhappy ones for almost all intellectuals in China, and Tsien hardly could have been an exception.

31

The scientists who went back to China from America returned to a world they had no part in making. Despite their complaints about the United States and all their woes among the Americans, real or imagined, they had enjoyed limitless academic freedom there. They had experienced the freedom to let their imaginations soar, to search, to pursue science for the sake of science. Now, back in the land of their birth, they were obliged to abide by the credo of Maoism. The culture they had absorbed in the West — the music, the arts and even aspects of science — soon would be officially labeled poisonous.

For those scientists whose talents could further Communist China's great power ambitions, however, the conditions in the beginning had been quite bearable. They had been given special privileges. Research materials were available in abundance. Money was earmarked liberally for their work. The Academy of Sciences took steps to encourage young intellectuals to follow scientific careers, even to the point of overlooking suspect bourgeois family backgrounds. The Twelve-Year Plan for a March on Science was the main preoccupation of the academy in the mid-1950s.

Then came even more encouragement. On February 27, 1957, Chairman Mao addressed a closed session of the Supreme State Conference. The title of his address was "On the Correct Handling of Contradictions among the People." The speech was not published then.[1] But a line from it was well known long before publication: "Let a hundred flowers bloom, let a hundred schools of thought contend."

This, indeed, was something new. Until then, no other school of thought except that of the Chinese version of Marxism-Leninism was likely to be tolerated. To the intellectuals, it seemed to promise a period when they might be able to speak their minds openly about the things they disliked in Mao's China. Many rose to the opportunity to criticize, at a time when there had been widespread grumbling among China's intellectuals. "Hundred Flowers Societies" blossomed everywhere, and the light of the debate attracted swarms of unsuspecting moths.

One such moth was "Jimmy" Chien, the protégé of Dr. Tsien Hsue-shen in the old Caltech days. Years after he disappeared into China, Jimmy Chien's name began to emerge in scientific journals. Western intelligence, monitoring Chinese broadcasts and combing Peking propaganda publications began to note increasing mention of Chien Wei-chang in his new role of rising figure on the stage of Communist Chinese science. By 1954, a year before his one-time mentor, Tsien, could leave America, Jimmy Chien had already become vice-president of Tsinghua University in Peking. The Chinese press referred to him as a jet propulsion specialist. At the age of forty-two he had become one of the youngest of a fifty-man national committee of the All China Association of Natural Sciences. Chien simultaneously managed to hold more than twenty different positions in the political-scientific upper stratum. But with the "Hundred Flowers," Jimmy Chien came to grief. Like many of his fellow intellectuals, Chien had taken Mao at his word.

"I will definitely not join the Communist party," Chien proclaimed loudly and publicly at a Peking meeting.[2] Evidently, though he had described himself in his martini-drinking days at Caltech as a sympathizer with Chinese communism, he had not been back in China sufficiently long to have been decontaminated after his stay abroad, and thus still was not a member of the Chinese Communist party.

The Chinese student movement, Chien went on — probably unsuspecting that he could be putting his neck into a noose — was in search of leadership. He contended that if teachers tried to seize that leadership, there would be big trouble.

"Parents of some students recently wrote me," said Chien, "asking me to dissuade their children from making trouble. I did, but the students were more determined . . . It looks like the eve of the May 4th movement.[3] They would not heed the advice of their parents in the same way as we would not accept the advice of our parents when we were students." [4]

It was the wrong thing to say at that time. The Hungarian Revolution had exploded in Europe only a year before. The leadership of that revolt against communism had been the intellectuals — the Petofi Club — students in search of leaders. Hungary and the Petofi Club had obviously shaken Mao severely, since in later years he and his supporters were to refer to it constantly. More than ever, after Hungary, Mao had eyed Chinese intellectuals with suspicion.

The Hundred Flowers period continued into the summer of 1957. There were student rallies, protest meetings, criticism meetings. In one, some of the leaders urged that the president of Tsinghua University resign and let the vice-president — Jimmy Chien — take his place. Students launched rumor campaigns, spread confusion among Chinese youth. They visited factories to agitate among the workers and urge them to rise up against the regime.

Then, suddenly and brutally, it all came to an end. The party made it clear that the Hundred Flowers period was over. The blossoms withered in the heat of a new rectification campaign in which "rightists" who had unmasked themselves in the period of open criticism now would pay the penalty.

"Especially heartbreaking must have been the experience of the intellectuals who, honestly and earnestly, had cast their lot in with the Communist regime but were denounced as rightists on account of over-enthusiastic 'blossoming,' " wrote a noted Chinese observer in Hong Kong.[5]

Peking's party press ran outraged accounts of what had been going on: such poison, for example, as a poem written by a young student named Yang Lu. What young Yang had written had smacked of the stuff the Petofi Club was made of — disillusion and even hatred of the regime.

I have never loved this world, nor has the world loved me;
Its filthy and foul breath I have never praised;
I have never knelt to its idolatrous dogmas,
Or smiling, obsequiously against my will, sung their praises
*   parrot fashion.*
Therefore the world cannot regard me as a fellow being.
I am not one of them, and although I am among them,
My thoughts are entirely different from theirs. . . .[6]

This was strong medicine. The party press protested that "all these key members of the reactionary group are youths in their early twenties and have spent about one third of their life in the new society, but it can be clearly seen from the facts described above that these rightists are still refusing to relinquish the interests of the dying class of exploiters." [7]

How Tsien Hsue-shen, Chao Chung-yao, Hua Lo-keng and others of the important scientists in the nuclear program fared at that time can only be guessed. There were indications that Hua had to be "rectified." But it is clear that Jimmy Chien, like thousands of others who had raised their voices in protest, faced punishment.

That year, Chien was purged. Chinese journals quoted his confession, entitled "I escaped from the imperialist trap." He conceded that he was "alarmingly behind on current developments in my field" and would require five to six years of intensive study to catch up.[8] This was palpable nonsense. Chien was well ahead of most in his field.

The "confession," however, could hardly be called abject. Chien commented, for example, that "a scientist will no longer be a scientist if he does not have sufficient time for research," a reference to the practice of overloading the relatively few senior scientists with work and thus, by depriving them of research time, damaging the whole scientific program.[9]

Chien, later, deplored the deterioration of teacher-student relationships in Chinese universities. "How could one teach the young people when they could turn around and wage a 'struggle' against the teachers? In the 'three-anti' and the anti-counterrevolutionary campaigns, students dug out minute details of their teachers' personal lives to expose their faults. When the teachers knew that what they said might be used against them, they became extremely wary in their speech." [10] This experience of the teachers was to be repeated, in an infinitely more frightening way, in the mid-1960s.

But Jimmy Chien had a well-honed talent for maneuvering himself out of trouble. Evidently he was able to do so again, because before long he appears once again to have been working at the side of his mentor and fellow Caltech alumnus, Tsien Hsue-shen. Tsien appears to have been able to wield considerable authority. If he was touched at all by the hunt for "rightists," it must have been only lightly. And now Chien once again would hitch his future to Tsien, and the two would work closely together in a program designed to provide China one day with an arsenal of nuclear-tipped missiles.

Physicist Chang Wen-yu, who had studied at Cambridge University in England, returned to China soon after Tsien Hsue-shen. Chang, too, found disillusionment. "I have been back from abroad for half a year," he said, "and the thing that impresses me most is that the academic atmosphere in the country is not strong enough. The concrete expression of this is that many people keep their mouths shut. . . ."

So far as the top men were concerned, the situation evidently eased soon after Mao's witch-hunt had found a sufficient number of scapegoats and cowed all "rightists." Once the scientists indicated they had a proper attitude toward politics — which meant mostly keeping their mouths shut on that score — the regime tended to leave them alone, particularly if they were engaged in nuclear research.

While the senior scientists went about their labors, concentrating their own talents and those of thousands of engineers and technicians on the goal of nuclear power, they were all but isolated from the gathering political storms which burst upon China one after another in the wake of the Hundred Flowers and Mao's subsequent Great Leap Forward.

32

Peking was becoming impatient, and once again, a delegation of military-scientific men traveled to Moscow in search of nuclear aid. Bowing to the urging of Mao, the Russians in October, 1957, signed an agreement on new defense technology, under which China was promised a sample atom bomb — a prototype — along with data on how to make it. But the Chinese evidently wanted even more than that.

Slowly, signs of strain between Moscow and Peking were surfacing. Perhaps Khrushchev was becoming nervous at the eagerness of the Chinese comrades. And Mao Tse-tung, at that particularly crucial time, picked a bad moment for a tactical error. He frightened Khrushchev.

Mao was in Moscow in November, 1957, ostensibly only to attend the fortieth anniversary celebration of the Bolshevik coup. He had much to say to Khrushchev — about de-Stalinization, about his own ambitions for China as a future world power, and about the 1956 revolutionary events in Communist Hungary. The Hungarian revolution against Communism obviously had frightened Mao. Frequently thereafter his followers insisted there were certain elements in Peking who would have liked something similar to happen in China.

Khrushchev already had been talking publicly about the power of nuclear weapons to destroy all mankind. No longer was he saying that only the capitalist world would perish in nuclear war. In Mao's eyes, that was heresy, and at the world Communist conference in Moscow that month, Mao declared: "If the worst came to the worst, and half of mankind died (in a nuclear war) the other half would remain, while imperialism would be razed to the ground, and the whole world would become socialist." [1] Russia had far more at stake than China, and the evidence was that Khrushchev was horrified.

The indications were that at about this time, the Russians began dragging their feet on promises to support Red China's nuclear ambitions. The Chinese, however, showed no signs of having abandoned hope of getting their hands on the promised sample A-bomb. Defense Minister Peng Teh-huai went to Moscow the following February and lavished praise on the Soviet armed forces, which he was sure would serve as example and shining inspiration for the Chinese People's Liberation Army. The Defense Minister before long would be haunted by those words.

A few months later, Foreign Minister Chen Yi announced publicly that China would have the bomb "soon." And in June, 1958, Foreign Minister Chen dedicated China's first heavy-duty reactor — seven to ten thousand kilowatt capacity — provided by the Russians under technology agreements. At the same time a Soviet-Chinese team completed a cyclotron which could accelerate atomic particles up to twenty-five million electron volts.

By this time, Red China, which could ill afford it, was devoting the equivalent of several hundred million dollars a year to its pursuit of the nuclear weapon. The Chinese nagging of Moscow was becoming more insistent. Khrushchev hustled off on a secret visit to Peking and talks with Mao. The Chinese party Chairman bluntly demanded that the Russians provide China with nuclear-tipped missiles — this in the wake of a dangerous crisis involving the shelling of Nationalist-held islands off Taiwan. Khrushchev argued: Why did China want to be a nuclear power? Did not China have assurance of Soviet protection?

All this would come out later, publicly, in outpourings of bitterness between Moscow and Peking. Events of 1958: the off-shore islands crisis, a crisis in the Middle East in which Peking found Khrushchev wanting in courage, and the Kremlin attitude toward Chinese ambitions in general, all fed latent anti-Russian feelings in the Chinese party. As the feud developed, the shadow of the nuclear bomb hung over it.

Trouble was brewing inside China, too. Many of those intellectuals who had been abroad, and particularly those who had been in the United States, were experiencing difficult times. It was only the beginning for them. The Great Leap Forward was going badly, and eventually would prove to be an economic debacle. It was becoming evident that there was infighting in the upper reaches of the Chinese Communist hierarchy, and this would surface at the Lushan conference in 1959. It was there that the first outlines emerged of a struggle for the power to determine China's future.

"Just before the bourgeois rightists began their fierce onslaught in 1957, they viciously attacked the socialist system by alleging that 'there is no system which is absolutely good,' " the Maoist leadership would reveal in later years. "At the Lushan party meeting in 1959, the big conspirator, careerist and warlord, Peng Teh-huai, who styled himself Hai Jui,[2] had vainly hoped to overthrow the leadership of the Chinese Communist party headed by Chairman Mao." [3]

In this there is an indication that in 1959, questions of China's military and nuclear future were contributing significantly to the internal political struggle in Peking. It became known later that Khrushchev had torn up the October, 1957 agreement which would have delivered the sample A-bomb to China, and he was not likely to be forgiven. Publicly the Chinese would accuse him of having set a price on compliance with the agreement: a measure of Soviet control over whatever the Russians might provide in the way of nuclear weaponry. Two months after Khrushchev's action, the Chinese party faced a crisis over policy. When the dust cleared, Mao Tse-tung had stepped down from his position as chairman of government, the equivalent to the presidency, and turned it over to his then heir-apparent, Liu Shao-chi. The evidence later would be that Mao's act was far from voluntary. He retained, however, his chairmanship of the party. And he managed, in the infighting, to bring down the powerful and influential Peng Teh-huai, who was relieved of his Defense Ministry post. It became clear to the outside world later that Peng had objected not only to the Great Leap, but to Mao's military policies and to Peking actions which contributed to the growing feud with Moscow. Marshal Peng was replaced by the skinny and saturnine Marshal Lin Piao.

The Russians eyed the events suspiciously. There were clear anti-Soviet overtones in the dismissal of Marshal Peng. Soviet policy toward China, particularly where it involved collaboration in the nuclear field, became more cautious. On Kremlin orders, Soviet scientists would maintain strict control over Soviet nuclear materials in China. But the Soviet scientists would not be in China much longer, in any case.

By the time Khrushchev returned from his spectacular 1959 visit to the United States and his "Spirit of Camp David" talks with President Dwight D. Eisenhower, Peking was blasting him enthusiastically, and the Soviet leader once again took off for Peking to argue with Mao, to advise him to tone down China's bellicosity. But the quarrel only became noisier.

Behind all the ideological thunderbolts emanating from Peking and Moscow was the rankling question of China's nuclear ambitions and Russia's growing opposition to them. Khrushchev became, to Peking, a "modern revisionist," a coward who was afraid of violent revolution. By this time Peking surely knew it was on its own so far as the bomb was concerned. It would be, as the propaganda put it, a case of "relying on one's own resources."

China had the resources, despite her economic reverses in the wake of Mao's disastrous Great Leap Forward. And it had the men to do the job: men like Chao, Wang and Chien to make the bomb, men like Tsien to marry it to a missile. Khrushchev had shut the barn door too late, for the horse had already escaped.

At Moscow in November, 1960, at another world Communist meeting, silver-haired Liu Shao-chi, chairman (president) of the Chinese People's Republic, raised a finger and announced to a hushed audience of Communist dignitaries: "China soon will become a nuclear power. We have four atomic reactors in operation. Such atomic reactors are not set up only for peace purposes, but they may also be used for war purposes." [4] His words echoed like a distant crack of doom.

The beginning of the end of Soviet-Chinese nuclear collaboration had been heralded the previous April when *People's Daily* published a Lenin's Birthday anniversary editorial, "Long Live Leninism," for the first time spelling out specific complaints against "modern revisionism." By now the facade of monolithic unity was developing deep cracks.

Khrushchev, by the end of 1960, had pulled all Soviet technicians out of China and had halted all technological aid, but by the time he acted there were "no problems China could not solve on the road to nuclear power." [5] She had the men and she had the materials.

The nuclear argument raged on through months and years of statements, letters and speeches, spilling out many political secrets between Moscow and Peking. Insults and verbal brickbats flew back and forth in profusion.

"No one can monopolize the right to speak on the question of nuclear weapons," growled the Chinese. [6] The Soviet Government, retorted Moscow, had years of experience with nuclear weapons. "The point is not that someone wants to monopolize the right to speak about nuclear weapons and to deny this right to others; the point is: whose pronouncements on such a question carry weight and whose sound like prattle?" [7]

Peking had to admit, the Russians insisted, that China was un-prepared to produce nuclear arms in quantity. China would be better advised to rely on Soviet protection and "devote its efforts to the development of the national economy."

"Let us grant that by overstraining its economy, the CPR will finally be able to produce a few atomic bombs. But how many such bombs in this case would be aimed by the imperialists at the CPR? Would the Chinese leaders feel themselves more secure, even though sitting on their own atomic bomb?" [8]

The quarrel ran on and on in that vein. Meanwhile, the feud was seeding a growing internal political crisis inside China and contributing to a situation which would foment upheaval in the Soviet Union as well. At the same time, the world Communist movement was in an uproar, also partly as a result of China's nuclear ambitions.[9]

Khrushchev by 1964 dropped all pretense that what was going on between Moscow and Peking was solely an ideological dispute. "If in the past," he protested, "some comrades thought that all this was merely a theoretical quarrel, then now there is absolutely no foundation for holding such an opinion. . . . This is not simply a theoretical quarrel and not merely an ideological polemic, but a far-reaching schismatic course aiming to impose political domination over the socialist camp and the worldwide Communist movement." [10]

As much as anything else, Khrushchev intimated, it was a nuclear-military argument. The exchanges made it clear that China's leaders felt the Soviet Union would not use its military might in the interests of spreading Communism at gunpoint and was trying to prevent the Chinese party from pursuing a policy which promised to surround China with nations it could consider safely submissive.

And then, with the quarrel at its most bombastic level, came two great upheavals, one political, the other technological. The Kremlin dismissed Khrushchev. Red China dropped its first atom bomb.

33

Peking erupted with celebration. Signs blossomed all over the capital, at bus stops, on factories, in shop windows: Nuclear Bomb Success, and youngsters danced in the streets.[1] Premier Chou En-lai, in a display of Chinese Communist logic, blandly announced that the atomic blast was "an important contribution to the defense of world peace." And in a slap at the Russians, he also described it as a "victory of the Chinese people relying on their own resources." [2]

In the United States there was mild public interest. Advance announcements that the blast was coming, and downgrading it, had eased the blow considerably. In Russia, the population was still reeling from the news of Khrushchev's tumble from power. There was little time to pay attention to China's bomb, which the press had dismissed with a curt one-sentence announcement.

The first Chinese atomic device was exploded from a slender tower four hundred feet high — the tower which spy planes had watched going up piece by piece. The blast hit the Takla Makan salt flats with brutal force and sent out shock waves picked up by seismographs thousands of miles away. When the debris was analyzed, both Americans and Russians were shocked.

To Dr. Ralph Lapp, who had been one of the important figures in America's Manhattan Project which developed the first U.S. atom bomb, China's entry into the Nuclear Club meant that "a new look at our deterrence" was required.[3] Peking might soon hold in its hands the power to threaten the world, not necessarily with its own arsenal but with its capability of attacking, for example, the Nationalist Chinese on Taiwan, which conceivably could lead to a thermonuclear war between the United States and the Soviet Union.

It was a chilling thought. However much the Russians and Chinese themselves might be fighting, Soviet interests clearly would be immediately at stake should China become involved in major conflict with the United States, and the world cataclysm could develop with the inevitability of Greek tragedy.

The Russians had known well in advance that the China explosion was coming. The Americans had certain knowledge of it. The Central Intelligence Agency had been watching the goings-on in Sinkiang for a long time.

Since the Russians had refused to send Chinese interceptor jets and missiles, it was easy for U-2 spy planes and other high-flying craft to photograph China's installations. The Takla Makan Desert is wide open. It was an easy subject for the cameras of the U-2s and orbiting satellites. Nationalist Chinese pilots had trained in the United States for the U-2 job.

For months, various spies in the skies watched heavy equipment hauled overland across China to the desert site. They had watched the blast tower being erected, piece by piece. The satellite devices were so efficient that on their passes over China they produced, from a hundred miles in the air, pictures in which one could read the names on street signs.

The satellites were sent into polar orbits from California. Their cameras recorded detailed pictures of enemy and friendly countries alike. The film was ejected over the Pacific in parachute devices and caught on the way down by specially-equipped C-130 cargo planes. The photographs were rushed to Washington, processed en route.

The perfection of this system had been an important breakthrough. It evidently was this to which the Chinese had referred when they complained that Khrushchev had received certain information which decided him to go ahead with the signing of a partial nuclear test ban. Not much could be kept hidden for long.

The U-2s, satellites and possibly photographic drone planes as well had, long before China's first explosion, established that a plutonium reactor center had been in operation near Paotow in Inner Mongolia.

The aerial spies spotted roads newly built in Sinkiang's desert, heavy traffic, new buildings and workmen's tents. Electronic ears later would be able to pick up the explosion, pinpoint the test site and estimate the size of the blast. Magnetic eyes would see disturbances in the earth's magnetic field. Radio direction finders, called feelers, would pick up signals which could time the blast to the exact second. Sophisticated instruments all around the world would analyze the impact on the ground as the device hit. Reconnaissance planes with air filters mounted on their wings would gather fallout debris. Samples would be examined in laboratories for more clues. There was little the Americans wouldn't know about the Chinese program, and what gaps there might be would be filled in by Chinese documents published by China's Academy of Sciences and smuggled out of the country by spies.

Red China was helpless to do anything about it, a fact which made Peking all the more furious with Moscow, which could have supplied the means for countering some of the American detection methods.

But the true description of the bomb and its meaning did not reach the American public at once. After the first news of the explosion, Americans still were reckoning that it would be a long time before China became an "efficient" nuclear power with a delivery system and with warheads married to missiles. If there was an immediate worry, it concerned the effect of the Chinese blast on backward nations which Peking was trying to impress and to the leadership of which Peking long had aspired.

The consensus of experts in the United States was that China might achieve a moderate stockpile equal to that of France by 1970; hydrogen bombs and perhaps medium-range bombers and missiles by 1975, a position roughly equivalent to Britain's in 1964. By 1980, almost anything could happen inside seething, overpopulated China.

The low yield of the first Chinese test had been as predicted. But if the blast itself was no surprise, there was surprise enough to come. It developed that the fissionable material was not plutonium, which is used in the simplest nuclear devices. Instead it was the rare isotope of uranium, U-235. The Americans discovered this by the examination of the radioactive fallout.

This evidence of advanced technology had a chilling effect, both in the West and in the Soviet Union. No longer was there a tendency to dismiss China's first blast lightly as primarily a propaganda stunt. The technology which had brought it about had been complex.

Indications were that China had in full operation a gaseous diffusion plant for the production of enriched uranium, and this meant a much more sophisticated technology than had been expected. The plant was at Lanchow in Kansu Province, seven hundred miles east of the testing area in Sinkiang. It was built in the early days of China's nuclear drive, with Soviet assistance.

Not many years before, Lanchow had been a smallish, remote city of two hundred thousand. In 1964, spy planes noted furious activity in the area. And the city had burgeoned into a teeming metropolis of a million and one of the most important industrial centers in China. It was a center for heavy machinery, chemicals and an oil refinery. There was plenty of power available from the hydroelectric installation constructed on the Yellow River nearby.

The walled city, lying in a valley hard by the Yellow River, is surrounded by towering hills of desert sand, over which camel caravans still plod along in the ancient way. A network of railroads links it with sources of supplies and with the Takla Makan site.

American chemists noted that enriched uranium produced by the Lanchow gaseous diffusion process provided a great amount of flexibility in nuclear technology. Enriched uranium would make possible the reactor production of tritium, which is a key ingredient in thermonuclear bombs. The Chinese thus might have been more clearly in sight of an H-bomb than the West had dreamed possible.

The United States had known for some time that China had a gaseous diffusion plant. But the process is expensive, requiring enormous quantities of electric power. China was willing to make the investment.

It meant that China could extract fissionable U-235 from the relatively nonfissionable U-238, and thus be able to stockpile low-yield bombs fairly quickly.

The H-bomb, by the reckoning of American experts, would be tougher to achieve, especially without any outside help from the Russians. But definitely the Chinese were on their way. The question was: when? [4]

In the United States and the Soviet Union, it was a time for sober reflection on just what had been wrought in China and how it had been done — primarily with Soviet and American aid.

By the time Soviet experts were pulled out of China, about ten thousand Soviet scientists in all had been involved in working with the Chinese in various branches of science. In the meantime, China between 1949 and 1960 had graduated two hundred and thirty thousand engineers and was planning for two million more graduates by 1967. They had the benefit of the knowledge passed on to them by the men who had gained it abroad.

China, by the time the Russians left, had a hundred thousand who could be called scientists and three hundred thousand who could claim to be engineers. It would have required only a small percentage of such an army to build a bomb. Many of the scientists and engineers had been superbly trained and were highly skilled. Moreover, they had ready access to raw materials for the bomb.

There would, however, have been a damaging shortage of senior scientists to work on such a program had it not been for the extremely able men like Drs. Chien, Wang, Chao, Tsien and others trained in the United States and Western Europe.

The bomb was a costly one from several standpoints. It was the result of a decade of concentrated effort at the cost of nobody knew how much hardship and privation for China's hungry millions, at the cost of alienating the Russian allies, at the cost of more isolation for China from the Communist world and the family of nations. But the politicians in Peking found excuses. From an ideological standpoint, the bomb was a must — more so in view of the American, Soviet and British treaty banning most types of testing, but Peking's Communist politicians had put it this way:

"Whether or not nuclear weapons help peace depends on who possesses them. It is detrimental to peace if they are in the hands of the imperialist countries." [5]

Peking seemed to be arguing that China did not really want the bomb and was doing all she was doing against her will. This was as much for the benefit of her own xenophobic people at home as for that of the Russians.

"Socialist countries do not want nuclear weapons. Nuclear weapons cannot be eaten. No one would be happier than we if nuclear weapons were thoroughly destroyed." [6]

The Russians were made all the more uncomfortable by the implications in the Chinese statements about prospective proliferation. China, from the words of her leaders, evidently cared little how many nations armed themselves with the bomb.

China's blast reverberated around the world. In Western Europe there was indignation. Many European nations could have had their own programs if they had wanted them badly enough. The press in Italy, which had the West's strongest and probably most influential Communist party, pictured China as ambitious and aggressive and a nation without respect for human life.

Possibly because of President Charles de Gaulle's influence, however, the indignation aroused in Western Europe by the initial shock soon died down. De Gaulle had no more major interests in Asia. He had not been party to the partial test-ban treaty. Thus he and France received the China bomb without any murmur or protest. France hardly could protest, since the French had been saying all along that the only proper nuclear deterrent was one's own.

In Britain, the official reaction of the ruling Labor party came in an expression of determination to stand by commitments to Southeast Asia and the Southeast Asia Treaty Organization.

In Australia and New Zealand, there was acute worry. China was far more imminent a threat to them than to Western Europe. Officially both countries condemned the China bomb as an outrage upon world opinion and a threat of proliferation. Australia, like Britain, pleaded against an "utterly foolish" political boycott of China.

For India, Ceylon and the Himalayan states, the explosion of China's bomb was the worst kind of news, particularly in view of the history of China's pressures on the Himalayan frontiers. The event provoked a debate in India's parliament and in the press on whether India, too, should have the bomb.

In Thailand, Prime Minister Thanom Kittikachorn's government expressed fear that the China bomb would encourage Communist subversion in all Southeast Asia.

There was political impact in Latin America. Even diplomats expressed themselves as impressed with China's feat, calling it a brilliant achievement for a backward nation and indicating they believed it would mean a realignment of military and political forces in the world.

Most of the Communist world was glumly silent about China's first blast. But not North Vietnam. Hanoi received the news of the bomb with jubilation. Hanoi Radio judged that China's bomb would be an "encouragement for the Vietnamese people in their sacred fight against U.S. aggression and for national salvation, as well as for the revolutionary peoples now struggling for self-liberation." [7]

Gradually, in the United States, the idea was accepted that there was now a real military threat to Asia in China's possession of the bomb, and this involved the United States, so deeply committed to the defense of Asia. Perhaps, the Asians worried, the United States might now seek a return to the policy of threatening "massive retaliation."

Either the Americans now would get into some sort of dialogue with Peking, thus implying recognition eventually, or see the threat of China to Asian and world peace grow apace. Sooner or later, then, both the Russians and the Americans probably would face the necessity of negotiating with Peking if there was to be any end to the arms race. And sooner or later, if China was to become a less dangerous member of the family of nations, Peking ought to be in the United Nations.

The big trouble was: Peking seemed completely disinterested in talking with either the Americans or the Russians, and equally disinterested in the United Nations.

34

Premier Chou En-lai gloated. "Have we not exploded an atom bomb? Has not the label, 'sick man of the east,' fastened on us by Westerners, been flung off? Why can't the proletariat of the East accomplish what the bourgeoisie of the West has been able to?" [1]

The Chinese had done it, he exulted, in spite of Khrushchev's perfidy in tearing up "several hundred agreements and contracts." As for the imperialists, "since China possesses nuclear weapons, things have begun to change," said Chou. Eventually, he implied, peace-loving China would force the war-loving ruling clique of Americans into an agreement to destroy all nuclear weapons.

Chou, who had visited Moscow a month after Khrushchev's fall, was unimpressed by the duumvirate which succeeded him: First Party Secretary Leonid Ilyich Brezhnev and Premier Alexei

Nikolayevich Kosygin. They were practicing "Khrushchevism without Khrushchev," and there was not "the slightest difference with Khrushchev on the question of the international Communist movement and the attitude toward China." But although Chou found reasons to boast publicly, he had many other reasons to worry privately. In 1965 signs of a forthcoming political explosion were clearly discernible. A New Year's message to the people from the Communist party, printed by *People's Daily*, complained of "some comrades among us who always consider themselves right and never imagine they can be wrong."

It was against a background of internal uneasiness in China, of confusion generated by the Moscow-Peking war of words and general world nervousness over a steadily intensifying war in Vietnam that the Red Chinese exploded their second atomic device.

Seven months had elapsed since the first device had been dropped from a tower onto the salt flats of Takla Makan. The second explosion, on May 14, 1965, was reported to be not much larger than the first — still only relatively little beyond that range of twenty-kiloton force equivalent to the first American blast at Alamogordo twenty years before. But there did seem to be a difference.

The fireball from Blast No. 2, films disclosed later, seemed lighter than the first in color. It took on the shape of a fiery sphere which appeared to separate from the stem of smoke like a decapitated mushroom.

The watching world noted with relief that the estimated force was not much greater than the first. But for the experts — and for the politicians whom they advised — there was reason enough to be concerned.

The second blast brought indications that the Chinese scientists had been making fairly swift progress on the road to an H-bomb. The experts judged that the Chinese had the capacity by this time to test a dozen times a year if they so chose.

Now the experts around the world began revising their estimates of the Chinese timetable. Blast No. 2 indicated the Chinese could have medium-range ballistic missiles with nuclear warheads well before 1970. Possibly the H-bomb would soon be in Chinese hands.

This was a sobering thought. It had taken the United States seven years from the first atomic bomb to produce the first H-bomb. It had taken the British five years and the Russians four.

China's nuclear program meant a prospect of mounting trouble on the home front which would have to be met by downgrading the needs of the population. The program represented a huge investment for so poor, hungry and backward a nation.

Indeed, nuclear weaponry had seemed to be leaping ahead of development of the armed forces, which still lacked the means or the equipment to measure up to the requirements of a burgeoning atomic power. Already, experienced China-watchers could detect signs of strain within the officer corps of the People's Liberation Army. Even within the military field itself there had to be a certain amount of lively competition for what was available in the way of resources, to build up those conventional forces upon which China, in the long run, had to rely primarily for protection. Certainly China could not dream for many years of matching the United States in nuclear weapons. The distinct probability was that there would be sharp debate in the upper echelons of the People's Liberation Army about the rationing of the nation's resources between the conventional forces and the nuclear bomb-missile program.

There would be political fallout both at home and abroad. Abroad, the bomb was helping Red China to lose friends and contributing to the progressive isolation which, later on, the Great Proletarian Cultural Revolution would encourage even more. It would tend to worsen considerably the already severely strained relations between Peking and the Communist nations of the Soviet bloc.

On the whole, Americans did not appear to be particularly impressed or concerned by China's second test. This apparent lack of public concern disturbed some of the American experts. Dr. Lapp, the nuclear physics pioneer who had served the U.S. War Department as adviser and had been a former director of the Atomic Energy Research and Development Board in the Defense Department, remarked that he felt it unfortunate that the second Chinese blast had seemed to worry U.S. officials so little.[2]

To Lo Jui-ching, then the chief of staff of China's army — and soon to be purged for an alleged attempt at a military coup d'etat against Mao — the test was "a realistic preparation for nuclear war, so that we shall be in a position to cope with the situation successfully."[3]

And for Asia, the second Chinese explosion was an indication that time was growing short. The blasts raised China's potential for mischief and blackmail. Once again, protests rained in on Peking from Asians, even from representatives of the extreme left. To these, the Chinese replied that the Peking regime regarded the test as a "victory for all Asian, African and Latin American peoples" because it destroyed the idea that only advanced nations could develop such weapons. This, too, was a clue to the prestige and nationalist factors in the Chinese leaders' urge to develop the bomb.

Whatever furor the blast produced, however, would fade fairly soon. In the interim, Sinologists would discern outlines of a developing political convulsion inside China. Perhaps that would slow them down. But, upheaval or not, the West — and the Russians — would be in for a good deal more nervous watching.

Both the Soviet Union and the United States could expect that Peking would be more difficult to deal with, and, under a regime which had produced the explosions, perhaps much more dangerous. The Peking leadership had made it clear it did not go along with the idea that there might be such a thing as an accidental war. It saw its nuclear potential — however small at the time — as a counterdeterrent which could prevent the more powerful nations from interfering with China's policies, and Peking refused to accept the Kremlin plea, first voiced by Khrushchev, that small wars might lead to big ones. With a device deliverable by plane or missile, which the Chinese now could foresee in the immediate future, the Peking leaders would have a new shield for their activities in Asia and elsewhere. Perhaps Peking could hope, by striking fear into the hearts of other Asian leaders, it could accomplish politically at fairly little risk what it would not dare to attempt militarily.

Spectacular developments for the Communist movement were in the making. China was about to have two more explosions. Only one would be nuclear.

35

Two thousand years ago in the time of the Han Dynasty there was a popular parable about a man named Lord Yeh, who let everybody know that he was fond of dragons. Everything in and around his home was fashioned to remind him of dragons.

A dragon in heaven learned of all this and decided to descend to earth and pay a visit to Lord Yeh. And when Lord Yeh saw the huge dragon with its long tail, he ran off in a panic. The moral of the story is that Lord Yeh did not really love dragons at all. He just loved things that looked like dragons.

Mao Tse-tung pretended to love a dragon, too. Throughout his revolutionary career his dragon was the Chinese people — a mighty and powerful dragon. Mao counseled his followers never to be afraid of the dragon.

"There are those who speak daily of arousing the people, yet they are scared to death when the people do rise up," Mao had said in surveying the state of the peasant movement in Hunan Province in 1927.

But the day came when the dragon rose up and looked at Mao. And Mao, like Lord Yeh, became frightened and ran away.

The gathering storm had been hardly perceptible to the Western world until July, 1961. Even then the outlines were obscure. A clue to the puzzle had been a speech by Liu Shao-chi, Mao's successor as chairman of the People's Republic.

The key remark was buried in the Chinese press accounts. Liu had said: "There have been quite a few shortcomings in our work, which together with the natural calamities of the past two years have given rise to difficulties." [1]

The remark was important because it represented an abrupt reversal. A top leader was saying publicly that the party had been wrong, and by implication, that Mao Tse-tung had been wrong, that something might be wrong with the system. Liu was not blaming natural calamities alone for China's economic woes. He was blaming the party, too. That the criticism came from Liu was a matter of deep significance. It hinted at a struggle of ideas at the top, and perhaps even at a struggle for power.

And then in 1965 Mao was haunted by a four-hundred-year-old ghost. The ghost was that of Hai Jui, a mandarin official in the court of Emperor Chia Ching in the Ming dynasty. His name was celebrated in legend and opera throughout China down through the centuries. For many Chinese he was a symbol of championship of the oppressed. Now, Hai Jui's ghost was hovering over another cause celebré.

It was significant that the twentieth century furor over Hai Jui had begun in Shanghai, Mao Tse-tung's own stronghold. There, on November 10, 1965, Yao Wen-yuan, a veteran propagandist, published in the Shanghai newspaper *Wen Hui Pao* an article commenting on a historical drama about Hai Jui.[2] Mao was in residence in Shanghai at the time. The article was a violent denunciation of the play *Hai Jui Scolds the Emperor*, which had been written by Wu Han, a noted dramatist and historian. In addition, he was deputy mayor of Peking — that is, vice-chairman of the Peking municipal party committee, of which the powerful Peng Chen was the chairman. Peng, who ranked then at least seventh in the ruling Chinese party Politburo, at times had looked like a possible successor to Mao's mantle.

What had Wu Han done? In 1959, he had written an essay entitled "Hai Jui's Dismissal," and another entitled simply "On Hai Jui." Obviously there was some powerful force behind all this, because both essays were published in *People's Daily*, the party's chief newspaper, the first in June and the second in September. And then, on September 30, 1959, as if to represent a sardonic comment on the eve of the tenth anniversary of Communist power in China, the essay was presented as a play on the stage in Peking. It was enormously successful, with an appreciative audience who understood its meaning.

Wu Han became virtually a Hai Jui specialist. He published a small book, the *Story of Hai Jui*, and yet another drama, published in 1961 and performed by the Peking Opera House in February of that year, with the full approval of the Propaganda Department of the Communist party Central Committee.

Something was very wrong. The essay and play without question were sharp indictments of Mao Tse-tung and his policies. In the first of the essays Wu, evidently with the approval of the propaganda powers, had published this passage:

"Now the people have to pay more taxes than ever before, everywhere. Yet you (the emperor) spend a lot of money on superstition and religion. And you spend more and more money every day. As a result, the people have become very poor. In the past ten years or so, every family has become practically penniless.

"For a long time, the nation has not been satisfied with you. All officials, in and out of the capital, know that your mind is not right, that you are too arbitrary, that you are perverse. You think that you alone are right. You refuse to accept criticism and your mistakes are many.

"The present problem is that the emperor is wrong, and the duty of the official is not clear. This is the most serious thing in the country. If we do not talk about it, what should we talk about?" [3]

Considering who Hai Jui was and what his reputation was as a champion of a people oppressed by government, a champion of returning lands to peasants and redressing the evils imposed on them by village officials, and a champion of those unjustly accused, this was heady wine in Peking.

Hai Jui had devoted himself to the cause of reducing taxes on the poor and helping the peasants against the depredations of the gentry and imperial officials. Hai Jui died in 1587 at the age of seventy-three and his death was mourned by the populace more than it would mourn the death of the son of heaven, the emperor, himself. The modern "son of heaven" was Mao Tse-tung, and the privileged officials of the modern celestial empire were party cadres who did as they pleased with the peasants, and often were bitterly hated in return.

Wu was indulging in what the angry supporters of Mao — once they had sufficient strength to do so — would call Aesopism. That is an old Communist sin — the sin of speaking in parables and allegories to get over a point damaging to the regime. Wu's points were devastating.

One of the nine scenes in his drama portrayed the "return of land to the peasants." Yet another had been built on the theme of "rehabilitation of innocent people from prison." Few could escape the meaning of all this. It was a cry of angry protest against Mao's Great Leap Forward, a demand for its abandonment, a plea for the rehabilitation of all those who had been lured into criticizing Mao's system and then banished as "rightists."

It would become abundantly clear later on that the drama about the dismissal of Hai Jui was meant to point up the injustice of Chairman Mao's dismissal of Marshal Peng Teh-huai as defense minister. It became clear, too, that a powerful element among the Chinese professional military leaders — as opposed to those who supported Mao's notions of a proletarianized army — sympathized with and supported Marshal Peng.

For such a strong protest to be launched there had to be strong support. The fact that Mao could do nothing to stop the publication and production of the Hai Jui pieces suggested that the protesters had influential protection in high places.

A torrent of abusive propaganda directed against Wu Han attempted to hide the real reasons for the assault. The real reasons were that Mao now sought to reassert his dictatorial authority and that he was being opposed by elements in the highest stratum of the party.

Wu was assailed for having presented a lofty official of the Ming dynasty as a humane and beloved person. According to all the tenets of Marxist-Leninist dogma as interpreted by Mao, this could not be so. It was historically incorrect and it was ideologically incorrect to intimate that an imperial official could be anything other than an oppressor of the people.

The baying pack was led, significantly, by *Liberation Army Daily* (Chiehfang Chun Pao), the newspaper of Lin Piao's Defense Ministry. It saw Wu's literary efforts as a threat from China's intellectuals to the future of the revolution as Mao had envisioned it.

As Hai Jui had challenged the emperor four hundred years before, essayist and playwright Wu Han, with the protection of his chief, Mayor Peng Chen, now was challenging the supremacy of Mao. Indirectly, the essay and play were proposing the end of the people's communes, the return of commune land to the peasants for private cultivation and the restoration of Peng Teh-huai as China's military chief. Implicitly, it was a broad indictment of Mao Tse-tung and praise for those who had been purged for opposing him.

There was no denying the damage the Great Leap had done to China. High party officials admitted it indirectly, and while they laid the major share of the blame to "natural calamities," some also hinted that the party and its policies were much at fault. The worst of the trouble evidently was between the years 1959 and 1962. Nevertheless, the three Red banners: "the general line, the Great Leap Forward and the people's communes," would continue to be the slogan for "socialist construction of China," Premier Chou En-lai informed the National People's Congress.[4]

This was bitter news for the Chinese people. It was a signal that the battle lines for a struggle were being drawn. Liu Shao-chi would represent the pragmatists and experts, Chou the "revolutionary leftists" and Mao Tse-tung. Chou, with his education, culture and polish, ordinarily would have qualified as an "expert," but in this case he was "Red" before "expert."

By 1962, there had been some degree of recovery in the economy. Mao and his supporters soon would do more than simply reinstate the general line. They would eventually feel free to demand that all the personal interests of the Chinese citizen be subordinated unconditionally to the interests of the state. The concept of "self" had to be eliminated. There would be no nonsense about raising living standards, and anybody who proposed such a thing would be judged guilty of "economism" [5] and treated accordingly.

By late 1965, it appeared likely that President Liu and Mayor Peng Chen were allies. They seemed to have firm control of the party's lower-level bureaucrats. They had dominating influence in the trade unions of which Liu had been the architect, and the Young Communist League, eight million strong, which Peng had built and which he had directed and dominated over the years. All this seemed to add up to a formidable power base.

Despite differences at upper levels, Mao still wielded enormous power and authority in the fact alone that he was Mao, founder of the revolution and symbol of Chinese Communist triumph. But he would need help. For this help, he turned to the frail Lin Piao. The Defense Minister, his skinny frame often wracked by a tubercular cough, responded.

Lin began to grow in stature and power. Behind him, apparently, were other influential figures: the suave and able Premier Chou, the Russian-hating Chen Yi who was vice-premier and foreign minister,[6] and the apparatus of the government. From all appearances, the crippled Teng Hsiao-ping, general secretary of the party, tried for a time to remain neutral, and for a time there had been an uneasy truce between the two camps. There had been no clear sign of any widespread disunity among the top leaders, military and political, until November 1965, when Mao faded out of the Peking picture. He had gone to Shanghai, Mao's favorite retreat when there was trouble in Peking.

And meanwhile, in Peking, the truce was broken by the sudden onslaught against Wu Han. By implication, this attack was directed at the mighty Peng Chen himself. The developments ripped apart the Chinese leadership. The top people in the party, the government and the army were choosing sides. On one side were Mao and Lin Piao, now regularly dubbed in the press as "Comrade Mao Tse-tung's close comrade-in-arms." On the other side was Liu Shao-chi, who by then had the support of the party Secretary-General, Teng Hsiao-ping.

Defense Minister Lin by no means had the undivided loyalty of the officer corps. In May, 1965, he had affronted the bemedaled professional military leaders by his decision to abolish all ranks. There would be no more marshals, no more generals, no more admirals.

Defense Minister Lin was the apostle of "people's war." In September, 1965, he established himself as chief interpreter of Mao by publishing his celebrated essay, "Long Live the Victory of People's War." This elaborated the Mao principles that "political power proceeds from the barrel of a gun," and that revolutionary war must arise with the peasantry and gradually strangle the cities. Lin's essay applied Mao's principle on a world scale: the advanced countries were the cities, the backward countries were the peasantry.

So far as foreign policy had been concerned, there had seemed on the surface to be little division in the top ranks of China's leadership. Peng Chen, for example, had been one of the loudest and most enthusiastic detractors of the "Khrushchev revisionists."

As for Lo Jui-ching, at that time a figure to reckon with as army chief of staff and member of the powerful Communist party secretariat, he dutifully echoed the party line to the end, belaboring "U.S. imperialism," denouncing the "Khrushchev revisionists kowtowing to U.S. imperialism's nuclear blackmail," and even accusing the perfidious Russians of "spreading everywhere the fear of the horrors of war and nuclear weapons." Only a revisionist could look upon the horrors of war and nuclear weapons as something to fear.

None of this saved either Lo or Peng Chen.

A climactic struggle was about to begin, and these events eased anxiety in the West. To the watching world it seemed that China's Communist party was about to come apart at the seams. Was China, after all, really such a threat? Could a nation so torn by political struggle continue to push forward at a rapid pace on the scientific front and challenge the mighty nuclear nations? China's scientists answered the question.

36

An enormous sheet of fire seared the sky almost ten thousand feet above the wastes of the Takla Makan Desert.[1] Quickly the fire was enveloped in a vast dome of white smoke, and then, like a cauliflower being flattened, it began to assume a sort of oval shape.

It was May 9, 1966. A full year had gone by since the Chinese scientists had touched off their last atomic explosion. This time there was ominous meaning in the cloud.

First, the indications were that the Chinese had developed a thermonuclear device. That is, it appeared to have contained the ingredients which are used in the manufacture of hydrogen bombs. Second, the Chinese had been able to perfect a device compact enough to be dropped from a plane. They now would be able to stockpile "deliverable" weapons.

The force of the explosion was at least six times that of the previous two. It was in the range of a hundred and thirty kilotons of TNT. It indicated progress far more rapid than Western experts had anticipated.

The gaseous diffusion plant which U.S. intelligence had discovered at Lanchow had seemed smaller and less productive than those possessed by other nuclear nations. If U.S. estimates had been correct, the plant would have been able to process six thousand tons of uranium ore a day and produce enough fissionable material each month for two nuclear devices in the low-yield range — if the ore was of a relatively high grade.

But China seemed to be getting a bigger bang for its money than the other nuclear nations got when they were starting out.

The explosions had shown no evidence of tritium, which is expensive and hard to manufacture. Tritium is a triple-weight fuel for H-bombs and it requires enormous resources to produce it.

The Atomic Energy Commission in the United States, relying on reports of various detection devices, speculated that China's Blast No. 3 used a core of enriched uranium with quantities of lithium-6 as a liner. Lithium-6, a thermonuclear material, still would indicate a Poor Man's H-Bomb on the way. The French had used it in 1960. The Americans and Russians had experimented with it years before.

But Poor Man's H-Bombs could still be awesome weapons, even if not so effective as those of the Russians and Americans. With a uranium jacket, a Poor Man's H-Bomb would be a highly "dirty" superbomb, whose radioactive fallout would have a high contamination potential.

Poor Man's Bomb or not, it was notable that all three Chinese explosions to that date had used not plutonium, which would have been both easier and cheaper, but the U-235, which cannot be separated chemically from natural uranium.[2] There were two ways of extracting U-235 from U-238. One was by electromagnetic separation in which uranium ions accelerated by high-voltage electrodes moved in curved paths through a magnetic field. The U-235's path was directed toward a separate receiver. In the other method, gaseous diffusion, uranium hexafluoride gas was pumped through myriad cells divided by membranes. The U-235, being lighter, diffused more readily than the U-238 through the membrane.

Since all other four nuclear powers had utilized plutonium devices, it had been widely assumed China would do likewise. It was, relatively, a good deal easier to produce fissionable plutonium from natural uranium by chemical methods. Production of weapons-grade U-235 was far more complicated. It had required huge resources in Britain and the United States. France, at the time of China's third blast, had yet to reach the point where it had a U-235 plant ready to go into full production.

Had the Chinese scientists hit upon some new secrets? Had they discovered better, simpler methods of producing fissionable materials? Did all this mean that China's drive to become a major world nuclear power would be far more swift than anybody in the West had imagined? Had the Russians given the Chinese more than the West had suspected? The latter seemed unlikely in view of the Kremlin's attitude since 1959, which a change in Soviet regimes had failed to alter.

The answer seemed to be that, to a large extent, the Chinese scientists had done much of it on their own. They had, of course, had considerable and significant help in what their senior physicists had learned from the Americans and West Europeans, from what scores of able scientists had learned at the Dubna Institute in the Soviet Union where, even as late as the spring of 1965, a few Chinese were still in residence. The likelihood seemed to be that China had improved on the gaseous diffusion process at Lanchow, possibly combining it with the electromagnetic process. The electromagnetic process was the common property of all nations, since the United States had declassified the information on it as many as ten years before. Moreover, the Chinese could have learned a great deal from the Russians about the Soviet electromagnetic technology.[3]

The help the Russians had given the Chinese in the atoms for peace program had been a matter of political expediency. Moscow had extended such aid to other nations, including those of the Communist bloc in Europe. It could hardly have denied the same to China without acknowledging that there was, in reality, no such thing as a world Communist movement or a comity of "socialist" nations. Moreover, in the mid-1950s, Premier Khrushchev was badly in need of all the support he could get from foreign Communist parties, in view of his difficulties with Poland and Hungary and the impact on the Communist world of his de-Stalinization measures. So the Kremlin continued on a course which would save face for the present, though it led toward the result it could only fear.

More sinister than Communist China's achievement of three nuclear explosions was the Peking regime's presentation of this event to the Chinese people. The story of the first, second and third explosions had been carefully filmed in color, to be shown to audiences in movie theaters around the country. Eventually, the film turned up in Japan, obtained by the Tokyo Broadcasting System. The TBS acquired the film with the assistance of the moribund but still functioning Japan-China Friendship Association of Japanese leftists.[4]

The film, and other propaganda revolving about the tests, seemed designed to ease Chinese minds about nuclear war. The bomb was not so bad after all. The film could have been a Chinese Communist version of "How I Learned to Love the Bomb."

In one scene, a hen was shown leaving a cage, purportedly in the blast area, after the explosion. It was flapping its wings lustily and it topped off this remarkable show of durability by laying a perfect white egg among healthy and colorfully blooming flowers.

Other scenes depicted such things as rabbits hopping about happily among the patches of vividly green grass in the same area which was supposed to be struck by atomic explosion or presumably affected by heavy fallout. Evidently, the idea was to tell the Chinese people that the A-bomb would be no more terrifying than any other weapon if one took proper precautions.

For a Westerner, it was appalling to contemplate what the meaning of all this might be. It was no less appalling to learn that audiences in Red China, shown the films of the first three explosions, worked themselves up into states of high hilarity over the notion that China, too, had access to nuclear weapons.

During the showings, quotations from the little red book the *Thoughts of Mao Tse-tung,* would be flashed on the screen at irregular intervals. The audience would chant the quotations in unison, loudly and gaily.[5]

As shown on Japanese television screens, the film depicted the Chinese people as overjoyed at an official announcement by Premier Chou En-lai that the first explosion had been achieved. There were scenes of purported jubilant celebrations in Sinkiang Province, the site of the testing, and in a number of cities throughout the country.

Soldiers were shown fighting their way through dust storms in the Takla Makan Desert to reach the region near Lop Nor where the test took place. The film presented shots of the various gadgetry of nuclear installations, with special attention to eerily flashing lights. It showed nothing of any technological importance which could not already have been known or surmised outside China.

But it did place much emphasis on the animals placed in cages in the test area, presumably to experiment with the effects of radiation on them. Dogs, cats, monkeys and chickens were shown first being placed in the cages and later purportedly emerging unharmed.

The net effect of all this was to make the sophisticated viewer wonder: At this stage, at least, was this burgeoning bomb of China's — as the French had insisted — more a political bomb than a military one? Was the major purpose to assert the prestige of China? The cheers which greeted the explosions — even though demonstrations might have been ordered officially from high places — strongly indicated the role nationalism had played in China's nuclear drive.

Of course, even though China's leaders might have been motivated primarily by political and prestige purposes, the existence of a Chinese nuclear potential still would have considerable military meaning. It did not mean that China would use the weapon carelessly. Indeed, the Chinese leaders — despite all the Western worrying to the contrary — had given every indication all along that they were prudent and cautious men when it came to challenging a greater power.

The film seemed intended to heighten an impression among its viewers that a fierce enemy was waiting to lunge at the Chinese throat and that a wise Communist party and Great Leader had taken steps to protect the nation. The pictures of Explosion No. 2 reinforced this impression.

Immediately after this blast, the film suggested, there were elaborate military exercises in the blast area, as if to indicate that the atomic explosion was much less terrifying than it might have seemed. This would have been in line with that Mao Tse-tung dictum that nuclear weapons were paper tigers and that the future would be decided not by such weapons, but by men.

Two months in advance of China's third explosion, Secretary of Defense McNamara appeared before the Joint Congressional Committee on Atomic Energy and offered a prediction: that within two or three years, Communist China would be capable of launching a nuclear attack on countries within seven hundred miles of her borders. This meant that China soon would have the means of delivering her atomic weapon. But he found any threat to the United States still a long way in the future.

"Since a significant Chinese Communist nuclear threat to the continental United States is not expected to develop earlier than the 1975–1980 period," he said, "that threat can be omitted from this particular analysis [of the prospects of nuclear war]."

However, the McNamara estimate did make it appear that the United States now believed China would progress at a pace much swifter than had been expected.[6] McNamara reflected a good measure of respect for China's capabilities in the field. "That the nuclear program was able to continue in spite of a very severe economic crisis is testimony to the determination of the Chinese to produce modern weapons," he told the committee. "Although the results may be slow in coming, there is no reason to suppose that the Chinese cannot in time produce medium-range or even long-range ballistic missile systems and arm them with thermonuclear warheads." [7]

The secretary took note of a "widespread desire" among Asian nations for some sort of accommodation with China which was coupled with "perceptibly rising concern" over Peking's belligerence and incipient nuclear power. He estimated that the Chinese possibly could develop and deploy a small force of ICBMs by the middle to the latter part of the 1970s. Even such a small force might seem attractive to Peking as a token — highly visible — of threat to the United States.

But in McNamara's opinion it remained a "primitive threat" until the mid-1970s. So far as China was concerned, no U.S. decision on a deployment against the Chinese threat would be necessary (in 1966) because "the lead time required for the Chinese to deploy their offensive system is greater than the lead time required for us to deploy our defensive system."

"A light antiballistic missile system using exatmospheric interceptors and terminal defenses at a small number of cities offers promise of a highly effective defense against small ballistic missile attacks of the sort the Chinese Communists might be capable of launching within the next decade," McNamara concluded. This would "remain highly effective against the Chinese Communist threat for some time."

The chairman of the Joint Chiefs of Staff, General Earle Wheeler, backed up the secretary. There would be plenty of time with regard to a Chinese threat because "I don't believe they are going to have any capability to do very much before the mid-1970s."

But if the U.S. government was thinking in terms of the Chinese deliberately posing a direct threat to continental United States, it may have been making a serious miscalculation. The chances were that the Chinese were by no means intending to pose a palpable, open threat. To do so in the face of U.S. power would be to invite their own destruction.

The Chinese aim seemed to have much more to do with a long range and cautious strategy of eventually forcing the U.S. presence out of Asia. This, conceivably, could be done with medium-range nuclear-tipped missiles which could make China's neighbors so nervous that they would bring political pressures on their governments to push the United States out. That could be accomplished in the tested Communist way: employment of mass pressure, born of fear, on governments in the Far East.

China was able to permit her scientists to push ahead swiftly with the program. Yet the program was threatened on all sides by difficulties arising from the backlash of the developing political upheaval in Peking and the obvious heavy economic cost of the nuclear program.

In Kansu Province, site of the Lanchow industrial complex and the gaseous diffusion plant which fed the nuclear program, and an area of extreme importance to Peking, there were reports of rising opposition to the regime and of a terror campaign to keep it in check. And in Sinkiang there were reports of frontier clashes with the Russians, of rising Chinese suspicions of local nationalism among the minority peoples, of persecutions of the non-Chinese and of floods of refugees across the border into Soviet Kazakhstan.

The stories of these escapees would not come out in detail until more than two years after China's nuclear debut, when Moscow finally decided to use them in an anti-Mao propaganda campaign.[8]

Astonishingly, Red China's riotous difficulties and profound political and economic upheavals did not seem to interfere with the steady progress of the nuclear program, even though the areas directly concerned with that program reported some of the most serious troubles.

Some Americans probably believed, in the early summer of 1966, that the incredible events which took place in Peking and throughout China would spell the end of the country's threat to the rest of Asia and to world peace. Perhaps those who had been inclined to scoff soon would begin to wonder whether the time had not arrived to pray.

37

Mao and his supporters had not one, but three bomb programs to nurture.

One was the "spiritual atom bomb," the description Mao modestly applied to his thinking. Its purported aim was to provide a beacon which some day would lead revolutionaries toward the obedient robot world Mao seemed to envision.

Another was the Great Proletarian Cultural Revolution, Mao's political atom bomb, which would produce "willing oxen," as Chinese propaganda put it. Every man and woman would be a soldier who would respond automatically to whatever orders might come from the top and would want for nothing except to "forget self" for the sake of labor and the state.

And the third, of course, was military. One of its basic aims was to gain for China the prestige of a major world power and to pay rich dividends from its potential for blackmail in Asia and the backward world.

Preparations apparently were made before Mao launched the terror against the intellectuals and his political opponents. It must have taken some weeks to mobilize teen-age students and indoctrinate them for their role as Red Guards.[1]

In France, and later in Communist nations, revolution seemed always destined to devour its children. In China, the children devoured the revolution.

The first phase of the upheaval was begun in Peking in November, 1965, while Mao hid out in Shanghai, waiting for the storm to subside. It nearly brought China, with its seven hundred and fifty millions, its chronic mass hunger and its staggering internal problems, to full-scale civil war. Evidence pieced together later suggested that at one point in mid-summer, opposing divisions of the People's Liberation Army were on the move.

Peng Chen, the powerful Politburo figure who ranked seventh in the hierarchy, had fallen in May, 1966, from his post as mayor of Peking — chairman of the municipal Communist party committee. With his fall it could be assumed that a struggle for power in China was about to begin in earnest.

Mao and Defense Minister Lin Piao, now emerging as heir-apparent, began a savage attack on the intellectuals. The assault on "specialists," "authorities" and "scholars" was followed by twin offensives: one on the Peking daily press and the other on Peking University. A reshuffled municipal party committee in the capital fired the staffs of their newspapers: the *Pei Jung Jih Pao* (*Peking Daily*, not to be confused with the party paper, *People's Daily*); *Pei Jung Wan Pao* (*Peking Evening News*) and *Chien-hsien* (*Frontline Journal*). The power of Teng To and his allies, who ran those newspapers, was being broken.

The other prong of the offensive was aimed at the university to "tear aside the bourgeois mask of liberty, equality and fraternity," as *People's Daily* put it. The targets were "a handful of representatives of the bourgeoisie who wormed their way into our party, deliberately hid the class nature of the struggle and twisted this serious political struggle into a 'purely academic problem' and an 'exchange of different opinions.' " [2]

"When the anti-party, anti-socialist gang feverishly attacked the party in order to give it a heavy blow on the head and pour dogs' blood on its head in the hopes of overthrowing the party leadership," *People's Daily* thundered at the intellectuals, "you bosses behind scenes gave them the green light, beat the drum for them, summoned the wind and the waves, forgot yourselves in your excitement and acclaimed them in the belief that good days were in store for you, just around the corner."

It was a call to battle. First blood already had been drawn by the Mao-Lin Piao forces with the overthrow of Peng Chen. Now Teng To and his allies evidently had been beaten down, too, for *People's Daily* noted that the opposition, "like all reactionaries were simply paper tigers."

Nobody, the opposition was warned, could oppose Mao. Anyone who did would be brought down, "whoever he may be, whatever high position he may hold, however much of a veteran he may be; the only possible result is the loss of his standing and reputation." [3]

That was meant for the ears of President Liu Shao-chi and any of his allies in the inner circle of the Politburo. It was an ultimatum. Now the Mao forces sent mobs of youngsters on a wild rampage against Peking University. The siege was brief.

Many in Peking University had bitter memories of 1957 and the "blooming and contending" of the period of Mao's Hundred Flowers. Many had been hurt by Mao's stratagem, had seen their friends and colleagues humiliated and punished for divisive reasoning. One who remembered was Lu Ping, rector of the University, who had served Mao in 1957 by quashing a student revolt against the leader's thinking. Lu became head of the university by 1960. Evidently he lived to regret his actions against the students and their Hundred Flowers Society. He was on the other side, now.

Mao's group threw Lu Ping out of the University, branding

him and his deputy "anti-party elements" who had rejected Mao Tse-tung. Mao's forces accused them of trying to win over the younger generation. With the dominating Politburo authority in their hands, they issued a decree through the agency of the newly reshuffled Peking municipal party committee, firing Lu Ping as rector and party secretary of the University, along with his deputy, on charges of having tried to "drag along the young students to follow the landlord class and the bourgeoisie to their doom," of various "revisionist" policies and of having told students that "honest officials were important and corrupt officials were bad." Lu Ping and his deputy even recommended to students the play and essay about Hai Jui and his resistance to the emperor.

Reaction inside Peking University was one of stubborn resistance to the pressure, but the Mao forces had their loyalists, a nucleus of "revolutionary students" inside the University.[4] To these was assigned the task of producing the time-tested *tatse pao*, the wall newspapers or "big character posters" which called upon the youngsters to rise up in rebellion and "smash the black gang to pieces." Students supporting the rector fought back ferociously. It was an intramural war between "rightists" and "leftists." Studies were forgotten in the turmoil.

Thousands of young students who had been sent out to villages for "socialist education" suddenly were recalled to the University to "struggle against the black gang." The youngsters were told they had been tricked, that they had been sent to the villages by the rector himself, so that the loyal support within the University for the great leader and helmsman, Chairman Mao, would be broken up.

The battle raged for a week. It was bloody. Evidently there was a large body of anti-party feeling not only among students but particularly among the teachers. It was time for a demonstration of terror.

The opportunity came for the Maoists during a riotous mass rally. Red Guard students, just out of secondary schools, howled for the blood of a nineteen-year-old boy named Yang Kuo-ching.

A month before, the head of a delegation of journalists from Mali and his wife had been injured in Peking in a scuffle. Now the pro-Mao authorities decided that had been part of a plot to damage China's reputation abroad among friendly nations. They selected young Yang as the scapegoat.

A kangaroo court of Red Guards "tried" Yang before the screaming mob. It found him guilty of "counterrevolutionary activities." Solemnly, the head of China's Supreme People's Court, Yang Hsiu-feng, announced that the young man was guilty of undermining the class struggle. The head of the Supreme Court sentenced the boy to death. Immediately after the sentence, the young man was hauled to the execution grounds and, while the youngsters cheered, was shot in the back of the head.[5]

For Mao's taste, there were too many pragmatists among the scholars and teachers. As for the eight million strong Young Communist League, too many in it had tendencies toward individualism. "Young" Communists were too old and mature for the Mao-Lin program. They had been organized and indoctrinated under the wings of Liu Shao-chi and Peng Chen, and now the YCL was a threat to Mao. He ordered it dissolved and its leaders dismissed.[6]

Now Mao attacked the whole educational system. It needed "reform." The system had to be changed, starting with entrance examinations for enrollment of students in higher learning institutions. More proletarians and peasants should qualify and fewer young people whose parents or grandparents had been "bourgeois." To pave the way, enrollment would be postponed completely for half a year.

It meant complete suspension of all secondary and higher education — in fact, all education. It released younger students of secondary schools and colleges from obligation to study anything except *Thoughts of Mao Tse-tung*. It extended a license to the young for reckless cruelty. They would be a potent weapon of terror in the hands of the Mao-Lin faction.

What now would happen to the nuclear program? The citadels of learning would be the prime targets of the Red Guard attack, all over the country. Any who might be considered enemies of "the proletarian educational line" would be butts of violent abuse by mobs of teen-agers. Every province underwent an educational purge.

Why did Mao consider it all necessary?

"Chairman Mao told us long ago that everything reactionary is the same: if you don't hit it, it won't fall. . . . This applies to everything in the old world. We want to build the new world, so we must destroy the old; we want to create the new ideology and culture of socialism and communism, so we must subject the old bourgeois ideology and culture and the influence they exert to thoroughgoing criticism and clear them out." [7]

Mao, in his waning years, wondering about his niche in Chinese history, evidently intended to mold China into the pattern he had chosen for it, and indeed the Red Guards at their enormous mass rallies seemed too powerful for any barrier designed to prevent them from cutting a path of devastation.

People's Daily officially proclaimed that what had been Mao's cultural revolution had been transformed into the Great Proletarian Cultural Revolution. Its aim would be destruction first, because, it said, without destruction there could be no construction. It would foreshadow "a development of the socialist revolution by leaps and bounds and a new big leap forward in China's socialist construction." [8]

That was it, then. The Great Leap had failed. Powerful elements in the party had turned against it and demanded its abandonment. Mao bided his time until he was strong enough to act. Now there would be a new Great Leap, when the enemy finally was routed.

Mao continued to live in Shanghai, awaiting the developments in Peking. His enemies were everywhere. For Mao and Lin Piao, it appeared that a bloody road would lie ahead. Mao at that point could not even be certain how much support he had within the People's Liberation Army, and Mao and Lin set out to secure the armed forces under their control. They launched an attack on a "handful of representatives of the bourgeoisie who worked their way into our armed forces, dominated some of our cultural departments for a period of time," said *Liberation Army Daily*.[9]

The crisis within the armed forces came to a head swiftly.

The removal of Lo Jui-ching as Chief of Staff of the PLA did not become known until August 1, 1966 — August First Army Day — but the chances are that he was deposed well before that and replaced by Yang Cheng-wu, his deputy.

Lo probably was deposed in July, since it was at that time, as a careful study of documents indicated, that China came closest to civil war.[10] Mao was still in Shanghai, apparently with Defense Minister Lin Piao, when the crisis reached its peak and there was widespread disaffection among higher officers of the PLA. Chinese party documents which became available later indicated that Lo had issued orders to a division in northwest China to move down toward the Peking-Tientsin area. At the same time, Defense Minister Lin is believed to have ordered a division to move north toward Peking, from Shanghai. He is believed to have told his division commander to make contact with the commander of Lo's division and order him to remain outside the Peking-Tientsin area. Somehow, the stratagem worked. Had it not, civil war might have erupted.

That was the end of Lo. He was headed for humiliation and disgrace. And the star of Lin Piao rose even higher. Now there could be no question any more that he was second in the party only to Mao himself.

38

A madness engulfed China and the watching world wondered: what would happen now to the nuclear weapons program? Would it slow down? Would it come to a halt because of persecution of the intellectuals? What would happen to the scientists running the program?

Mao, all the evidence showed, distrusted any with "bourgeois" backgrounds — and all his senior scientists had come from families who had been well-to-do before communism, who had money enough to send their sons abroad for education. All the senior scientists had been contaminated by contact with the United States and other Western nations. Some, like Tsien Hsue-shen, Chao Chung-yao, Wang Kan-chang and Hua Lo-keng, had been abroad for long periods of years. Mao feared all of them.

Some — Hua, "Jimmy" Chien and others — had been caught in the Hundred Flowers crackdown. But the evidence indicated they suffered little, subjected only to a brief reeducation and routine, formal confessions. They did not have to move "into the mountains and fields," as the slogan had it, to learn humility and submission through corrective labor and to mould themselves into proper proletarians. Mao could attack most intellectuals — but not the physicists. Those he needed.

Few scientists would be likely to believe that Mao Tse-tung's thinking could produce nuclear weapons, even though for the record they were required to "regard Chairman Mao's writings as the supreme guide in all work." They could take with tongue in cheek the order to "give prominence to politics" in all their work, and another order admonishing them to "avoid imitating pure bourgeois research."

Vice-Premier Nieh Jung-jen, who had studied nuclear physics

in Europe, was in military-political command of the superweapons program. Small, aging but wiry, the durable Nieh was the model of a modern Chinese hater of "revisionists and U.S. imperialists."

On the eve of the fateful Central Committee Plenum, Nieh had presided over the 1966 Summer Physics Colloquium of the Peking Symposium and made the major address to an international gathering of scientists from properly "anti-imperialist" areas. He assured them that China's pursuit of nuclear weapons was for peace alone. But, said Nieh, "The U.S. imperialists have recklessly used scientific achievements to manufacture weapons of mass extermination and conduct sanguinary suppression of the revolutionary struggles of the peoples of Asia, Africa, Latin America and the rest of the world." [1]

Nieh's news for Chinese scientists was bad. He informed them they must realize "the question of developing science is first and foremost a political question.

"Through the present Great Cultural Revolution, the broad masses of intellectuals and scientists will the better arm their minds with Mao Tse-tung's thoughts, change their world outlook and raise their socialist consciousness. Thus they will be able to advance along the road of being Red and expert, dare to make revolution and be good at making revolution in scientific and technological work, to obtain fruitful results in scientific experimentation and the better serve the people wholeheartedly."

The Chinese physicists knew where they stood. Within that framework they could continue their research unmolested unless and until they came under suspicion. All of Peking's leaders seemed in agreement on one point: the nuclear program must go on.

Yet, whatever care the party sought to take of the nuclear scientists, the Cultural Revolution campaign was bound to throw the scholars into a state of confusion. Senior scientists with ties abroad and scores of technicians would have to fall within the category of those who were suspect. They could hardly be optimistic about the outlook. It would be only human for them to adopt protective coloring, the passive attitude of doing nothing and staying out of trouble, an attitude not uncommon in countries ruled by totalitarian dictatorships.

Men like missileman Tsien and physicist Chao, after years on American campuses, could hardly have been happy at the sight of the cultural revolution as it assaulted education and scaled ludicrous heights.

Tsien, Chao, Wan Kan-chang, Chien San-chiang and others like them had made the nuclear bomb and put China on the road to missilery. They were expected to believe it would have been impossible without the *Thoughts of Mao Tse-tung*, which always accomplished miracles. Any who read the "three good old articles" — "The Foolish Old Man Who Moved the Mountain," "Serve the People," and "In Memory of Norman Bethune" — should be automatically capable of astonishing feats.

Little could be done in China without applying Mao's thinking. It was no wonder that "The East is Red" was the new national anthem. Its words made a citizen appreciate Chairman Mao:

> *From the Red East rises the sun,*
> *In China appears Mao Tse-tung,*
> *Who works for the people's welfare.*
> *He is the people's savior.*

The people's savior may have been responsible for a number of his beloved sons perishing in the waters of the Yangtze in the hot summer days just in advance of the August Central Committee Plenum and the mass madness it loosed.

Evidently, the party felt something had to be done about all the rumors concerning Mao. He had not been seen in Peking publicly for months. Some said he was ill. Some said he had died. And many, with some justification, speculated that he may have gone mad.

So Mao emerged from his Shanghai hideout. On July 16, he took a dip in the Yangtze River. The 72-year-old Mao, to hear the press and broadcasts tell it, had jumped into the Yangtze, swum ten miles, and broken a few world swimming records. The swim dominated China's propaganda for days. Clearly, it was meant to demonstrate that the old man's health was good enough to permit him to carry on his cultural revolution-cum-purge to the end. He had been swimming to the melody of "Shui Tiao Ke Tou," his own poem, which went:

> *I care not that the wind blows and the waves beat,*
> *It is better than idly strolling in the courtyard.*

After sixty-five minutes, the intrepid Chairman yielded to the entreaties of fellow swimmers to board the waiting boat, but "he was vigorous and showed no sign of fatigue." Swims were hastily organized by anxious party functionaries. The Physical Culture and Sports Commission called for a mass campaign throughout the country, with swimmers carrying flags and quotation-bearing placards calling for "struggle against the class enemy." Some may have drowned in the process, but it was for a worthy cause.[2]

The message of Mao's swim was important. It implied that Chairman Mao was healthy and ready to do battle in Peking with his political opponents. And two weeks after the swim, the Central Committee opened its notorious 11th Plenum where, at the pinnacle of Chinese power, a new cast of characters was waiting to dominate the stage.

One was Chen Po-ta, once Mao's speech-writer [3] and his private secretary. An aloof, ascetic teetotaler, he was a veteran propagandist and chief editor of *Red Flag* (Hung Chi), the principal theoretical journal of the party. At sixty-two, Chen suddenly emerged as the chief administrator of the Great Proletarian Cultural Revolution. The Central Committee named him head of its "Cultural Revolution Group."

Another new face was that of Tao Chu, a rough individual who had bossed the South Central Bureau of the party, one of the most difficult of political assignments. Square-jawed, his gray hair cropped in military style, Tao Chu was known as a ruthless though able administrator who also had been a vice-premier. Now he became chief of the party's propaganda department, replacing the fallen Lu Ting-yi. At one time he had been a watchdog for Lin Piao, as head of the political department of the Fourth Field Army when, in 1949, it had been driving against Chiang Kai-shek's remnants.

At the time, President Liu Shao-chi still was much in evidence, occupying an honored position at party functions, still identified as vice-chairman of the Central Committee and chairman of the Chinese People's Republic. Party Secretary Teng Hsiao-ping was at his side at the mass rally which heard Tao Chu's maiden speech as a newly admitted member of the upper Politburo.

The August Plenum marked the mid-point of the party's critical "Fifty Days" which had begun in June, when Liu Shao-chi, according to the evidence, came close to establishing control over the nation with a group which would have opposed many of the seemingly irrational policies of Chairman Mao and Vice-Chairman Lin Piao.

However, the combined efforts of Lin Piao, Chen Po-ta, Tao Chu and the sinister Kang Sheng, the latter with a long history of secret police activity, were enough to stop Liu to the extent where it was once again safe for Mao to return from Shanghai after his long exile of eight months.

Lin Piao clearly was the anointed heir-apparent to Mao. The anointment must have come on the first day of the August Plenum, though it was not publicly announced for another year. Lin quickly took steps to guarantee his safety, including a purge of the armed forces he commanded as Defense Minister.

The propaganda attending this purge was revealing. It disclosed that the first decisive conflict within the armed forces had occurred during the Chinese intervention in the Korean war, when certain advocates of modernization in the military began to force through a program to produce a professional army with ranks and modern equipment in the style of Western armed forces. At that time it still was a "people's army" without uniforms, medals or titles. Before long, the professionals had their way. Ranks were introduced on the Soviet model. Uniforms were decorated with medals. Officers bore the titles of Marshal, Senior General, Admiral and down through the ranks.

The second major clash had come in 1959, when Mao threw Peng Teh-huai out of his Defense Minister post and turned the armed forces over to Lin, who reestablished the "people's army" and in 1965 abolished all ranks. This was a Mao-Lin victory over the professionals who did not want to alienate the Soviet Union, and who, apparently, still were hopeful at that time of Soviet help on the nuclear program.

The third key struggle inside the army continued to the eve of the August Plenum.[4] Once again, a group in the army had tried to do away with the "people's army" concept and work toward modernization, which was counter to "Chairman Mao's proletarian military line." One of these obviously was Lo Jui-ching, who was purged as chief of staff. There must have been many, many more. Mao's group wanted no potential Oriental Bonaparte. It felt safest with a "people's army." [5]

In an atmosphere of high tension, the Central Committee went into its fateful Plenum on August 1. After a week of deliberations, and probably of intense squabbling, the Plenum produced its communiqué, a declaration of war. "The handful of people in power who took the capitalist road" from that time forward, throughout many months of incessant turmoil, would be targets of "proletarian revolutionaries."

When the dominant wing of the party was ready to send teenage Red Guards on an incredible binge of violence against those Mao distrusted, care was taken to warn them away from the important scientists. Said instruction number twelve of the sixteen-instruction communiqué:

"As regards scientists, technicians and ordinary members of working staffs, as long as they are patriotic, work energetically, are not against the party and socialism and maintain no illicit relations with any foreign country, we should in the present move-ment continue to apply the policy of 'unity, criticism, unity.' Special care should be taken of those scientists and scientific and technical personnel who have made contribution. Efforts should be made to help them gradually transform their world outlook and style of work." [6]

The scientists who were working on nuclear programs, in par-ticular, were to be relatively safe from harassment. This policy, while it offered a measure of protection to scientists doing prac-tical work in areas affecting China's world position, was, in the long run, bound to react against science as a whole. It would not stop the development of bombs and missiles, but it would seriously impede science in other fields which could raise the living stan-dard and productivity of the Chinese people. The Communists were willing to pay a price for nuclear muscle. The rest of the celebrated twelve-year "March on Science" was going to suffer.

Watchers abroad calculated that up to the time the Cultural Revolution broke out, Red China, starting almost from scratch, had been able to build a total research and development force of up to 475,000, of whom 53,000 were scientists and engineers, the rest technical workers and nontechnical personnel. They concen-trated on the "development" — the practical aspect — of "research and development." [7]

39

The insanity burst like a sudden midsummer thunderstorm, a few days after the Central Committee Plenum ended.

The "iron broom" as Chen Po-ta, chief of the Central Com-

mittee's Cultural Revolution Group, called the Red Guard movement, swept across China, inspired by a line from a Mao Tse-tung
poem: "The golden monkey wrathfully swings his massive cudgel
and clears the jade-like firmament of dust." The battle cry was
published time and again in the party press.

"Smash all kinds of freaks and monsters," Chen Po-ta exhorted
the youngsters, and by the millions they responded with reckless
enthusiasm, tracking down the "four olds" — old art, culture, customs and habits — smashing anything and everything that recalled
the past.

Crowds, frightened, watched in silence as the youngsters dev-
astated private homes, broke windows, smashed furniture, threw
jewelry, clothing and shoes considered "bourgeois" into the
streets. The silent people watched while the blood-lusting youth
grabbed the owners, dragged them into the streets and beat them
with sticks, then adorned them with paper signs reading "capitalist" or "counterrevolutionary" and paraded them away to unknown destinations.

Ancient men and women trudged along wearing dunce caps,
prodded forward by the teen-agers. Teachers, writers, scientists
and other intellectuals were subjected to weird humiliations. Some
were driven to suicide. Some were believed to have died under
the torture.

Foreigners did not escape. One mob broke into a building
where about a hundred foreign diplomatic families lived and hung
a huge portrait of Mao Tse-tung on each door. Another mob
smashed into the century-old Roman Catholic Sacred Heart Academy in Peking, insulted the French nuns, hoisted a red flag, installed a bust of Mao and plastered the walls with signs reading
"Foreign Devils, Get Out" and "Chase Out the Running Dogs of
Imperialism." The school was not for Chinese but for the children
of foreigners.

At the corner of Wang Fu Chang Street, a concentration point
was set up by the Red Guards to collect jewelry and other valuable objects confiscated from private homes and apartments. The

objects included bathtubs, living room furniture and a variety of odd items — even including collections of seashells — all of which were considered bourgeois luxuries.

All citizens were told to prove their loyalty to Mao by displaying pictures of him in homes and boards with his quotations in windows. Some, in self-protection, wore quotations on their clothing. Hardly a bicycle, rickshaw or taxi in town lacked its big card displaying a Mao quotation. Shops selling Mao pictures ran out of stock. Every bus driver was told: put up a picture of Mao — or else. Neon signs carrying advertisements were required to substitute quotations from Mao's thoughts.

The Red Guards demanded that "all newly built bicycles, cars, trains and planes should carry tablets with quotations of Mao."

Hordes of youngsters burst into stores and cleaned them out of perfumes, face powders, face creams and other cosmetics, and required all this to be replaced with harsh scrubbing soap. The Red Guards demanded an end to the manufacture of such things because "cosmetics and perfumery serve the bourgeoisie and the beauties."

Barbershops took a particularly bad beating. Red Guards raided one after another in a number of cities, on the prowl for boys or girls who might have gotten fancy bourgeois haircuts. They were seized, had their heads shaven clean on the spot, and then were paraded through the streets wearing signs, jeered by howling mobs.

The demonstrators called for "abolition of such old customs as visits to relatives and the buying of sweets and fruits for this purpose. All people," they proclaimed, "bearing feudal and bourgeois names must on their own initiative go to the people's police stations and have them changed. On leaving their homes, landowners, counterrevolutionaries, subversive elements, right-wing elements and capitalists must wear the sign bearing the inscription 'scum' and the masses must see to this."

The teen-agers went on a nationwide rampage of name-changing.[1] The Kailan Coal Mines of Hope Province dutifully changed their name to "The Anti-Imperialist Coal Mines." A druggist in Nanchang was forced to name his shop the "Down with the Bourgeoisie Drug Store," another had to call his establishment the "Red Heart Drug Store." A photographer suddenly found he was running the "Anti-Revisionism Photo Studio." A grocer changed his shop's title to "The East Wind Food Store."

Revisionist and bourgeois phonograph records and sheet music had to go. This included Bach, Mozart, and Beethoven, and such Russians as the classical Tchaikovsky and the modern Shostakovich. Most book stores were told they could sell only the works of Mao Tse-tung. Art stores, threatened by the rampaging teenagers, threw out all the classical paintings and substituted portraits of Mao.

Sunglasses were adjudged bourgeois. Chess was too Russian, but even Chinese checkers was found to be bourgeois, decadent and feudal.

Red Guards demanded that traffic lights be changed. Since red was a revolutionary color, traffic ought to "go" on red and stop on green.

Drinkers were told: don't drink. Smokers were told: don't smoke. Both Mao Tse-tung and Chou En-lai were chain smokers, but that was none of the masses' business. Restaurants were told to serve only cheap meals suitable for workers and peasants.

In Canton, a mass rally of Red Guards and "revolutionary teachers" gathered at the Huanghuakang Cemetery. They decided that the statue of the Goddess of Liberty had to be torn down and the goddess herself put on trial. "Goddess of Liberty, Go to Hell," screamed a poster.

New songs were published for the Red Guards. Some of the new hit-parade titles: "The Works of Chairman Mao Shine with Golden Rays"; "The Books of Chairman Mao are the Treasure of the Revolution"; "The Hearts of the Shepherds and the Ideas of Mao Tse-tung are Closely Related"; "Best of All, We Like to Read the Works of Chairman Mao"; "Chairman Mao Is Dearer Than Father and Mother to Us"; "Politics to the Forefront";

"The Workers, Peasants and Soldiers are in the Van of the Revolution."

On the afternoon of August 25, according to a Hsinhua Chinese-language broadcast, "a revolutionary fire was ignited in the Central Institute of Arts to destroy the sculptures of emperors, kings, generals, ministers, scholars and beauties, images of Buddha and niches for the Buddha sculptures. The revolutionary students and teachers of the institute said, 'What we have destroyed and crushed are not only a few sculptures, but the whole old world.'"

The institute got, in return, "a color portrait of Chairman Mao."

The party press goaded the youngsters to even more destruction to pave the way for the establishment of the "four news."

The Red Guards had their way in almost everything. But when they demanded that Peking change its name to Tung Fang Hung — The East Is Red — the idea failed to catch on.

In Moscow, *Pravda* noted, with masterly understatement, that "these are unusual days in Peking." [2] Just how unusual the situation was came forcefully home to the Russians almost as soon as the Red Guards were unleashed for their mission of destruction.

It was a bright August morning. The Soviet Chargé d'Affaires in Peking, a ploddingly earnest man named Rozdukhov, set forth from his embassy to go to the airport to see off a visitor to Peking, Vice-President Kamanga of Zambia. The Zambian visitor was going from Peking to Moscow, where attempts most likely would be made to eradicate the effects of his Peking sojourn.

Rozdukhov stepped into a big, black limousine whose fenders were adorned with flags of the Soviet Union.

He drove as far as the high iron-grill gate of the Soviet Embassy compound, and there encountered an astonishing sight which shook his orderly bureaucratic soul. Across the road was an enormous portrait of Mao Tse-tung, completely blocking the right-of-way. And around the sign milled thousands of shouting, jeering youths in khaki uniforms with red armbands, breast badges and neckerchiefs, sweating from their exertions and enthusiasm.

The street sign had been changed. The street where the Soviet Embassy compound was located had been known as the Street of the Growing Prestige. Now that name was covered up and a huge sign in red characters proclaimed it as Street of the Struggle against Revisionism.

Swiftly, the yelling Red Guards surrounded the Soviet car and began pounding on it, shouting threats at the revisionists seated inside and making motions indicating they were going to overturn it.

Rozdukhov finally shrugged his shoulders, muttered a resigned "Nichyevo" and ordered his driver to turn back to the embassy. At the airport, Vice-President Kamanga of Zambia looked in vain for a Soviet representative, while he listened to the blandishments of Premier Chou En-lai, who seemed that day to be in a particularly good mood.

An angry protest came from Moscow against this "act of hooliganism," which it insisted had been carried out with the full knowledge of the Chinese government, and which was seriously hampering the "normal work of the embassy." The Peking government rejected Moscow's protest.

In a fierce blast at Moscow, *People's Daily*, the official voice of the Chinese party, called the Soviet leaders "the termites of the working class and the scum of revolutionary ranks." [3]

The Russians, their patience stretched taut, continued to exercise restraint. A statement of the Soviet Communist party Central Committee noted that despite all the difficulties, "the Communist party of the Soviet Union will continue to promote further the line of strengthening friendship with the Chinese Communists and with the multimillion Chinese people." [4] Moscow seemed to be betting — or hoping — that the Maoists would lose.

The Red Guard took delight in harassing the Soviet Embassy day after day. One day teen-agers from the Peking Institute of General Medicine trudged to the embassy carrying a big character poster which they hung on the fence. It read:

"New hatreds have been cut into our hearts. We shall not

forget them — not in a hundred, a thousand, or ten thousand years. One day when the time comes, we shall cut the skin off you, we shall tear out your sinews, we shall burn your corpses and disperse your ashes in the wind."

Then they set up loudspeakers and blasted the same message repeatedly toward the windows of the Soviet Embassy.

Red Guards were pouring into Peking from all parts of the country, aimless kids on the prowl, with no need to study anything but the little red book of Mao's thoughts, eager for a binge to let off youthful steam, ever ready to inflict the weirdest cruelty on real or imagined enemies, constantly incited by the Maoist press.

In a state in which old gods were being destroyed, worship of Mao was the substitute religion. The religious fervor had gone out of the old Soviet-line Communists, for whom politics had become a dull routine, a way of making a living. In Europe and the West in general, the old-line Muscovite Communists had become almost bourgeois in their outlook. Not so those in still struggling, backward China, with their visions of transforming the world, their need for fanatic belief in a redeemer.

Even, so it seemed, the scientific mind could become captive of the fanaticism. No more striking example of this could be found than that of a woman scientist who, herself, had played an important role in China's nuclear march. Perhaps, occasionally, she looked back wistfully to her life of gentility in New England. But her commitment to Chairman Mao had been a deep one. For her, there could be no turning back.

40

The blonde, who once wore her flowing hair in braids as a child in Vermont, was an incongruous sight on the streets of Peking. Now in her middle forties, Joan Chase Hinton amply filled the drab blue suit of a devout member of the Chinese Communist party. She worked to produce a "big character poster," [1] grimly fashioning denunciations of those who failed to bow before Chairman Mao. With equal zeal, Joan Hinton's perspiring husband labored at her side. The two were fulfilling vows to oppose all that their native America symbolized.

It was a strange climax for a career of undisputed scientific genius. Willingly or otherwise, Joan had been caught up in the feverish madness of the great Chinese political convulsion. The party had been well pleased with her contributions to China's nuclear ambition, and now with the propaganda value of her poster-painting.

"As a young woman, Joan Hinton's dream had been to dedicate herself to science," said the New China News agency (Hsinhua). "But this was shattered by the murderous explosion of the atom bombs over Hiroshima and Nagasaki.

"She was attracted by the gunfire of China's liberation war. Realizing that in the U.S.A. science serves only the interests of the imperialists, she came to China, her heart brimming with revolutionary enthusiasm, at the close of 1948 when the whole country was being rapidly liberated." [2] The following spring, Hsinhua related, Joan Hinton reached Yenan, the cave-pocked citadel of Mao Tse-tung's Communist forces.

Joan was the daughter of Mrs. Carmelita Hinton, a remarkable schoolteacher from Omaha who founded the famous Putney School in Vermont in 1935. Mother Hinton created a sensation in U.S. preparatory school circles, extending John Dewey's revolution in elementary schools to the secondary schools. Prominent parents flocked to the Vermont school to expose their children to Hinton's progressive education.

At the University of Chicago, Joan's talent for science earned her honors as a physicist. Her abilities attracted the attention of top scientists, including Enrico Fermi. She went with other brilliant students to Los Alamos as a research assistant on the Manhattan Project, the super-secret U.S. drive to build the world's first atom bomb.[3] Joan witnessed the first A-bomb explosion. The sight of this fiery mushroom monster chilled Joan Hinton — and changed her life.

"Ever since that morning," she recalled, "when we sat on a hillock south of Albuquerque and felt the heat of that bomb twenty-five miles away, something had started to stir in me."

Hiroshima and Nagasaki, Joan said, had shattered her.

"As one who touched with my own hands the very bomb which was dropped on Nagasaki, I feel a deep sense of guilt and shame at the part I played in this crime against humanity as a whole, and this crime against the Japanese in particular." [4]

In 1948, Joan had journeyed to China, telling the passport office she had a job with the Chinese Welfare Fund.[5] A year later she married an American, Erwin (Sidney) Engst, who reached China as an agriculturalist with a United Nations relief agency. That was the year the Communists seized full control of China. Joan's conversion to the Red cause was immediate and emotional.

She related to the Chinese press that her first job in China was laboring in an iron factory in the mountains of Shensi. She claimed they "melted up American-made hand grenades, shells, wings from crashed planes sent from America to Chiang Kai-shek, steel and aluminum weapons sent by America to kill them, and made them into cooking pots, plows and saws." [6]

It was after this that Joan married the American and with him settled on an animal breeding farm in Inner Mongolia. After living there two years, she wrote, she had "only seen one thing Russian; that is, ten Soviet stallions given to our farm for breeding purposes. The silent eyes of these ten stallions tell more to the Mongolian horsemen than any amount of insinuating speeches of Acheson [the U.S. Secretary of State] ever could."

The Mongolian people, Joan went on, "are not afraid of words, they only believe in what they see. And what do they see as far as America is concerned? Again, it is not empty words of friendship which impress them. It is bombing planes, guns and tanks given to the Kuomintang. In our farm's cornfield are two old craters from American-made bombs. No amount of speeches from American diplomats can erase these holes and the people do not easily forget.

"The people of China want peace. The people of the world want peace, including the people of America."

Joan then made an appeal to pacifism among U.S. scientists.

"Though I suppose I have been away too long to still be considered a member of the American scientists, yet I personally still feel as though I am one of you. I have written you to let you know at least the story of one of your members.

"One person refusing to work on secret projects, refusing to work on war, of course, does no good. But all of you at home united together have a very special strength in your hands.

"I only want to say to you: Use your strength, use whatever you can to work actively for peace and against war. As long as there is war, science will never be free. Are we scientists going to spend our lives in slavery for madmen who want to destroy the world? At home one gets frightened. Listening to so much war talk one begins to believe that if we do not prepare for war the other side will and then we will be destroyed.

"But now I have been living on the other side for some time and know for sure that this is a lot of lies, that China wants peace and is working for peace with all she has. She will never attack America, nor will any of her allies. If you people would only believe this, if you could only see for yourselves as I am seeing them, I am sure you would not hesitate for a minute to work for peace with every ounce of strength you have." [7]

As she suggested, perhaps Joan Hinton had been away too long from the land of her birth. But she had not altogether thrown off the memory of the old days in America. A few travelers who went to Red China in the mid-1950s and saw Joan Hinton made note of this, finding her anxious for gossip from home. But if she was wistful about her memories, she bent not an inch in her devotion to the notion that everything done by a Communist leadership was done for peace, and that everything done by an American leadership was evil and aimed toward war.

Radio Peking, indeed, presented Joan to the world as an angel of peace. It broadcast a speech she made at one of the early Communist-sponsored Asian and Pacific Peace Conferences and, with evident satisfaction, noted that Joan had been given a standing ovation for what she had said.

"I am ashamed," Joan told that audience, "to admit it took the horror of the bombings of Hiroshima and Nagasaki to shock me out of my ivory tower of complacency.

"I shake the hands of all those who have refused to join in this deadly work and say: Let us work even harder to force the outlawing of atomic bombs, bacteriological warfare and all weapons of mass destruction." [8]

When China exploded its first atom bomb, Joan Hinton probably chose to believe it was done in the name of world peace. Intelligence reports placed her in a nuclear research center at Paotow in China's Inner Mongolia. [9] She had been reported in contact with Bruno Pontecorvo, the physicist who had defected from Britain to Russia and who seemed to have been a big help to the Chinese nuclear program. So, probably, was China's version of St. Joan.

41

Tien An Men Square, between the time of the August Plenum announcements and China's National Day, October 1, 1966, was the scene of nine enormous rallies, each involving a crowd of more than a million, each more noisily colorful than its predecessor.

Mao Tse-tung appeared in person, but spoke at none of them. Lin Piao, now invariably called "close comrade-in-arms of Chairman Mao," spoke at all of them, and he was like an old-time religious revivalist exhorting the faithful to confess and convert.

At each succeeding rally, there were significant changes in the name lists and the positions of prominence of the leaders on the tribune. But at the August 31 rally, the Maoist faction had yet another method of demonstrating how far President Liu Shao-chi had fallen from his preeminent place as Mao's heir apparent.

The top leaders arrived for the rally in automobiles. In the first were Mao, Lin, Ho Lung (who later would break with both) and Yang Cheng-wu,* the new army chief of staff. In the second were Premier Chou En-lai, Tao Chu (the meteorically rising newcomer to the inner circle), Nieh Jung-chen who bossed China's nuclear program, and Chiang Ching, Mao's fourth wife, who was about to emerge as a power in her own right. In the third car were Teng Hsiao-ping, the party secretary general, Kang Sheng, the rising secret police expert, Foreign Minister Chen Yi, and finally Liu.

By this time, Liu had slipped into the eighth place in the

---

* Yang Cheng-wu himself was denounced by street demonstrators in 1968, amid signs that he, too, was on the way out.

Politburo name lists. Already, he could be upstaged by Chiang Ching, who had been named "deputy head of the cultural revolution group under the party Central Committee." Chiang Ching, a onetime struggling Shanghai actress, had the signal honor on August 31 of proclaiming the rally opened and receiving revolutionary students and teachers from all parts of the country, to whom she gave a "proletarian salute and extended a warm welcome," as Hsinhua put it.

Chiang Ching proved to be a fire-eater. Few could have been more violent in demands for vengeance, more vituperative in denunciation of the "class enemy," more vindictive in attacks on those who once had occupied respected positions.

There is an old saying in China: "When the woman comes, the nation decays." One could wonder: was this another instance of Chinese history repeating itself through a distorted mirror? Did not emperors of old, when they were in trouble, put forward their wives to carry on their political wars and turn to favorite generals to shield them from political enemies? Was Chiang Ching destined to become a female gray eminence, a shadow empress?

Chairman Mao himself arrived at the rally wearing an olive green army uniform, as if to signify to the milling million in the square his reliance upon Lin Piao and the People's Liberation Army. Indeed, by this time, the propaganda was full of injunctions about the importance of the army and of "learning from the army." The armed forces — that section of its officer corps which remained loyal to Lin Piao — would be an important factor should the Great Proletarian Cultural Revolution get out of hand, and it had been showing signs of doing just that.

Despite obvious dangers, those controlling the party's Central Committee went right on encouraging excesses. Either the Central Committee was contradicting its own orders and warnings against Red Guard excesses, or there was a difference of opinion at the top level. The latter seemed the more likely. Despite some precautionary words from Premier Chou and others that the Red Guards should beware of going too far, *Red Flag* and *People's*

Daily in mid-September published identical editorials praising the Red Guards' work in the Cultural Revolution. It appeared that matters must have been approaching a climax. The Maoist revolutionaries were told the time was ripe to strike down "the handful of persons in authority taking the capitalist road" and to "seize state power." [1]

This, in fact, proved the beginning of a long struggle for the seizure of power in cities and provinces around the country. Holdouts against the Maoist faction had been strongly entrenched. This was notably true in Sinkiang Province, for example, where a major clash probably took place in September of 1966.

On National Day, October 1, commemorating Communist capture of the China mainland, another monster rally was assembled in Tien An Men Square, this time with 1.5 million people taking part — the biggest yet of the mass meetings. Strangely enough, the official press coverage indicated a place of honor for Liu Shaochi, suggesting that the president had won back some ground in a see-saw struggle for power with the Mao-Lin Piao faction. He was listed first after Mao and Lin among those who mounted to the tribune to the cheers of the mighty throng. As customary, Lin Piao made the principal address. This time it was brief, containing a few perfunctory swipes at the Americans and a few at "modern revisionism within the leadership of the Communist party of the Soviet Union."

And while all this was going on — and China seemed sliding toward internal disaster — the nuclear scientists labored, relatively undisturbed. They were about to be heard from again. And America was about to remember Tsien Hsue-shen, the missile specialist from California Institute of Technology.

42

Now came the day Tsien Hsue-shen would repay the Americans with interest. It was another of those bright and balmy October days in Peking when the announcement came, and the Chinese press bubbled with glee.

"The United States imperialists and the modern revisionists both lost their bearings and their tongues for some time. . . . The latest miracle created by the Chinese people under the guidance of Mao Tse-tung's thinking has made all oppressed people proud and happy and left the imperialists, modern revisionists and reactionaries in all countries crestfallen," cried *People's Daily*. Before the President of the United States, Lyndon B. Johnson, left for Manila and a summit conference of America's Pacific allies, the newspaper gloated, he did not dream that while he was only half way on his tour he would run into the "guided missile–nuclear weapon test of the Chinese people."

Tsien Hsue-shen's genius, and the knowledge he had brought back from America, had now produced a triumph of propaganda for his native China and her Communist leaders. President Johnson was in Malaysia at that moment, issuing resounding pronouncements on the future of all Asia and the depth of the American commitment to it. At that moment in history came a Chinese declaration of Peking's own claim on Asia's future.

"On October 27, 1966," read the communiqué, "China successfully conducted over its own territory a guided missile–nuclear weapon test. The guided missile flew normally and the nuclear warhead accurately hit the target at the appointed distance, effecting a nuclear explosion." [1]

This was Blast No. 4. There could be no question that Dr.

Tsien had joined the nuclear warhead to a rocket. The timing indeed seemed calculated to jar the nerves of the Nuclear Club's oldest member. Tsien's missile carried a defiant message, a warning that such arms would be a deterrent to any American interference with what China might do in Asia.

President Johnson responded quickly to the challenge. At Kuala Lumpur, the U.S. President put it this way:

"We can only regard the pursuit of national nuclear power by too large a part of the underdeveloped world as a tragic fact, for bread is the need of millions who face starvation every day, and bombs are too often purchased at the price of bread. . . .

"We have already declared that nations which do not seek national nuclear weapons can be sure that they will have our strong support if they need it, against any threat of nuclear blackmail. We hope that mainland China, like other developing nations, will concentrate its resources on economic development. In this way a truly modern China can emerge on the mainland. For a peaceful China has nothing to fear from any of us. A peaceful China can expect friendship and cooperation.

"A reckless China can expect vigilance and strength." [2]

Asia was shaken by the implications of a Chinese nuclear-tipped missile. In Japan, experts at the Nomura Research Institute speculated that the Chinese had achieved a major breakthrough in rocket development. China's nuclear missile would bring Japan, Okinawa and the rest of China's near neighbors easily within range. Western experts had estimated that the range of the Chinese missile was between four hundred and six hundred miles and that it had carried a warhead with a punch of twenty kilotons.

43

The Red Guards, on whose young shoulders rested Mao Tse-tung's Great Cultural Revolution, danced in the streets.[1] They tolled gongs and beat drums. They marched in cheering, unruly crowds to headquarters of the Communist party Central Committee near the Square of Heavenly Peace and staged a noisy celebration. They stacked hundreds of giant-sized messages of congratulation beneath a big floodlit portrait of Mao. Over and over they shouted "Long live Chairman Mao" and "Long live the Great Proletarian Cultural Revolution."

Outside the building of the newspaper *People's Daily* people formed long lines to receive — once again free of charge — extra editions of the official party paper. The special midnight issue carried a huge headline in red characters: "HAPPY NEWS!"

The "happy news" of December 28, 1966, was that Communist China had conducted a fifth nuclear test. The announcement gave no information on the device tested. In the United States, the Atomic Energy Commission disclosed that monitoring devices had placed the yield at "a few hundred kilotons." Experts in Washington viewed it as a major stride toward the hydrogen bomb.

Once again, Defense Minister Lin Piao basked in the light of the nuclear test. Because of the test and what it portended, People's Liberation Army men were told to pledge themselves "to respond to Comrade Lin Piao's call for more effective study and application of Chairman Mao's works."

Lin long before had ordered the PLA to arm itself with "the spiritual atom bomb" of Mao's thinking, behind which he could exercise control. Now he was promising them real nuclear weapons and, evidently, while bowing in the direction of the Buddha-like image of Mao, was claiming the lion's share of the credit for himself.

A constant repetition of the line that China would not be first to use the bomb and China's call after the first blast for a summit meeting on prohibition of nuclear weapons, were tokens of Peking's caution. Peking apparently did not want the idea to get abroad that she had any intention of threatening any major power — least of all the United States — with her nuclear development program. Red China was far too vulnerable for such a risk. But the Peking regime seemed highly pleased that Americans "admitted" their concern that "China has been able to shorten the timespan between its tests with such rapidity and that its fifth test followed the fourth in only two months."

It seemed obvious by now that the United States had underestimated the potential of the Chinese in the nuclear weapons field. The Russians had done likewise, perhaps even to a greater extent. China's goal of thermonuclear capability now was clearly in sight.

The Atomic Energy Commission speculated that Explosion No. 5 was an experiment with a triple-stage bomb. Analysis of the debris indicated this. It even contained some ordinary U-238 as a fissionable material.

This meant that China's latest explosion had been the "dirtiest" type with high contamination potential in the radioactive fallout. The indications were that the explosive power had been obtained from fission-fusion-fission reaction in three stages: first, the explosion of the fission trigger; second, the generation of intense heat to ignite the thermonuclear materials, and third, the fusion reaction giving off neutrons and causing the U-238 atoms to split. Normally, U-238 does not fission. But in this complex process it is exposed to extremely high-energy neutrons and its fission greatly increases the power of a thermonuclear weapon. At the same time, it makes the weapon extremely "dirty." The drawback to the triple-stage bomb is that it is bulky and hard to deliver by bomber. The United States had tested such a bomb as far back as 1954 at

Bikini and it had produced the heaviest of fallouts. The Russians, too, conducted similar tests in 1961–1962.

The reaction around the world among non-Communist nations and even in most of the Communist ones, was one of dismay. Both scented danger. As the Yugoslav Communists put it:

"The fifth Chinese nuclear explosion shows that modern China, which is in the grip of convulsions and twists of internal contradictions and conflicts, is seeking a way out through an absolute militarization of the country. Judging by all the signs, it is trying to impose itself on the world and to achieve at least some of its great-state and nationalist aims, which are becoming more and more obvious." [2]

China had brought "a sense of insecurity and offensive threat, not only to India but to many neighboring countries," commented P. K. Banerjee, minister of the Indian Embassy in Washington.

But in Communist North Vietnam, President Ho Chi Minh once again hailed a Chinese nuclear test as a "great contribution to the cause of safeguarding the peace of the world." [3] Just how sincere he was about it was open to question, since the North Vietnamese long had shown signs of worry that, in their war with the United States, they might be over-helped by their big neighbor to the point where Vietnam might cease to exist.

Nevertheless, Hanoi radio itself insisted that the Vietnamese were joyous at the news of the nuclear successes which, it said, "resulted from the correct leadership exerted by the Chinese Communist party headed by Mao Tse-tung." It extended "warmest congratulations." This was bending over backwards. The Russians, from whom Hanoi was getting the most important of its military and economic aid, were apt to be a good deal less than enchanted by a salute to the Chinese party's "correct leadership."

The Russians, no less than the rest of the watching world, were bewildered. The Chinese explosions had come, one after another, each more menacing-looking than its predecessor, while China was involved in an internal uproar which seemed to threaten her with national calamity. [4]

But there was always the silver lining, the bright side of things. China still could only underkill. The Americans and Russians could overkill. The latter had what the Pentagon, in that curious jargon which is all its own, called Assured Destruction capability, and also had Damage Limiting capability. In Defense Secretary McNamara's 1967 Budget Statement, the terms were invariably capitalized.

China would be less a problem to the United States than the Russians because the Russians had Damage Limiting capability to pose against the American's Assured Destruction capability. China had little in the way of Damage Limiting capability. But it did have seven hundred million people, and killing them could pose a problem. The Pentagon had discovered something else, however, which might console the American people. It was called Lead Time.

"With respect to the protection of the U.S. against a possible Red Chinese nuclear attack, the Lead Time required for China to develop a significant ICBM force is greater than that required for deployment of our defense — therefore the Chinese threat in itself would not dictate the production of an ABM (anti-ballistic missile) system at this time."

There was even better news than that for the Americans. If the Chinese should strike first with nuclear weapons, the United States might lose only a million people — if it had the ABMs proposed in the Pentagon program. If it did not have the ABMs it could lose up to ten million. An "austere defense probably could preclude damage in the 1970s almost entirely." But:

"As the Chinese force grows to the level it might achieve by 1980–1985, additions and improvements might be required, but relatively modest additional outlays could probably limit the Chinese damage potential to low levels well beyond 1985."

In fact, "it is not clear that we need an ABM defense against China. In any event," said McNamara, once again seeing the brighter side, "the lead time for deployment of a significant

Chinese offensive force is longer than that required for U.S. ABM deployment." [5]

China, in the Pentagon's view, would require many more tests before achieving truly operational capability with medium or intermediate range missiles. But Washington acknowledged that the nuclear weapons and missiles programs were being developed with the highest priority in China. The Pentagon already was thinking in terms of the possibility of a Chinese space launch or a long-range ballistic missile launching in the near future. There would not, however, be a "significant" number of operational ICBMs before the mid-1970s.

Other experts were speculating that by 1972, Red China might have an operational force of a hundred or more ICBMs capable of reaching U.S. targets, provided the political turmoil in China did not seriously impede the program. Up to that time, it had not appeared to have done so. And so far as sophistication in weaponry was concerned, China already had surprised the Americans. She might do so once again.

44

While the scientists were busy with China's fifth nuclear explosion, Chiang Ching, Mao's fourth wife, was detonating her very own "immensely powerful spiritual atom bomb," as *People's Daily* put it. In fact, she touched off a series of explosions, one after another, whose political repercussions were louder than the echo from the western desert.

Mme Mao prepared the young Red Guards for a joyous campaign of cruelty by making a fiery address which the youngsters extolled in wall newspapers as "a revolutionary torch in the field of literature and art, an order for mobilization, a signal for the campaign, a timely rain and a guiding lamp." Chiang Ching, they announced, was their inspiration for daring feats of revolutionary patriotism.

Fired up by that speech, a group of eighty Red Guards held a meeting in a government ministry building, to receive their instructions. From there, they marched to the home of Peng Chen, the deposed Peking mayor and Politburo member, gathering swarms of yelling youth on the way.[1] Their operation had the look of a well-organized and carefully executed plan. All the details had been taken care of, including the supply of a truck, in advance, from some person high in authority. The truck was important to what was about to take place.

The youngsters, waving their little red books of Mao's thoughts, burst suddenly into Peng Chen's home.

"When we dragged Peng Chen from his bed," gloated a wall newspaper, "he really looked like a paper tiger." They dragged him across the courtyard and threw him into the waiting truck.

Peng, cringing from a combination of fear and shame, was driven in humiliation through the streets, his head bowed, a placard across his chest condemning him as a revisionist. They hauled him before a howling mob of a hundred thousand young kangaroo court judges and pronounced him a "criminal revisionist, a counterrevolutionary plotter and a political careerist, the leader of the struggle against Chairman Mao and the ideas of Mao Tsetung." He had, they announced, "attempted to take over the power in the party, army and state."

Peng Chen was by no means alone in his agony. The young Guardists at the same time raided the homes of high officials of the Peking municipal party committee. It was the beginning of a riotous but organized attack on all elements in high places suspected of heresy. In the predawn hours of December 24 in Cheng-tu, capital of Szechwan Province, Red Guards from the

Peking Institute of Aviation sent especially for the task, invaded the home of Peng Teh-huai, Lin Piao's predecessor as Defense Minister, and placed him under "arrest," although it was likely he had been under at least house arrest all along.

"This bald-headed Khrushchev," as a Peking Red Guard wall newspaper called him, was taken to Peking from Cheng-tu and on December 27 subjected to another kangaroo court of tens of thousands of youngsters who chanted criticisms at him, accused him of being a bourgeois, a revisionist and a counterrevolutionary.[2]

Then another extremely influential figure came under Red Guard attack. He was Ho Lung, who had the rank equivalent to armed forces marshal, was a vice-premier, member of the party secretariat and the ruling Politburo and an old revolutionary comrade of Mao. The seventy-two-year-old soldier was a dangerous target for the Maoists, because his influence in the armed forces was extensive. If any man could rally support for a stand against the cultural revolution, it was likely to be one such as Ho Lung. Nevertheless, he was so severely attacked that he is believed to have slipped quietly out of Peking, in flight, possibly to the hills of Szechwan, perhaps to work out means of organizing resistance with other dissident army figures.[3]

Then it was the turn of the tough Tao Chu. No one had risen so high, so fast, as Tao had in the early stages of the Cultural Revolution, when he was whisked away from his South Central Bureau job to become propaganda chief in place of the purged Lu Ting-yi. His name soon ranked fourth in the name lists of the Politburo, after Mao, Lin Piao and Premier Chou En-lai.

Suddenly and inexplicably fallen from favor, Tao Chu was dragged through the streets of Peking and made defendant in yet another kangaroo court of Red Guards. It was possible that Tao was one more victim of the vengeful Mme Mao. The Red Guards quoted Mao's wife as having told them that "Tao Chu attended Central Committee meetings, but never sided with the proletarian revolutionary line represented by Mao Tse-tung." According to Mme Mao, Tao Chu was "loyal to the line represented by Liu Shao-chi and Teng Hsiao-ping, and is connected with enlarging the Liu-Teng faction." If it could happen to Tao, it could happen to almost anyone.

By early January, the confusion in Peking — indeed, in much of China — was enormous. It was soon to be compounded by what was called the January Revolution.

"A revolution," Mao Tse-tung once said — and this was quoted time and again that January — "is not a dinner party, or writing an essay, or painting a picture or doing embroidery. It cannot be so refined, so leisurely, so restrained and magnanimous. A revolution is an insurrection, an act of violence by which one class overthrows another."

There was nothing refined, leisurely or magnanimous about the Great Proletarian Cultural Revolution. It was a major explosion whose tremendous force rocked China. The dominant faction had opened a Pandora's box, and it would not be easy to close it. It is one thing to start a revolution, quite another to keep it under control. But the Mao-Lin faction did seem in January to be gathering strength as it moved against clearly stubborn resistance which was pulling the Communist party structure to pieces.

The evidence of this strength was in the brutality of the attacks on men who long had been considered unassailable: President Liu, General Secretary Teng and many another. The cheerleaders for the cultural revolution were Chen Po-ta, the dour man who had accompanied Mao on his Moscow visits as a private secretary, and Mao's wife, who was Chen's deputy. She, more than any other leader, openly demanded cruelty and ruthlessness toward those labeled enemies of proletarian dictatorship.

The Chinese have an old expression: "Don't hit dogs in the water." It is the equivalent of "Don't kick a man when he's down." But now the Maoists were being exhorted to hit both "dogs in the water and dogs not yet in the water," the latter those resistance elements in the party apparatus who had not been brought to shame.

Things were beginning to look black for President Liu. His celebrated pamphlet, "On Self-Education of the Communist," also called "How to Be a Good Communist," was singled out for heavy attack, although once it had been a bible for aspiring Communists. One of the sins of the book, it was discovered, was that it quoted from ten classics of Marxism, which was more times than it had quoted from the works of Mao Tse-tung.

President Liu and Secretary Teng still seemed to have strong support among the provincial cadres of the party, and their tormentors had not yet been able to clear the top ranks of the party of opposition elements. *Red Flag*, the theoretical journal, seemed to confirm this with an editorial rapping those who disagreed with Lin Piao as "bad eggs of the Khrushchev type" and "a time bomb planted in our party." [4]

"Hit Liu Shao-chi on the head!" screamed the wall posters. There was a sudden eruption of mobile loudspeakers, blaring out the latest words of Chiang Ching — Mao's ubiquitous wife — demanding that all opponents of her husband's thinking be arrested immediately.

Just in advance of the January Revolution, wall newspapers appeared in Peking with what were supposed to be the "confessions" of President Liu and Secretary Teng. Even if the texts were genuine, the "confessions" seemed unlikely to satisfy the Maoists. Perhaps the two had agreed to some sort of confession to restore some appearance of unity in the party at a time when continued uproar might invite national catastrophe. But the confessions did not go all the way in conceding that all Mao had been attempting to do was right and everything about the opposition was wrong.

Teng Hsiao-ping's "confession" represented him as completely supporting "the instructions given by Chairman Mao Tse-tung and Comrade Lin Piao." It said "Comrade Liu Shao-chi and I should take a direct responsibility for the mistakes committed in various districts and various fields after the eleventh plenary session." [5]

As Communist confessions go, that was not much of a confession. The one attributed to Liu was much longer, a rambling document which accused him of "crimes" dating all the way back to 1946, and particularly of misdeeds in mid-1966 as the Cultural Revolution was gaining momentum. It recalled that he had presided over the daily work of the party central while Mao was absent from Peking prior to July 18. That had been a critical time. Mao had been in Shanghai then, waiting for the smoke to clear in Peking. Perhaps Liu had been within a shade of taking over power.

The purported confession also dragged in Wang Kuang-mei, Liu's wife, suggesting once again the hand of Mme Mao. Mme Liu, too, evidently had committed political "crimes."

The "confession" recalled the opening session, August 1, of the Eleventh Plenum at which there was discussion of Liu's "mistakes." It said:

"A unanimous decision came at this time naming Comrade Lin Piao as Chairman Mao's first aide and his successor. Comrade Lin Piao and other comrades are all better and greater than I am. I am firmly resolved to abide by the rules as a member of the party and not engage in two-faced maneuvers."

That was the first time up to then that there had been any public attempt to announce the anointment of Lin Piao as Mao's heir.

The confession never appeared in the official press. It seemed highly unlikely that Liu, who could regard himself as having an equal claim with Mao to having fathered the Chinese Communist party and its revolution, accepted all the nonsense he was supposed to have written in his confession about Mao's greatness and the necessity "to learn from Comrade Lin Piao."

Legally, Liu could not be removed as Chairman of the Republic — president — without the convocation of a party congress. If Lin and Mao were going to bring him down, they would have to try to do it illegally until such time as they felt confident enough to call a congress.

There had been no party congress for more than ten years,

although under the rules one should have been held in the early 1960s. It seemed likely the Mao-Lin group did not dare convene a congress for fear of finding themselves in the minority. Thus it would be necessary first to eliminate the opposition by whatever means possible. So the attacks on Liu and Secretary Teng rose in intensity — still confined to wall newspapers.

The January Revolution was in fact a convulsion. It brought chaos to virtually every Chinese provincial capital as Mao's "revolutionary rebels" and Red Guards set out to "seize the power from the handful of persons in authority in the party who took the capitalist road."

Shanghai, China's largest city, was hit hard. The situation for a time there verged on civil war, by official Chinese account. Peking Radio broadcast angry complaints that "bourgeois" forces in Shanghai had sabotaged power and water supplies and cut off transport. Resistance to the Red Guards mounted hourly. It seemed that for a time, in the uproar, the participants could not distinguish friend from foe.

Many other cities underwent similar trouble. There were work stoppages, sabotage and transport interruptions. In Peking, an aircraft factory stopped work because of pitched battles between Red Guards and workers. In Nanking, scores were reported killed and hundreds wounded in clashes between Maoists and supporters of the newly-fallen Tao Chu. Fighting spread to many areas of China and was reported to have reached serious proportions in Kiangsu Province, with tens of thousands involved. All rail traffic between Hankow and Peking was cut off for two days while Red Guards went on new rampages. Posters in Peking reported clashes between the youngsters and peasants in the Shanghai area and many areas of the hinterland. The government was flirting with paralysis.

There were at the time thirteen of Premier Chou En-lai's fifteen deputy premiers who had come under Red Guard attack, and Chou himself complained it made the day-to-day business of government extremely difficult. The opposition fought back with wall posters of its own — what the Red Guards later would discover had been "counterrevolutionary black leaflets."

One wall poster in Peking reported six persons handed over to security officials because their leaflets had criticized Kang Sheng. The six were "sent before the masses" for denunciation before being dispatched to the mercies of Kang Sheng's own security squad. Kang Sheng was a formidable power in the Mao-Lin establishment. His real name was either Chang Shao-ching or Chao Yung. A native of Shantung in 1903, he had been a Communist since the early 1920s and a student of intelligence methods, in which he received basic training from Moscow's NKVD. Stalin, some say, once had expressed admiration for Kang as a student of secret police administration.[6] His talents would now serve Mao well, and he ranked high in the new inner circle.

The January Revolution had a look of desperation, a campaign to save the Cultural Revolution from catastrophe. Mao's supporters everywhere were exhorted to "seize power" from the entrenched party bureaucracy at provincial and municipal levels.

There had to be "destruction before construction." The targets of destruction were "despicable swine who wormed their way into the party . . . and colluded with landlords, rich peasants, counterrevolutionaries, bad elements and rightists to carry out ferocious counterattacks."

But the January Revolution failed to bring down Liu Shao-chi. Indeed, as the contest swirled into the spring, the opposition appeared to gather new strength.

The Mao-Lin faction did wrest control in some areas, but at a heavy cost. It included the cost of a wrecked party apparatus. Where the Maoists took over, enormous oath-taking rallies were held by the "revolutionary rebels," Red Guards and army personnel to pledge allegiance to Chairman Mao. A typical pledge was the one adopted in Kiangsi Province:

"Chairman Mao, our dearest, dearest, great leader, the reddest, reddest, reddest sun in our hearts, great leader, teacher, commander and helmsman, our dearest, dearest red commander in chief, we loyally wish you eternal life." [7]

The South Central area of the country seemed at times almost detached from the rest and under control of dissidents. One of the most serious outbreaks occurred in Wuhan, the big triple city in Hupeh on the Yangtze — scene of Mao's celebrated swim — and the economic heart of China. An organization under the control of dissident army men and calling itself the Million Brave Soldiers appeared to have nearly seized control of the vital area for President Liu.

Mao and Lin seemed in danger. Their main enemies were still in operation, refusing to surrender.

Liu Shao-chi in mid-July was reported to have made yet another confession in the form of a "statement of self-examination," but it was denounced as a hoax and "another poisonous arrow aimed at Chairman Mao and the party Central Committee . . . and unbridled provocation against the proletarian revolutionaries and a manifesto to incite a handful of counterrevolutionary revisionists for a new counteroffensive." Once again, the press did not use Liu's name. [8]

Tao Chu, despite the ferocity of the attacks on him, remained much in evidence as a potential menace to Lin Piao's leadership claims. Perhaps Peng Teh-huai and Lo Jui-ching, too, were not entirely out of the picture, despite Red Guard poster reports of attempted suicides.

In Shanghai, where the January Revolution began and through the summer the most turbulent of China's cities, the newspaper *Wen Hui Pao* indicated that Tao Chu was still operating somewhere in his stronghold area, South Central China. [9]

Something close to anarchy must have been reigning in the late summer of 1967 in areas like Wuhan, South Central China, Mao's native Province of Hunan and in Honan Province, the breadbasket of China. Serious disturbances continued in Shantung and Kwangtung Provinces. Frequent outbreaks were reported in Canton and Shanghai. The battle was far from over. [10]

If Lin Piao's predecessor as Defense Minister, Peng Teh-huai, and the deposed army chief of staff, Lo Jui-ching, had been safely put away by the Lin-Mao forces, the influence of their examples still may have remained a threat within the ranks of the armed forces. This could have explained the virulence of renewed attacks on the two at a time of deepening crisis. The top theoretical journal of the Chinese party, *Red Flag*, produced a long diatribe against the two.[11] It supported the suspicion that Peng and Lo opposed proletarianization of the army and had hoped to modernize it.

"Peng Teh-huai remarked nonsensically that 'the achievement of the armed forces in military training and the mastery of military techniques by cadres at various levels are the basic criteria for judging the fighting power of our army today and in the future,'" *Red Flag* protested. "Lo Jui-ching used large-scale military contests to disparage politics. . . . In fact, Peng Teh-huai, Lo Jui-ching and their ilk have always opposed proletarian politics but have practiced putting bourgeois reactionary politics first. . . . With the support of the top party person in authority taking the capitalist road (President Liu), Peng Teh-huai and Lo Jui-ching have engaged in the army in fostering personal forces, establishing their personal authority, winning over defectors and renegades, forming private parties and making secret contacts with a foreign power in an insidious attempt to usurp the party and the army." (This probably referred to Marshal Peng's opposition to estrangement from Moscow.)

"Peng Teh-huai gathered a group of class aliens who infiltrated the party and some speculators, counterrevolutionaries, unreformed old military officers and other demons and freaks, to form an anti-party clique and a counterrevolutionary military club. In the case of Lo Jui-ching, he colluded with such counterrevolutionary revisionists as Peng Chen (the fallen Peking mayor), Lu Ting-yi (the deposed propaganda chief) and Yang Shang-kun (an ousted Russian-educated party secretary) to form an anti-party conspiratorial clique. . . . In short, Peng Teh-huai, Lo Jui-ching and their ilk, who were agents of China's Khrushchev in the army, have tried their utmost to reform our army with counterrevolutionary revisionism and bourgeois tricks in order to usurp our military leadership. If they succeeded in this conspiracy and were given the arms in their hands, our country would have changed color and we would have lost our country and party, as well as our lives."

After this startling suggestion that a top-level struggle to the death had been raging, *Red Flag* extravagantly extolled Lin Piao as having made outstanding contributions to averting the Peng-Lo threat.

The frail, consumptive Lin was not necessarily emerging as a Red Napoleon, but a suggestion of army preeminence over the party seemed to be stirring widespread apprehension and pointing China toward a dangerous road.

Outside observers, including the Russians, looked on with a mixture of wonderment and fright, noting that China's peasants were becoming restless, that hungry people were on the prowl.

But once again, China was a paradox. For all the confusion and violence, the nuclear bomb program continued, as if in complete isolation from the reality of China's torment. Whatever happened to the politicians seemed to have little effect on scientists and engineers. Nothing halted progress on the bomb.

45

Four huge, brightly colored balloons soared into the blue sky over the Takla Makan Desert. From the balloons trailed long red and white banners bearing slogans: "Long Live Our Great Chairman

Mao," "Long Live the Invincible Thought of Mao Tse-tung," "Long Live the Chinese Communist Party," "Long Live the Great Proletarian Cultural Revolution."

Army officers solemnly ran up a five-star Red Flag. Commanders snapped orders. Army personnel, technicians, engineers and scientists obediently lined up and in loud voices recited quotations from the *Thoughts of Mao Tse-tung*.[1]

"What we need is an enthusiastic but calm state of mind and intense but orderly work," they chanted in unison. "Our duty is to hold ourselves responsible to the people."

The chanting over, scientists and engineers checked the complex equipment one last time. Each screw, each tiny electronic part, each welded joint was examined with meticulous care. Key men stationed themselves inside the control center. Signal lights blinked furiously. Soldiers donned protective suits, masks and goggles. Army officers took up their vigil at observation posts. Over a loudspeaker, a voice announced, like the crack of doom: "The world-shaking moment has arrived."

For a tense second the men waited, awestruck even at the thought of what was to come.

Man-made lightning clawed at the hot, blue sky. Enormous thunder rocked the desert earth below. A great ball of flame appeared, turning the air hideous with reds and purples.

The burning ball disappeared. A mushroom cloud rose skyward. Poisoned air drifted eastward toward the Sea of Japan.

On that morning, June 17, 1967, Communist China exploded her first hydrogen bomb, achieving full membership in the Nuclear Club. With it, she shook the world and changed it drastically.

As the thunder died away, the test-site personnel recited new quotations from Mao Tse-tung. Some, at the prodding of their group leaders, burst into song, "Sailing the Seas Depends on the Helmsmen." Others clustered about an enormous portrait of Mao and shouted quotations at the tops of their voices. Some danced with tears in their eyes and waved their little red books of

Mao's thoughts, according to florid accounts in Peking's press.

The news reached Peking at midnight and there, according to the news agency Hsinhua, it brought the population into the streets for jubilation. Said Hsinhua:

"People set off firecrackers, beat drums and gongs and cheered, 'Long Live Our Great Leader, Chairman Mao!'"

All the credit for the H-bomb was given to Mao's thinking. Somebody dredged up what Mao was supposed to have said, by odd coincidence, nine years before: "I think it is entirely possible for some atom and hydrogen bombs to be made in ten years' time." If Mao had said it, he hit it on the nose.[2] If he hadn't said it, who was to be the wiser?

Once again, as in all the other tests, the scientists came last when it was time to pass out credit.[3]

"It has taken China only two years and eight months to cover the entire course from its first A-bomb explosion in October, 1964, to the successful H-bomb test," said *People's Daily*. "To do the same thing, however, it took the U.S.A. seven years and four months, the Soviet Union four years and Britain four years and seven months. China's speed, therefore, is the fastest in the world."

The figures were correct. Peking did not bother to mention France, still without an H-bomb.

46

What Tsien Hsue-shen, the rocketry genius from the California Institute of Technology, and his American- and European-trained aides accomplished in China — a delivery system for its nuclear weapons — became a basic and critical problem for American security and for world peace. Within three years from the time of her first H-bomb explosion, China could have a stockpile of a hundred hydrogen bombs. Soon she would be in a position to launch an intercontinental missile and get into the space race with a satellite orbiting alongside Russian and American artificial moons.

China already had passed France in the nuclear arms race and was moving into position to overtake Britain and become the third of the nuclear powers, behind the United States and the Soviet Union. She had profited hugely from U.S. and Soviet pioneering in the field, and certainly from the scientific know-how her sons — like Drs. Chao and Tsien, Hua Lo-keng, Wang Kan-chang and others — had gained in the United States and the Soviet Union. Perhaps, some speculated, the Chinese had even outdone their benefactors and found a quicker way to concentrate U-235, possibly a centrifuging process.

The West had been warned many years before against waking the sleeping giant that was China. Now the giant was awake, and restless. A China dominated by those who professed unfailing faith in "people's wars of national liberation" would be a dangerous China, whether or not its leaders were bent on geographical expansion.

A U.S. congressional committee, a month after the Chinese H-blast, estimated China could be capable of launching a hydrogen bomb on the United States within four years and noted that America lacked effective means of repelling such an attack.[1]

It seemed to outsiders that China was in the hands of an irrational regime. This aroused widespread concern among Americans and brought pressure for the development of ABMs — anti-ballistic missiles. The program could have consequences far beyond ministering to American nervousness. In using the threat of China to rationalize military development and deployment of ABMs, the Americans were frightening their friends in the Far East who might then, in spite of their own distaste for it, themselves use the threat of China to demand American help for their own nuclear development.

Secretary of Defense McNamara did, indeed, cite the threat of China in proposing a "relatively inexpensive" system of ABMs. It would, he said, be insane and suicidal for China to attempt an attack on the United States, "but one can conceive conditions under which China might miscalculate."

There was, McNamara found, evidence that China was devoting "very substantial resources to the development of both nuclear warheads and missile delivery systems" and that she would soon have medium range ballistic missiles and within a few short years an intercontinental ballistic missile capability." [2]

A high-placed U.S. official noted glumly that soon there would be "a beep-beep-beep from a Chinese satellite, and the press will translate this as meaning an intercontinental ballistic missile is on the way" to completion.

Senator Henry M. Jackson, the Washington Democrat, who had correctly predicted in October, 1965, that China would have an H-bomb in two years, also predicted a ballistic missile threat to both Southeast and Soviet Asia. And, he added, China "will have enough bombs and missiles to be a real threat to life in the United States and North America" by the mid-1970s. [3]

"We've got to have a public gut feeling that all this spells big trouble," said Representative Craig Hosmer of California, a Republican member of the Joint Committee on Atomic Energy. [4]

And Dr. Ralph Lapp, the Manhattan Project man, estimated that by 1970 Red China would have a hundred H-bombs if they used their U-235 production for triggers, which seemed a likely course.

Americans were made no more comfortable a month after the H-bomb explosion when the deposed Nikita S. Khrushchev supplied some chilling thoughts about Mao Tse-tung's philosophy. In a widely publicized television interview [5] smuggled out of the Soviet Union, Khrushchev represented Mao as having begged him to provoke war with the United States. Khrushchev at the time —

it was 1959 — already had been horrified by previously expressed Mao sentiments about the relative unimportance of widespread nuclear slaughter. Now he was again shocked. He told Mao, he recalled later, that all the divisions China could produce — and China had manpower to spare — would be meaningless against a few powerful nuclear-tipped weapons. "He thought I was a coward," snorted Khrushchev. And, from the tone of subsequent Peking propaganda, that probably was just what Mao thought.

On December 24, 1967, two days before Mao's seventy-fourth birthday, the Atomic Energy Commission in Washington announced the detection of a low-yield atomic explosion by the Chinese in the area of Lop Nor in Sinkiang. Strangely, this time Peking was silent. This was all the more striking by contrast with the extravagant publicity given to the previous six explosions, and it provoked speculation. Western scientists were able to determine that the Chinese had used a nuclear fission device of low yield, with a twenty-kiloton strength, or roughly equivalent to that of the first Sinkiang test in 1964. The explosion was in the air, probably in the neighborhood of fifteen hundred feet.

Some speculated that the test was a failure, or at least that something had gone wrong. Some suggested the test had been premature, and should have been timed two days later for Mao's birthday. Possibly, too, the test had been conducted in defiance of orders from the central authorities in Peking. In support of this latter theory, it was argued that the Communist leaders feared the reaction, both at home and abroad, to additional explosions at that time, and had wanted to postpone testing for a while. On the other hand, the Peking leaders may have simply decided, now that China had achieved H-bomb status, to impose secrecy on further developments for a variety of reasons, not excluding a regard for world sentiment.

It may have been, too, that since the test was a small one, possibly a preparation for something bigger, that the authorities decided to make no announcement, preferring to await more spectacular developments. The haste China had been displaying in her nuclear program up to then would seem to have precluded the theory that its leaders were skittish about world opinion. They had seemed to exhibit, on the contrary, keen anxiety to perfect some sort of deterrent which would keep the Americans and Russians at bay while China pursued her political ambitions in Asia.

As month after month went by without yet another Chinese explosion, the West began to wonder what was the matter. Already Western experts were pushing back the Chinese timetable. Possibly there had been greater technical problems than the West suspected, or possibly the Great Proletarian Cultural Revolution had, indeed, interfered with the science program. There had been no sign, after the apparent failure of the December, 1967, shot that the Chinese scientists had experimented with a booster for an intercontinental ballistic missile. Perhaps, some speculated, the Chinese were merely holding off to await a propitious date and thus get the most propaganda profit possible from the psychological impact. Meanwhile, the Chinese did not let up on their propaganda pressure on the nations of Asia.

"War can be avoided, since China's development of the hydrogen bomb has made resorting to nuclear weapons virtually impossible," Chinese Foreign Minister Chen Yi remarked to a visiting Japanese politician a few weeks after the H-bomb exploded. And he added: "The simplest and safest solution to the Okinawan problem is the removal of U.S. military facilities there." [6]

The meaning was clear. This was a hint of blackmail to come, a hint of the pressure China probably intended to bring to bear against governments through frightening neighboring populations. The implication was that if the U.S. forces withdrew from Asia, so would the threat of a conflict which might mean the use of nuclear weapons.

Once again, Peking stressed the Mao–Lin Piao doctrine that all politics should proceed from the barrel of a gun, that revolution should begin in the countryside and gradually strangle the cities.[7]

The orchestration of Chinese propaganda suggested the idea of using the nuclear arsenal to carry out a strategy of making nations on China's periphery her hostages. Peking could continue to be cautious with regard to tempting U.S. — or Soviet — power and still hope to make significant gains by the implicit threat of her arsenal and indeed of her potential to bring the nuclear might of the superpowers down on Asia. Before long China could hope that popular opinion in weaker Asian countries would bring pressure on governments to demand the withdrawal of U.S. forces.

China's nuclear potential also produced agonizing problems for the Russians. More and more, Peking was an infuriating problem for Moscow, which openly accused the Red Chinese of trying to set the non-white world against the white, with China as the champion of all colored people.[8]

Peking propaganda constantly badgered and harassed the Kremlin. Red China banished Soviet diplomats and the Russians responded in kind. Sino-Soviet relations were never at a lower ebb since communism had taken over the mainland.

China — which had publicly and officially laid claim to six hundred thousand square miles of Soviet territory as having been taken by "unfair treaties" in the past — stirred up frequent troubles along frontiers all the way from the Soviet Far East to Sinkiang in the west.

Moscow, meanwhile, pumped inflammatory, separatist propaganda into the non-Han areas of China, particularly into the Sinkiang-Uighur Autonomous Region. It was as if Moscow's interest had quickened in border prospects, as if the Kremlin was speculating that perhaps China might be dismembered. Perhaps warlords would emerge — Communist warlords who would construct friendly buffers for the U.S.S.R.

Whatever the motivation, Moscow decided to tell, from its own point of view, what had been going on all that time in Sinkiang, the nuclear test province rich in uranium and other rare ores, and in other non-Chinese areas under Peking.

"Communists and anyone else who disagrees with the Peking

dictator's course are being killed," indignantly reported Moscow's Radio Peace and Progress.[9] "The national minorities in China and all non-Chinese people are being bitterly persecuted by the chauvinistic Mao clique.

"Radio Station Peace and Progress has many letters from people who managed to escape from the so-called Red Guard. It is hard to read these letters without anger. The following is the statement of Balkhash Bafin, a former PLA lieutenant-colonel, graduate of the central national school in Peking and holder of three orders and five medals of China. He is now a citizen of Soviet Kazakhstan.

"From day to day, the campaign against all honest Communists in Sinkiang increased. Arrests began. The Kazakh national intellectuals were ridiculously accused of trying to set up Kazakh rule and to unite all the Kazakhs of China, Mongolia and the Soviet Union under them.

"This ridiculous claim about the setting up of Kazakh rule first appeared with the failure of the creation of the new history of the Kazakhs, the Uighurs and the Kirghiz of Sinkiang Province. The Chinese Communist party leaders and the Chinese government figured that this new history would prove one thing, namely, that the Uighurs, Kazakhs and Kirghiz are all Chinese, and consequently they have one motherland stretching from the southern part of China and to the Aral Sea. In other words, the new history was needed to uphold the Kazakhs, Uighurs and Kirghiz who live in China.

"But the intellectuals, the Communists of Sinkiang, did not fall for this lie. Peking then declared that the residents of Sinkiang had two hearts — one yellow Russian heart and the other a red Chinese heart.

" 'We will trample on the yellow heart,' said Peking."

The broadcast went on: "They say that millions of Chinese have moved into Sinkiang, that the local population is being driven off their ancient lands and herded deeper into China onto lifeless deserts. Forced assimilation is taking place. Kazakh, Uighur and

Kirghiz girls are taken away from their parents and for fear of death are forced to marry Chinese.

"The leaders of the so-called Red Guards say that Chinese blood must predominate in the veins of every person. The Red Guards destroy everything: books, record players and records, furniture and dishes. They cut off the braids of the women and girls and forbid the wearing of national clothes. This is the truth as reported by eyewitnesses. This is the truth about the activities of Mao and his gang which completely contradicts the interests of socialism and the national policy of the Communists."

Sinkiang-Uighur Autonomous Region, it would seem, was a dangerous place for China's nuclear installations. It had a border of fifteen hundred miles with the Soviet Union. Chinese rule historically had been unpopular there and there had been rebellions in the past, notably among the Moslems. Frequently in the past, after Sinkiang had come under direct Chinese rule as a result of the Sun Yat-sen revolution, its governors had acted like local independent warlords. The Chinese hold always had been tenuous. It would make a tempting target for Soviet subversion.

Whatever happened, China was going to be an enormous problem for a long time for both the Soviet Union and the United States. Both were looking at one of the world's most puzzling paradoxes. Here was a country of seven hundred and fifty million people, growing at the rate of fifteen million each year, under the sort of government which made prognostication a futile exercise. It was a country whose regime badly needed an outside enemy — indeed, a ring of outside enemies — to excuse the measures it hoped to carry out internally. China needed peace, but Peking did not want the appearance of peace, at least not while the country remained a have-not in comparison with the Western world. China had a huge standing army but virtually no navy, nuclear bombs but an obsolete air force, nuclear missiles but a shortage of heavy conventional armament. She was a backward nation, yet at the same time a leading industrial nation. Her city populations in every province were vastly affected by political and social upheavals, but enormous numbers of peasants in the hinterland, far removed from the bigger cities, were virtually untouched by them.

Early in 1968 there were vague signs that the violence of the Cultural Revolution was beginning to ebb. Some in the regime — notable among them Premier Chou En-lai — appeared to be exerting considerable effort to moderate the force of the movement launched by Mao. Although the internal propaganda continued to be violent in tone, the Red Guards were less and less boisterous. Perhaps they were exhausted, and perhaps Chou and others in the inner circle of power in Peking had taken firm measures to insure control over them, if only in the long-term interests of national security.

It would be no surprise, either, if after all the loud denunciations of the opposition and all the confusion, the two sides in the power struggle reached some form of compromise which would permit China to present a more respectable appearance to the outside world. Perhaps this might happen when Mao finally relinquishes the chairmanship of the party.

The time may come when China will have a regime which will appear more rational and more approachable. As one U.S. Government China-watcher expressed it, advances in science and technology, among them satellite communications, tend to pull nations more closely together. Those which cooperate in these advances can expect to move ahead faster than those which, like today's China, try to go it alone. Thus, there might be pressure on China to join a community of powers for a better, more peaceful world.[10]

While the words of the Chinese Communist regime and of its press and radio have been consistently belligerent in recent years, it probably would be unwise for the rest of the world to take them literally. The Chinese traditionally have had a penchant for exploding firecrackers. There is detectable in the pyrotechnics of their words a defensive attitude. China's leaders are aware the country faces enormous problems which are growing steadily: a population increasing at the rate of fifteen million a year, the needs for food, education, training, industrialization, modernization of science other than in the nuclear field, and most of all the problem of resolving conflicts inside China which have led to political chaos and threaten economic disaster as well.

There is no reason to doubt that China eventually will be the dominant power in Asia. It has all the resources and the energetic and clever people necessary for that objective. In the long run, China's achievement of nuclear status may lead, perhaps, under leaders yet to emerge, to a less explosive world.

Despite reckless-sounding words, it seems unlikely that the Chinese Communist leaders underestimate the awesome responsibility involved in ownership of nuclear weapons. Thus, one conclusion from the story of China's march to nuclear power seems to be inescapable: that the prescription for dealing with China requires a large measure of patience, more than any other one ingredient. The Soviet Union, when it was have-not, had leaders who could be loudly bellicose. But as the Russians' living standards improved, the Soviet stance became less warlike. The Russians had reached a point where they had much to lose in armed conflict. It is not improbable that China, despite her gigantic problems, will go through a somewhat similar development, in her own, Chinese way.

But understanding and collaboration must work both ways. The Peking regime under Mao and Lin Piao in the 1960s steadily isolated itself and became more and more unapproachable. There is rising anxiety in the West for better communication with Peking, but "if seven hundred and fifty million Chinese people are to be kept isolated from the international community, the full responsibility rests solely on the de facto government in Peking," said a report of a panel of U.S. students of policy.[11]

As of now, humanity has only a few short years to consider its future and, in fact, whether it has a future at all. It has only a few years to consider what it will do about "people's wars," about agreement on nuclear weapons control, on nuclear testing, on nuclear proliferation. It has only a few years to consider what it will do about including China in a search for the answers. It has only a few years to consider what it will do about enormous spending for weapons nations dare not use.

47

Tsien Hsue-shen, Chao Chung-yao, Hua Lo-king, "Jimmy" Chien, Hsiao Chien and scores of other Chinese scientists who had plumbed the mysteries of nuclear power and rocket propulsion on American campuses may have had some satisfaction from the knowledge they had contributed enormously to a Communist Chinese program which now was a deep source of concern to the Americans. Most of them probably felt they had reason to be bitter about their experiences in the United States. But it was just as likely that most of them, too, felt that they had come the full circle. The anti-foreign, anti-Oriental, anti-intellectual hysteria they had witnessed in America was mild compared with what they now encountered in their motherland.

They were finding that not even the top scientists, the ones most important to China's nuclear ambitions, could consider themselves safe from the wild excesses of the cultural revolution. The Chinese Academy of Sciences, citadel of Chinese Communist research, found itself in mid-1967 invaded by proletarian revolutionaries. Someone had ordered a "mass campaign for revolutionary repudiation" to "launch ferocious attacks on China's Khrushchev and his agents in the Chinese Academy of Sciences." The revolutionary rebels extorted "repentance statements" from those in the academy suspected of being lukewarm toward Mao Tse-tung's thinking.[1]

"The proletarian revolutionaries and the revolutionary masses of the Chinese Academy of Sciences have held frequent symposiums of scientists to urge them to join the great revolutionary repudiation campaign and reform their world views in the course of the struggle," the nation was informed.

Perhaps the physicists and those in the higher strata of China's nuclear research program could escape some of this, but surely they could hardly regard it with equanimity. Already, the Cultural Revolution had done enormous damage to Chinese education. Schools, colleges and universities had been closed for more than a year, and even those which were able to reopen in mid-1967 were engulfed in revolutionary confusion. What would happen to the young scientific cadres who one day would be needed to fill out the ranks of China's army of scientists?

Not even the scientists involved directly in the nuclear program were entirely free from persecution by the anti-intellectual young Maoist rebels. One such was Hua Lo-keng, the mathematician from the University of Illinois. At the height of the Cultural Revolution, he suddenly found himself denounced. Hua, then fifty-six and head of the Mathematics Institute of the Academy of Sciences, already had been given a large measure of credit by European Communists for his role in China's nuclear program.

Red Guards in Peking put up posters accusing Hua of having once admired Chiang Kai-shek in the pre-Communist days. On one of the busiest streets of the capital, the youngsters denounced Hua and all those who gave him credit for helping produce the China bomb. They called him anti-socialist, said he had opposed Mao's Great Leap Forward, that he had spoken favorably about the Soviet scientific system and had attacked Chinese "policies of self-reliance." [2] Hua may have been an exception among the nuclear scientists, though that is by no means certain, in view of the fact that all the top scientists had "bourgeois" backgrounds.

Chao Chung-yao seemed to have fared reasonably well from

the time he returned to China from California. One of the few non-Communists ever to tour Chinese nuclear installations or see China's supersecret bases reported on Chao's fortunes as recently as late 1964, just in advance of the first Chinese atomic explosion. The visitor was Mark Oliphant, a physics professor from the Australian National University at Canberra, a member of a delegation from the Australian Academy of Sciences which had accepted an invitation from the Chinese Academy. Oliphant, guided through the Institute of Atomic Energy No. 1, found installed there Chao Chung-yao and his assistant, Hsiao Chien — the young physicist who had fled Pasadena just before Chao slipped away.

Chao and Hsiao, both of whom spoke fluent, easy English, gave Oliphant a tour of the laboratories and engaged him in a leisurely talk over pots of fragrant green tea. The Australian scientist visited other institutes and even gave a lecture at the Science Center. And he had lively discussions with the Chinese.

"I asked bluntly," the professor wrote, "what was China's attitude toward nuclear weapons, and when did they expect to make their first test? The reply was that China had to have nuclear weapons to defend herself against U.S. imperialism, especially as she could no longer rely on the help of the Soviets."

Oliphant went on to visit Atomic Energy Institute No. 2, located at the foot of the hills near the site where the Peking Man was discovered. About twelve miles out of Peking, Oliphant's car was stopped at a checkpoint. Foreigners, even diplomats, ordinarily were not allowed beyond that point. Military guards stood watch at the gates of the Institute and all building entrances. Oliphant asked the whereabouts of the institute director and other nuclear physicists whose names he knew.

"I was told they were 'out west,' " he reported.

"Out west" meant the Takla Makan Desert, where the nuclear test site was located. China was ready to make the leap into the nuclear age.[3]

And what about Tsien Hsue-shen? By the time the Cultural Revolution descended upon China, Tsien's American-born son

was eighteen years old and his American-born daughter was six-
teen. This was the age of the Red Guards. The two Tsien children
possibly could have been dragooned into service, as happened to
other educated children who were required to mount guard on
their parents and denounce their elders at any suspicion of "bourgeois" leanings. Dr. and Mrs. Tsien were lovers of Western music,
of such composers as Bach, Mozart and Beethoven. All such music
had been denounced as "poisonous weeds."

Perhaps the Tsiens, with their position of importance and their
privileges, escaped much of that. But they could hardly have rel-
ished the prospect of what was going on around them. Tsien, like
his American-educated colleagues in science, was watching a
Chinese brand of McCarthyism, immeasurably more violent and
cruel than what he had experienced in America.

Would Tsien have been the type of man to tolerate the Cultural Revolution? "Well," said a man who had known him well,
"it would all depend upon what he thought was right for China
in particular. I would think he would be a moderate, that he had
begun to appreciate Western culture to a great extent, that he
would support what he thought was for the good of China and
would be resigned about it. But he would disapprove of it if he
thought it would make China weaker."

From time to time, word of Tsien leaked out of China. He had
been installed in an apartment which could be considered luxurious by Peking standards. There was even a piano on which his
wife, Yin, could play for him the classics they both loved so much.

The Russians professed belief that Tsien was responsible for
China's ownership of a nuclear missile. A Moscow Radio broadcast in April, 1967, needling the Chinese Communist brethren,
noted Tsien's role as "the designer of the Chinese missiles."

"The point is that he held a key post in this field in the United
States until recently," said Moscow. "The administration then
allowed him to go to China, a moving situation: the paper tiger
helps his enemy create nuclear weapons carriers." [4]

It was convenient for Moscow to say Tsien was a "recent" acquisition of Peking. The point was to accuse China and the Americans of collaborating against communism. Peking was accusing Moscow of the same thing. Moscow knew precisely when and how Tsien went home.

Moscow Radio Peace and Progress on April 16, 1968, broadcasting in Mandarin to China, gave a much more accurate account of Tsien's departure date, although this time implying that some sort of imperialist plot against the Soviet Union was involved in permitting the scientist to return to China.

"Mao Tse-tung and his clique are short of experienced and well-trained experts in rocketry and atomic physics," it said. "Therefore, they prefer to choose the ready path of clandestine bargaining with the imperialists. Dear friends, judge for yourselves. The 'father of the Chinese atomic bomb' is Professor Tsien Hsue-shen, son of a rich Shanghai merchant who lived in the United States for a long time. After graduating from the Massachusetts Institute of Technology, he joined the military service. He quickly became a colonel in the U.S. Air Force and head of the rocket division of the U.S. National Defense Scientific Committee and adviser to the U.S. Navy. He later headed the research group of jet generators at the California Institute of Technology. Toward the end of World War II, Tsien Hsue-shen, together with other U.S. agents, went to Europe to round up Hitler's rocket technicians and to ship them to the United States.

"How did this high-ranking U.S. military officer, who was closely connected with nuclear and rocketry research, end up in People's China? The story is that after one of the secret sessions of the Sino-American ambassadorial meetings in Warsaw, Professor Tsien Hsue-shen was given permission to leave the United States for Peking. He carried with him large quantities of scientific data. This was in 1955, a time when noted U.S. scientists like Oppenheimer were persecuted because of the leftist inclinations of their associates.

"Back in China, Tsien Hsue-shen was appointed to the Chinese Academy of Sciences and was put in charge of the Institute of

Dynamics which, under the National Scientific Committee, carries out research in rocketry and nuclear physics. About forty scientists and experts are taking part in the implementation of the program of rocketry and nuclear physics, all of which had at one time or another received training in the United States and West European Countries."

Moscow's interpretation was a free-wheeling one, designed for the ears of Chinese listeners. But the question it posed was a good one for Americans to ponder: "How did this high-ranking U.S. military officer, who was closely connected with nuclear and rocketry research, end up in People's China?"

Sometimes friends abroad got direct word from Tsien. One word was in the form of a curt rejection of a nomination to an international astronautical organization because, Tsien pointed out, the Chiang Kai-shek regime in Taiwan already was a member. Another word came after American friends informed Tsien of the death of his old idol and mentor, Dr. von Kármán. He sent a brief cable to Caltech, expressing his grief.

That was all — except for one Christmas card, postmarked Peking, and received by Dean Watson of Caltech. The card was decorated with a typical Chinese drawing of a delicate spray of flowers. In his precise hand, Tsien had written:

"This is a flower that blooms in adversity."

Section Notes

Bibliography

Appendix

SECTION NOTES

This book covers a period of almost fifty years. The material in the first twenty-nine sections comes from interviews, official records of government proceedings and the newspapers of the period. The descriptions of events in sections four, five and six are based on investigations on the scenes on behalf of the authors by Japanese correspondents. The material in section eight and those following concerning Chinese scientists is based on exhaustive interviews with dozens of persons in California and elsewhere who were familiar with the characters involved or who played important roles in the story.

A great amount of the source material for the remainder of the book is the official press of the People's Republic of China, the official press of the Soviet Union and other Communist nations, and the reports of foreign correspondents stationed in China. None of the descriptions of the events should be attributed to the imaginations of the authors. On the contrary, these descriptions come directly, in all cases, either from the official Chinese press and radio or from non-Chinese witnesses. Lack of space has forbidden any attempt to make a detailed study or projection of Communist Chinese foreign policy. This book, primarily, concerns the nuclear weapon and its impact upon the people and nations who contributed to China's development of it.

Prologue

1. *The Travels of Marco Polo.*

2. "It is a struggle between wholly alien civilizations, a gigantic protest against the dominant civilization of the West," wrote a 1958 visitor to China, who found there deep-rooted feelings, concealed for years under a veil of courtesy, of "an immense hatred for the West which has been constantly swelling for generations." Amaury de Reincourt, *The Soul of China*, p. 265.

3. The bitterness spilled out in a nuclear dialogue between Moscow and Peking which began early in 1963 and continued through 1964, a series of open letters and statements exposing what had been Peking's nuclear demands and the Soviet responses to them.

4. Among the things that were going on, for example, was an apparent Soviet attempt to exact a price from China for nuclear help, referred to by Peking in a statement to the Soviet Government distributed Sept. 1, 1963, by the New China News Agency. It served notice Peking would not pay the price of permitting Soviet supervision and control of its nuclear program.

5. The China-watcher referred to here is a high-placed American expert who asked not to be identified by name or position.

Section 2.

1. Liao Cheng-chih's appearance and demeanor at Peking Airport was described in detail for the authors by Japanese correspondents who were on hand with him awaiting the arrival of the visitors.

2. Whatever strains the event produced between the Communist Chinese and the Japanese Socialists, Liao Cheng-chih was not made to suffer for it. At least into 1968, references to him in the official press indicated he retained his high standing and positions.

Section 3.

1. For the detailed description of what went on in the Hsin Chiao, the authors are indebted to Canadian and Japanese correspondents who participated in these events. The scenes in the hotel are as recollected by Tonio Matsuno, Peking Bureau Chief for *Asahi Shimbun* of Tokyo. The scenes at the foreign office and in Peking's streets were described by Charles Taylor of the Toronto *Globe,* Matsuno and others of the correspondents then based in Peking.

2. New China News Agency, Oct. 16, 1964.

3. Interview with the American journalist Anna Louise Strong, Aug. 20, 1946. This Mao remark was repeated time and again in the Chinese press after the first Chinese nuclear explosion.

4. "The Chinese bomb is a people's bomb, a freedom bomb," said a *People's Daily* headline on May 16, 1965. Frequent references were made in the press from time to time to the peaceful role of the Chinese weapon.

5. *Asahi Shimbun,* Tokyo, from Peking, Oct. 18, 1964.

Section 7.

1. *Aviation Week,* Oct. 26, 1964, quoted McNamara under a headline, "McNamara Minimizes Red China Atom Test." On another page, the magazine commented: "Democratic Administration officials initially all but dis-

missed the Red China blast . . . as a crude experiment with no modern means of delivering later weapons."

2. "In the opinion of Administration officials, the test had more psychological and diplomatic than military significance," said a Washington dispatch of the *New York Times* on Oct. 17, 1964.

The *Bulletin of the Atomic Scientists* commented in December: "There is a generous amount of ambiguity in almost everything the Administration has said on the subject. Sometimes official statements are ambiguous because a government feels it would be indelicate to state bluntly what it is getting at. But often, they are ambiguous for the same reason that private statements are often ambiguous — simply because the people making the statements are not clear in their own minds about what it is they really want to say."

3. *Department of State Bulletin*, Oct. 19, 1964.

4. Ibid. The President also noted that China had used scarce resources to "produce a crude nuclear device which can only produce a sense of insecurity of the Chinese people."

5. Quoted by *Aviation Week*, Oct. 26, 1964. Almost three years later Dr. Lapp would tell an Associated Press interviewer that the speed of the Chinese nuclear development surprised some U.S. experts, and would mention "the arrogance and egotism of U.S. physicists who didn't want to believe anyone could develop weapons faster than the United States did." Dr. Lapp was not alone in his concern. Dr. Philip Abelson of the Carnegie Institute in Washington predicted in the *New York Times*, Oct. 30, 1964, the Chinese would have a hydrogen bomb by the end of the decade. On April 29, 1965, the *New York Times* quoted Dr. Harold C. Urey as saying Peking could develop a nuclear delivery system in five years.

Section 10.

1. *The Wind and Beyond*, p. 309.

Section 11.

1. The material on the Suicide Squad's experiments with jet propulsion comes principally from Frank Malina's own account: "The Jet Propulsion Laboratory: Its Origins and First Decade of Work," *Spaceflight*, Vol. VI, Nos. 5 and 6 and "Characteristics of the Rocket Motor Unit, Based on the Theory of Perfect Gases," *Journal of the Franklin Institute*.

2. Ibid.

3. Ibid.

4. *The Wind and Beyond*, p. 243.

Section 12.

1. Tsien's words in these pages are taken verbatim from his testimony later before U.S. Immigration authorities.
2. Dr. Weinbaum himself told the authors he failed to recollect driving with Tsien, but Tsien was insistent on the point.

Section 14.

1. Malina, "The Jet Propulsion Laboratory: Its Origins and First Decade of Work," *Spaceflight*, Vol. VI, Nos. 5 and 6.
2. Ibid.
3. *The Wind and Beyond*, p. 308.

Section 16.

1. *Science in the News*, January, 1950. The Tsien speech received wide publicity across the United States.
2. *Time*, Dec. 12, 1949.

Section 17.

1. *New York Times*, May 11, 1952, in a review of cases of Chinese scientists in the United States, reported: "The case of the professor of mathematics who taught at the University of Illinois is indicative of what happens to American-trained Chinese scholars once they return. After receiving several letters, half-promising, half-threatening, the professor agreed to go back to China." This account dovetails with information obtained by the authors in Hong Kong, taken from local press reports of the period. Hua's assignment was announced by Peking Radio.

Section 25.

1. *The Wind and Beyond*, p. 313.
2. *Ibid.*

Section Notes

Section 26.

1. "Chinese Students in the United States, 1949–1955," *Institute of International Education New Bulletin*, Mar., 1956.
2. *Scientific American*, Feb., 1961, p. 68. A group of Chinese students seeking to be returned home in mid-1955 complained bitterly of immigration procedures they had experienced during their stay, "including arrests, threats of deportation and notices to leave the country" (*New York Times*, June 4, 1955).
3. *New York Times*, Mar. 9, 1951. This account estimated there were about 3,600 university students in the United States at that time doing graduate work at their own expense in the large state universities.
4. Dr. Chih Meng, director of the China Institute of America, expressed fear at the time that "some may get discouraged and accept the Communist invitation to return" (*New York Times*, May 11, 1952).
5. *New York Times*, May 11, 1952.

Section 27.

1. "On the missile side, the [nuclear] program is headed by Tsien Hsue-shen . . . with the help of Chien Wei-chang. . . . No one doubts the quality of talent that Peking has been able to assemble" (Dick Wilson, "China's Nuclear Effort," *Far Eastern Economic Review*, Hong Kong, Aug. 19, 1965, p. 328).

Section 29.

1. Los Angeles *Times*, Sept. 13, 1955. Moscow radio had a more Machiavellian explanation of the reason for Tsien's repatriation. It argued that he was sent back because the United States had no fear of Communist China and had, instead, been convinced through secret diplomacy that China would never attack the United States. Moscow Radio Peace and Progress, in a Mandarin language broadcast to China on Jan. 8, 1968, put it this way:

"Are you familiar with the incident of Tsien Hsue-shen? Prior to his return to China, papers in various countries had carried frequent reports about this genius scientist. One paper reported that a session of the Warsaw-Sino-U.S. ambassadorial meeting had played a decisive role in the fate of Tsien Hsue-shen.

"Tsien Hsue-shen had lived in the United States since 1935 (sic) and was a renowned rocket expert. A few years ago (sic) according to the report of a French paper *Current Affairs*, this well-known rocket expert was repatriated to the CPR as a result of a Sino-U.S. ambassadorial talk in Warsaw. You may ask how this happened.

The CHINA CLOUD

"Why should the U.S. imperialists offer this valuable expert to Mao Tse-tung, knowing full well that he possessed important secrets on the manufacture of military rockets? By repatriating Tsien Hsue-shen to Peking, Maoist propaganda could convince the people that Peking is in the forefront of all so-called anti-imperialist struggles. Furthermore, the imperialists do not believe Peking's statement that it wants to thoroughly defeat the so-called paper tiger."

2. Los Angeles *Times*, Sept. 14, 1955.

3. The press interview given by Tsien is reconstructed from the files of Union Research in Hong Kong. The Hong Kong scenes described in this chapter are based on interviews with persons who were present.

4. Information on the arrival of Tsien in Peking was provided by Hong Kong researchers from files of that period.

5. "Chinese scientists were promised heaven and earth and rapid promotion if they . . . came back from overseas" (*Time*, May 9, 1955).

"In material life, the leading Chinese natural scientists have been better off than their colleagues in the social sciences. . . . When the Communist rule became effective, they advertised, on several occasions, their special treatment toward scientists. . . . The love of science was one of 'five virtues' as was the promotion of these leading scientists" (Alfred Lee Chang, "Scientists in Communist China," *Science*, June 4, 1954).

6. A. Kashin, "The Atom and China," *Asian Review* (New Series), April, 1962.

7. "Certainly the quality (of Chinese scientists trained in Dubna) is not as good as those educated in the United States. Students who went to America before the Communists got power went because of their own merits. Students sent by the Communists to the Soviet Union were selected on the basis of reliability rather than ability" (Dr. Wang, Chi-hsiang, American-trained scientist who defected from Communist China, in an interview with *U.S. News and World Report*, Nov. 7, 1958). His opinion is supported by many other observers. A considerable number of the Chinese at Dubna were of high caliber, however, and in the last six months of 1960, before the Moscow-Peking rift began to interfere, one third of the published physicists' researches there were Chinese. Most of these appeared to be men who had received training in the non-Communist world. See T. Y. Wu of the National Research Council, Ottawa, Canada, writing in the *Journal* of the American Association for the Advancement of Science, 1961.

8. His old associate, Frank Malina, told an Associated Press interviewer in France in 1967 that he had no way of knowing what Tsien might be doing in China, but "the level of technology in China must have been almost nil when he arrived." Tsien, said Malina, was considered by Dr. von Kármán to be the most brilliant pupil he ever had. "He was," said Malina, "a good theoretical man and a good practical man and he used to outwork all of us."

Section Notes

Section 30.

1. Associated Press, Moscow dispatch, Aug. 26, 1957. Tsien seems to have been a frequent visitor to Dubna. He has been quoted in the Soviet press from time to time and has written for at least one Soviet journal.

1. "When I was in the Soviet Union," Dr. Frederick Lindvall, chairman of the Caltech Engineering Division, told the authors, "just after the Sputnik thing . . . one of [our] group, thumbing through a Soviet picture magazine, came across an article written by Tsien. . . . The article was pitched in praise of the accomplishments of Russian launch capability."

Section 31.

1. The speech was not made public until mid-June, 1957, when the New China News Agency broadcast a full text. The agency, in an introductory note, explained that there had been "revisions" in it since February when the speech was delivered.

2. Roderick MacFarquhar, *The Hundred Flowers Campaign*, p. 168.

3. The May 4th Movement of 1919 developed as a student protest against the Versailles Treaty, which turned over former German rights in China to Japan. Students in Shantung Province began widespread demonstrations demanding that China push for a big power role in the world. This movement was, in effect, an extension of the Yi Ho Tuan Movement of the Boxer Rebellion days, and its counterpart, the female Hung Teng Chao (Red Lanterns). The cry then was "kill the foreigners and destroy the Ching Dynasty." Chairman Mao evidently gave thoughtful study to both the Yi Ho Tuan and May 4th Movements, weighing the effectiveness of youngsters as political instruments. "Our most respected and beloved great leader Chairman Mao," said the Shanghai newspaper *Wen Hui Pao*, April 14, 1967, "has highly assessed the Yi Ho Tuan Movement and commended the revolutionary rebel spirit of the heroic Hung Teng Chao daughters." Thus, the Red Guards in turn seemed a development of the other youth movements of the past.

4. MacFarquhar, *The Hundred Flowers Campaign*, p. 169.

5. Theodore H. E. Chen, *Thought Reform of the Chinese Intellectuals*, p. 191.

6. MacFarquhar, *The Hundred Flowers Campaign*, p. 136, quoting the New China News Agency, July 12, 1957.

7. Ibid.

8. Theodore H. E. Chen, *Thought Reform of the Chinese Intellectuals*, p. 191.

9. Chu-yuan Cheng of the University of Michigan. *Scientific Engineering Manpower in Communist China, 1949–1963.*

10. Kwangming *Daily* of May 15, 1957.

Section 32.

1. In the Peking-Moscow quarrel throughout the 1960s the Soviet press quoted this line on many occasions, as if attempting to portray Mao to the rest of the Communist world as a dangerously reckless leader.

2. This is a reference to Hai Jui, the mandarin of ancient times who, legend says, defied the emperor on behalf of the people and thus became a hero to them.

3. Statement by a spokesman for the Chinese Government. The statement was distributed Aug. 31, 1963, by the New China News Agency and was a reply to a Soviet statement of Aug. 1, 1963.

4. New China News Agency, Nov. 24, 1960.

5. General Electric Corp, *Report on China's Economic Plan*, 1960.

6. *People's Daily*, Aug. 15, 1963.

7. Statement by the Soviet Government replying to the statement of the Chinese Government of Aug. 15, 1963 (Soviet News Agency Tass, Aug. 20, 1963).

8. Ibid.

9. "In 1960, Khrushchev abruptly and perfidiously tore up several hundred agreements and contracts, withdrew the Soviet experts working in China and cut off the supply of important items of equipment, thus seriously upsetting our original plan for national economic development and adding greatly to our difficulties" (Premier Chou En-lai, quoted by *People's Daily*, Dec. 30, 1964).

10. *Pravda*, May 5, 1964.

Section 33.

1. The scenes in Peking at the time of the first explosion were described by Japanese correspondents based there.

2. New China News Agency, Oct. 17, 1964.

3. *Aviation Week*, Oct. 26, 1964, p. 29.

4. Dr. Chu-yuan Cheng of the University of Michigan, a noted observer of Communist Chinese affairs, predicted at this time that China would have a nuclear warhead missile in 1967. He hit it right on target.

5. New China News Agency, quoting a Government spokesman, Aug. 15, 1963.

6. Ibid.

7. Hanoi Radio, Oct. 17, 1964.

Section Notes

Section 34.

1. Chou En-lai, speech to Third National People's Congress, Dee. 30, 1964, New China News Agency.
2. Quoted in *Life*, May 28, 1965.
3. Quoted by *People's Daily*.

Section 35.

1. Tung Chi-ping and Humphrey Evans, *The Thought Revolution* (1966).
2. Yao Wen-yuan was soon to become better known to students of Chinese affairs. According to the evidence, he served as a sort of ghost-writer to Mao's fourth wife, Chiang Ching in her role as deputy chief of the cultural revolution group. Thus it is significant that this original broadside was signed by Yao, for it seems to indicate inspiration from the highest sources.
3. *People's Daily*, June 16, 1959. This could hardly have been published in the Communist party's central newspaper without approval from the highest leaders. Chou Yang and Lu Ting-yi, then top members of the propaganda apparatus, later were among the first targets of the Maoist purge.
4. *People's Daily*, Apr. 16, 1962.
5. In the Chinese Communist definition, economism is the sin of buying loyalty by promising and providing economic benefits. "It is a form of bribery that caters to the psychology of a few backward people among the masses . . . inviting them to disregard the interests of the state . . . and pursue only personal and short-term interests" (*Liberation Army Daily*, Jan. 1, 1967).
6. Chen Yi later was criticized in Red Guard posters in the cultural revolution, but so were some others of the Mao group from time to time. It appeared from the cultural revolution group's own complaints that the opposition was using posters too, to sow confusion. Chen Yi apparently was in no real danger at that time.

Section 36.

1. The material in this chapter comes from a wide variety of sources and publications, including the U.S. Atomic Energy Commission, the *Bulletin of the Atomic Scientists, China Quarterly, Current History,* the Institute of Strategic Studies in London, the *Far Eastern Economic Review* and others.
2. Arnold Kramish, "The Great Chinese Bomb Puzzle and a Solution," *Fortune,* June, 1966.
3. Ibid.

4. Associated Press, Feb. 17, 1967.

5. Scenes like these were described abundantly in the official Chinese Communist press.

6. *New York Times*, Mar. 8, 1966.

7. Department of Defense, transcript of testimony.

8. Moscow Radio Peace and Progress was a principal outlet for propaganda against the Peking regime in this period.

Section 37.

1. In Taiwan, intelligence officials interviewed refugee youngsters from the mainland who told how they were enlisted and of the long and arduous trips necessary to get them to Peking on time for the Aug., 1966, meeting of the Central Committee which officially launched their movement.

2. *People's Daily*, June 4, 1966.

3. Ibid.

4. The events in Peking University were abundantly described by both the official party press and the reports of Communist and non-Communist correspondents based in the capital.

5. The Yang episode is reconstructed from reports in the official press.

6. New China News Agency, June 15, 1966.

7. *People's Daily*, June 8, 1966.

8. Ibid.

9. *Liberation Army Daily*, June 8, 1966.

10. This is not the independent interpretation of the authors. It is supported by top specialists with whom the authors conferred. A reported speech by Defense Minister Lin Piao to the Politburo, referring to the period, noted he "detected the smell of gunpowder in the struggle with Lo Jui-ching."

Section 38.

1. *China Reconstructs* (an official publication designed for propaganda abroad), report on the July 23–31 Colloquium (Oct., 1966).

2. Foreigners in China, including some from Communist countries, reported that "hundreds" of youngsters perished in attempts to swim the Yangtze. Their reports may have been exaggerated.

3. Kai-yu Hsu, in *Chou En-lai, China's Gray Eminence* (p. 226), refers to Mao's "speech-writer Chen Po-ta." Chen probably had little to do with shaping Mao's ideas, but as his secretary he had probably been required to set those ideas down on paper in organized form.

4. *Liberation Army Daily*, Aug. 1, 1966, provided this rundown on the succession of party crises and purges.

Section Notes

5. The ouster of Lo Jui-ching, which probably took place in July, became known to the outside world with the publication of a name list of officials at a ceremonial banquet. *People's Daily*, Aug. 1, 1966, identified a new "acting chief of staff."

6. *People's Daily*, Aug. 13, 1966.

7. Leo A. Orleans, *Research and Development in Communist China*, Library of Congress, June 28, 1967.

Section 39.

1. *People's Daily*, Sept. 2, 1966, carried a long list of name changes enforced by the Red Guards. All reports in this chapter on Red Guard activities come from the official Chinese press, unless otherwise noted.

2. *Pravda*, Aug. 26, 1966.

3. *People's Daily*, Sept. 8, 1966.

4. Tass, Aug. 31, 1966.

Section 40.

1. New China News Agency, Mar. 23, 1967. The article, discussing Americans taking part in China in the cultural revolution, spoke of four who "erected a poster," and added that "two of the coauthors of this poster were Joan Hinton and her husband."

2. Ibid.

3. The U.S. Atomic Energy Commission in a news release dated Oct. 16, 1952, said Joan Hinton held only a minor position at Los Alamos and had nothing to do with the actual manufacture of the bomb, nor did she have clearance from the AEC for access to classified materials.

4. *The Worker*, newspaper of the U.S. Communist party, interview with Joan Hinton by its correspondent in Peking, Jan. 18, 1953.

5. Atomic Energy Commission release, Oct. 16, 1952.

6. The magazine *People's China*, Sept. 16, 1951, carried this material in the form of a letter bearing Miss Hinton's name, addressed to the Federation of American Scientists in Washington and urging American scientists not to work on war projects.

7. Ibid.

8. *The Worker*, Jan. 18, 1953.

9. Institute for Study of the U.S.S.R., Munich, *Bulletin* of August, 1961. This article cited "official Communist sources" as identifying Miss Hinton as among scientists working on nuclear weapons. She may have been stationed at the installations in Paotow.

The CHINA CLOUD

Section 41.

1. This chapter is based on reports of the official Chinese Communist press.

The Aug. 8, 1966, communiqué of the 11th Central Committee Plenum advised that "the main target of the present movement is those within the party who are in authority and who are taking the capitalist road."

Section 42.

1. New China News Agency, Oct. 27, 1966.
2. Associated Press, Oct. 30, 1966.

Section 43.

1. The scenes in this chapter are as described in official Chinese Communist press reports.
2. Belgrade Radio, Dec. 30, 1966.
3. Hanoi Radio, Dec. 29, 1966.
4. As early as September, 1966, there were indications that some in authority in Peking feared the effects of the cultural revolution explosion on the economy. There were constant exhortations on provincial radios for an end to "revolutionary activities" during the fall harvest season. *People's Daily*, Sept. 18, 1966, told the Red Guards, "You must go to the countryside and participate in productive labor and help in the autumn harvest." The army, too, was told to order soldiers into harvest work.
5. Statement of Secretary of Defense McNamara before the House Subcommittee on Department of Defense Appropriations for fiscal 1968–1972 and the 1968 budget.

Section 44.

1. The attacks on the homes of Peng Chen and Peng Teh-huai were reported in wall posters and relayed abroad by Peking-based foreign correspondents.
2. The former defense minister would be accused in the central press later as having colluded with "big conspirators, careerists and warlords . . . for 17 years in order to bring about the restoration of capitalism." He is said to have been "exposed" at the 1959 Lushan conference, the meeting generally believed to have brought a crisis in party affairs leading to the dismissal of Peng as defense minister and possibly the surrender by Mao of

the chairmanship of the government to Liu Shao-chi. The accusations against Peng Teh-huai were detailed in *Liberation Army Daily* as late as July 30, 1967. It said that if the conspiracy had been successful, "thousands of people would surely die, our party and army would degenerate and our country change political color."

3. In February, 1967, wall newspapers in Peking denounced the military commander of the Wan Hsien military district of Szechwan for declaring his troops would be loyal to Ho Lung. A Red Guard newspaper reaching Hong Kong in November, 1967, reported Ho Lung was leading anti-Mao resistance among army men in Szechwan.

4. *Red Flag*, Dec. 15, 1966.

5. *Sankei*, Tokyo, Dec. 27, 1966.

6. The authors could find no actual documentation of Stalin's admiration for Kang Sheng. The report comes from a number of "old China hands." See Associated Press, Tokyo dispatch, Aug. 24, 1966.

7. Kiangsi Province regional broadcast, Jan. 4, 1967.

8. *Heilungkiang Daily*, Manchuria, June 22, 1967, broadcast by provincial service.

9. The Shanghai newspaper *Wen Hui Pao*, July 28, 1967, said: "Tao Chu is an important and sinister leader in the headquarters of the bourgeoisie and a top agent in the South Central China of China's Khrushchev (Liu Shao-chi). Tao is the vanguard of the scheme of restoring capitalism. . . . The two-faced counterrevolutionary Tao Chu is the top party person in authority taking the capitalist road in South Central China. He is behind-the-scenes boss of all counterrevolutionaries and revisionists, big and small, in South Central China. The poisonous and evil influence of Tao Chu is deep-rooted and widespread in this area."

10. *People's Daily*, July 30, 1967 said: "Rats are running across the streets with everybody shouting 'Kill them, kill them!' . . . Any big shots or veterans who dare oppose Mao Tse-tung's thought . . . will definitely have their heads smashed in."

11. *Red Flag*, June 30, 1967.

Section 45.

1. *People's Daily*, June 18, 1967, carried a detailed description of these events. The description is that of the newspapers in China and has not been embellished by the authors. The provincial press was no less florid in its descriptions of the celebrations. It was not, however, until Oct. 1 that the Chinese Communist press carried photographs of the H-bomb explosion. One picture showed a group at the site, cheering the explosion and waving copies of the red-covered book of Mao Tse-tung's thoughts.

2. This quotation began appearing in the press immediately after the H-bomb explosion and thereafter reappeared frequently.

3. New China News Agency, June 18, 1967.

The CHINA CLOUD

Section 46.

1. Report of the Senate-House Atomic Energy Committee, July, 1967. "Conceivably," it said, the H-bomb "could be ready as early as 1970–71, but this would be a tight schedule and makes allowances for only minor difficulties and delays."
2. *New York Times*, Sept. 19, 1967.
3. Posture statement to Senate committees on defense appropriations. Defense Secretary McNamara saw no direct threat to the United States until the mid-1970s. He found it "unlikely that the Chinese could deploy a significant number of intercontinental ballistic missiles" before then.
4. Interviewed by the Associated Press, July, 1967.
5. National Broadcasting Company, July 11, 1967.
6. *Yomiuri*, Tokyo, July 8, 1967.
7. "This experience [referring to guerrilla warfare in Asia] has borne out the correctness of Mao Tse-tung's brilliant idea of establishing base areas in the countryside and using the countryside to encircle and finally capture the cities," said a New China News Agency broadcast of July 25, 1967. This is the strategy outlined in Lin Piao's *Long Live the Victory of People's War*, published in Sept., 1965.
8. "Mao and his cronies have even resorted to slogans urging colored peoples to unite against the whites," said Moscow Radio Peace and Progress on Sept. 2, 1967. European Communists long have suspected this. On June 5, 1966, the Yugoslav journal *Vjesnik* accused Peking of trying to create "a new bloc of those hungry and colored peoples" in a program planned for a long time and with great patience.
9. Moscow Radio Peace and Progress, Feb. 17, 1967.
10. Associated Press, Aug. 4, 1967.
11. United Nations Association of the U.S.A., "Report of National Policy Panel," Library of Congress, 1967.

Section 47.

1. Peking home service broadcast, Sept. 16, 1967.
2. Tanjug News Agency (Yugoslav) dispatch from Peking.
3. *Bulletin of the Atomic Scientists*, May, 1966.
4. Broadcast by Andrei Antonov, Moscow Radio, Apr. 2, 1967.

BIBLIOGRAPHY

Books

Chen, Theodore H. E. *Thought Reform of the Chinese Intellectuals.* Hong Kong: Hong Kong University, 1960.

Cheng, Chu-yuan. *China's Economy, 1949–1962.* South Orange, N.J.: Seton Hall University Press, 1963.

Cheng, Chu-yuan. *Scientific and Engineering Manpower in Communist China, 1949–1963.* (NSF 65–14). Washington: National Science Foundation, 1965.

Cow Tse-tsung. *The May Fourth Movement, Intellectual Revolution in Modern China.* Cambridge, Mass.: Harvard University Press, 1960.

Gould, Sidney H., ed. *Sciences in Communist China.* (Publ. 68.) Washington: American Association for Advancement of Science, 1961. (Papers read at the A.A.A.S. symposium in New York City, Dec. 26–27, 1960. See especially "Nuclear Physics" by T. Y. Wu, pp. 631–643; and "Science, Scientists and Politics" by Theodore Hsi-en Chen, pp. 59–102.)

Griffith, William E. *The Sino–Soviet Rift.* Cambridge, Mass.: M.I.T. Press, 1964.

Halperin, Morton H. *China and the Bomb.* New York: Praeger, 1965.

Hinton, Harold C. *Communist China's External Policy and Behavior as a Nuclear Power.* (IDA/HQ 63–1918.) Arlington, Va.: Institute for Defense Analyses, August, 1963.

Hsieh, Alice Langley. *Communist China's Strategy in the Nuclear Era.* Englewood Cliffs, N.J.: Prentice-Hall (Spectrum), 1962. (A Rand Corporation Research Study)

Hutheesing, Raja. *The Great Peace.* New York: Harper, 1953.

Kai Yu-hsu. *Chou En-lai, China's Gray Eminence.* New York: Doubleday, 1968.

MacFarquhar, Roderick. *The Hundred Flowers Campaign and the Chinese Intellectuals.* New York: Praeger, 1960.

Moorehead, Alan. *The Traitors.* New York: Scribner's, 1952.

O'Ballance, Edgar. *The Red Army of China.* New York: Praeger, 1962. (See especially pp. 218–219 on nuclear power.)

The CHINA CLOUD

Parry, Albert. *Russia's Rockets and Missiles.* New York: Doubleday, 1960.

Pilat, Oliver. *The Atom Spies.* New York: Putnam, 1952.

Polo, Marco. *The Travels of Marco Polo.* New York: Liveright, 1926.

Portisch, Hugo. *Red China Today.* Chicago: Quadrangle Books, 1966.

Riencourt, Amaury de. *The Soul of China.* New York: Coward-McCann, 1958.

Snow, Edgar P. *The Other Side of the River: Red China Today.* New York: Random House, 1962. (See Chapter 82, "China, the U.S., Russia and the Bomb," pp. 631–645.)

Sokolovsky, Vasily D. *Soviet Military Strategy.* Englewood Cliffs, N.J.: Prentice-Hall, 1963. (A Rand Corporation translation)

Taylor, Charles. *Reporter in Red China.* New York: Random House, 1966.

Tung Chi-ping and Humphrey Evans. *The Thought Revolution.* New York: Coward-McCann, 1966.

Von Kármán, Theodore, with Lee Edson. *The Wind and Beyond: Theodore von Kármán, Pioneer in Aviation and Pathfinder in Space.* Boston: Little, Brown, 1967.

Warner, Denis. *Hurricane from China.* New York: Macmillan, 1961.

Wu, Aitchen K. *China and the Soviet Union.* New York: John Day, 1956.

Wu, Y. L. *An Economic Survey of Communist China.* New York: Bookman Associates, 1956.

Periodical Articles

Abelson, P. H. Chinese A-Bomb. *Science,* Oct. 30, 1964, p. 601.

A–Bombs For All? It's Getting Closer. *U.S. News,* Dec. 7, 1964, p. 36.

Alsop, S. One Great Question: Whether to Permit Uncontrolled Spread of Nuclear Weapons. *Saturday Evening Post,* Nov. 14, 1964, p. 18.

And Now There Are Five. *Newsweek,* Oct. 26, 1964, p. 54.

Another Finger on the Button. *Christian Century,* Oct. 14, 1964, p. 1259.

Aron, Raymond. Spread of Nuclear Weapons. *Atlantic,* Jan. 1965, pp. 44–50. (Excerpt from *Great Debate: Theories of Nuclear Strategy.*)

Arrogant Dragon Becomes Atomic. *Senior Scholastic,* Nov. 18, 1964, p. 13.

Asia's Atomic Cloud. *Senior Scholastic,* Oct. 28, 1964, p. 23.

Barnett, A. Doak. The Inclusion of Communist China in an Arms-Control Programme. *Daedalus,* Fall 1960, pp. 831–845.

Beaton, Leonard. I.S.S. View. *Survival,* Jan.–Feb. 1965, pp. 2–4.

Blast at Lop Nor; First Chinese Atomic Test. *Time,* Oct. 30, 1964, p. 66.

Bobrow, Davis B. Chinese Views on Escalation. *Military Review,* Jan. 1966, pp. 60–67.

Bibliography

————. Peking's Military Calculus. *World Politics*, Jan. 1964, pp. 287–301.

Buckley, William F. Bipartisan Proposal? How to Eliminate Chinese Bomb. *National Review*, Dec. 29, 1964, p. 1143.

Burnham, James. Chinese Bomb. *National Review*, Oct. 20, 1964, p. 910.

Candlin, A. H. S. The Chinese Nuclear Threat. *Army Quarterly*, April 1966, pp. 50–60.

Census of Foreign Students in the U.S. *Institute of International Education News Bulletin*, Mar. 1952, pp. 34–35.

Chang, A. Z. Scientists in Communist China. *Science*, June 4, 1954, pp. 785–789.

Chen, T. H. America in the Eyes of Chinese Students. *China and America*, June 1949, pp. 3–9.

Chen, Theodore H. E. Role of Science in Communist China. *Foreign Policy Bulletin*, Feb. 15, 1961, p. 81+.

Cheng Chu-yuan. Progress of Nuclear Weapons in Communist China. *Military Review*, May 1965, pp. 9–15.

Chien San-chiang. See Tsien San-tsiang.

China and [Nuclear] Arms; Top Table Turning. *Economist*, Oct. 31, 1964, p. 475.

China and the Bomb. *Science Digest*, Dec. 1964, p. 37.

China as a Nuclear Power. *New Republic*, May 26, 1958, p. 5.

China: Bomb No. 2. *Newsweek*, May 24, 1965, p. 48.

China Nears an H–Bomb Test. *Business Week*, May 14, 1966, p. 39.

China 1965: Our Annual Survey. *Far Eastern Economic Review*, Sept. 30, 1965, pp. 607–630.

China 1966. *Far Eastern Economic Review*, Sept. 29, 1966, pp. 603–625.

China, Nuclear Weapons and Disarmament (Editorial translated from the Peking *People's Daily*, Nov. 22, 1964). *War/Peace Report*, Jan. 1965, pp. 3–5.

China Passes a New Test; Peking's Nuclear Missile Shot. *Business Week*, Nov. 5, 1966, pp. 39–41.

China Presses Scientists. *Science News Letter*, May 7, 1955, p. 301.

China — "Through a Glass Darkly" — The Science of China Watching. *Business Week*, Apr. 23, 1966, p. 60+.

China's Bomb. *Economist*, Oct. 24, 1964, p. 344; Dec. 5, 1964, p. 1114.

China's Bomb. *War/Peace Report*, Nov. 1964, pp. 10–11.

China's Push to Catch Up in Science. *Business Week*, Feb. 5, 1966, pp. 116–120.

China's Second Nuclear Test. *National Review*, June 1, 1965, p. 449.

China's Shot Tells a Startling Story. *Business Week*, Oct. 24, 1964, p. 144+.

China's Twelve-Year Science Program: Interview with Kuo Mo-jo, President of Academy of Science. *New Times*, Moscow, Dec. 12, 1957, pp. 12–13.

Chinese Bomb; Last Word? *Economist*, May 22, 1965, p. 897.

Chinese Scientists under Communist Pressure. *Chemical and Engineering News*, May 30, 1955, p. 2306.

Chinese Threat Seen Focused on Soviets [Drive for Nuclear Capability]. *Aviation Week*, Nov. 14, 1966, p. 29.

Ching Yi-hung. Mao's Nuclear Base and Prospects. *Free China Review*, July 1966, pp. 34–38, Formosa.

Close, Alexandra. Regional Affairs – China "Bombs or Trousers." *Far Eastern Economic Review*, Oct. 29, 1964, p. 237.

Cloud, W. Nuclear Detective Looks at China's Atom Bomb. *Popular Science Monthly*, Jan. 1965, pp. 19–20.

Coffey, J. I. Chinese and Ballistic Missile Defense. *Bulletin of the Atomic Scientists*, Dec. 1965, pp. 17–19.

Cohen, D. China Upsets the Applecart. *Science Digest*, Aug. 1965, pp. 27–29.

Cousins, Norman. China and the Bomb. *Saturday Review*, Nov. 28, 1964, p. 18+.

Crashing the N Club. *Time*, Mar. 9, 1962, p. 46+.

Discussion of Chinese Nuclear Weapons Development [Comment on Jan. issue]. *Bulletin of the Atomic Scientists*, April 1966, pp. 29–30.

Dubna Physicists Discuss Training of New Scientists. (Translated and condensed from *Izvestia*, Dec. 28, 1960). *Current Digest of the Soviet Press*, Jan. 25, 1961, pp. 18–20.

Evans, Gordon H. China and the Atom Bomb, Part I: *Royal United Service Institution Journal*, London, Feb. 1962, p. 30+. Part II: May 1962, pp. 130–134.

Evans, Gordon H. Communist China's A-Bomb Program. *New Leader*, Sept. 18, 1961, pp. 15–17.

Fallout Over Peking: China's Bombs, Both Nuclear and "Spiritual," Are Slowing Its Drive for Real Economic Power. *Economist*, May 14, 1966, pp. 678–679.

Fateful Firecracker; Chinese Explosion of Nuclear Device. *Time*, Oct. 23, 1964, p. 36.

Feld, B. T. On the Chinese Separation Technology. *Bulletin of the Atomic Scientists*, Sept. 1966, p. 33.

Fifth-Nation Problem. *Scientific American*, Dec. 1964, pp. 60–62.

Fire Arrow. *Time*, Nov. 4, 1966, p. 35.

Fix, Joseph E., III. China –the Nuclear Threat. *Air University Quarterly Review*, Mar–Apr. 1966, pp. 28–39.

Foreign Students in the U.S.: IIE's Annual Census. *Institute of International Education News Bulletin*, Feb. 1951, pp. 20–21.

Bibliography

Frank, L. A. Nuclear Weapons Development in China. *Bulletin of the Atomic Scientists*, Jan. 1966, pp. 12–15.

Garthoff, Raymond L. Sino-Soviet Military Relations. *Annals of the American Academy of Political and Social Science*, Sept. 1963, pp. 81–93.

Gittings, J. China's Military Strategy. *Nation*, Jan. 18, 1965, pp. 43–46.

Gittins, P. G. The Red Dragon of China: A Brief Review of Communist China as a Military Power. *Australian Army Journal*, May 1960, pp. 15–18.

Griffith, Samuel B. Communist China's Capacity to Make War. *Foreign Affairs*, Jan. 1965, pp. 217–236.

———. The Glorious Military Thought of Comrade Mao Tse-Tung. *Foreign Affairs*, July 1964, pp. 669–674.

Guillain, Robert. Ten Years of Secrecy. *Bulletin of the Atomic Scientists*, Feb. 1965, pp. 24–25.

Halle, L. J. Any Number Can Play Nuclear Chicken. *New York Times Magazine*, Nov. 28, 1964, p. 33+.

Halperin, Morton H. China and the Bomb. *China Quarterly*, Jan.–Mar. 1965, pp. 74–87.

———. Chinese Nuclear Strategy: The Early Post-Detonation Period. *Adelphi Papers*, May 1965, No. 18. Pub. by the Institute for Strategic Studies, London.

———. Chinese Nuclear Strategy, the Early Post-Detonation Period. *Asian Survey*, June 1965.

Harris, T. G. Chinese Bomb Menace. *Look*, Dec. 1, 1964, pp. 28–29.

Harris, William R. Chinese Nuclear Doctrine: The Decade Prior to Weapons Development (1945–1955). *China Quarterly*, Jan.–Mar. 1965, pp. 87–95.

H–Bomb Power Plant [Tsien Hsue-shen]. *Science News Letter*, Aug. 11, 1956, p. 84.

Hinton, Harold C. Communist China's Military Posture. *Current History*, Sept. 1962, pp. 149–155.

———. A Difference of Dangers. (Review of *China and the Bomb* by M. H. Halperin). *Saturday Review*, Apr. 17, 1965, p. 54.

Hsieh, Alice Langley. China, Russia and the Bomb. *New Leader*, Oct. 17, 1960, pp. 17–20.

———. Communist China and Nuclear Warfare. *China Quarterly*, Apr.–June 1960, pp. 1–12.

———. Communist China and Nuclear Warfare. *Survival*, July–Aug. 1960, pp. 142–148.

———. Sino-Soviet Nuclear Dialogue. *Bulletin of the Atomic Scientists*, Jan. 1965, pp. 16–21.

Hsinhua Statement of 10/16/64. *Survival*, Jan.–Feb. 1965, pp. 8–9.

How Dangerous Is Red China? *U.S. News*, Apr. 4, 1966, pp. 29–31.

How the Reds Learned about the Atom [Pontecorvo]. *U.S. News*, Mar. 11, 1955, p. 70+.

How They Reacted: When Nikita Khrushchev Fell and Peking Exploded Its Nuclear Bomb. *Newsweek*, Nov. 9, 1964, p. 57.

How U.S. Knows about China's A-Tests. *U.S. News*, May 23, 1966, p. 6.

How Vulnerable Is Red China? *U.S. News*, Feb. 14, 1966, pp. 38–41.

Hungdah Chiu. Communist China's Attitude Towards Nuclear Tests. *China Quarterly*, Jan.–Mar. 1965, pp. 96–107.

Immigration Regulations Governing Foreign Students in the U.S. *Higher Education*, Feb. 1, 1951, pp. 121–124.

In the Shock Wave of Red China's Second A–Bomb. *U.S. News*, May 24, 1965, p. 6.

Indispensable Camera – New Uses [photographic surveillance from satellites]. *Life*, Dec. 23, 1966, p. 100.

Inglis, David R. The Chinese Bombshell. *Bulletin of Atomic Scientists*, Feb. 1965, pp. 19–21.

Investigations: Facing Life [William Hinton]. *Time*, Aug. 9, 1954, p. 21.

Is Red China a Paper Tiger? *U.S. News*, Oct. 19, 1964, p. 76.

Jet Scientist [Tsien Hsue-shen] Deported to China. *Aviation Week*, Sept. 19, 1955, p. 17.

Johnson, C. China's "Manhattan Project." *New York Times Magazine*, Oct. 25, 1964, p. 23+.

Jonas, A. M. Atomic Energy in Soviet Bloc Nations. *Bulletin of the Atomic Scientists*, Nov. 1959, pp. 379–383.

Jones, Mervyn. China and the Bomb. *Survival*, July–Aug. 1960, pp. 149–150.

Just How Dangerous Is Red China? Interview with Japanese Official Just Back from Mainland. *U.S. News*, Oct. 24, 1966, pp. 84–86.

Kashin, A. The Atom and China. *Asian Review* (New Series), Apr. 1962, pp. 136–140. (Excerpts from the *Bulletin of the Institute for Study of USSR* [Institut po izucheniyu SSSR], Munich, Aug. 1961, pp. 17–24.)

———. The Atom and China. *Bulletin of the Institute for the Study of the USSR.*, Aug. 1961, pp. 17–24.

———. Chinese Military Doctrine. *Bulletin of the Institute for the Study of the USSR*, Nov. 1960, pp. 36–44. Pub. by Institut po izucheniyu SSSR, Munich.

Kennan, G. F. Fresh Look at Our China Policy. *New York Times Magazine*, Nov. 22, 1964, p. 27+.

Kent, Nikolai. Joint Atomic Research in the Eastern Bloc. *Bulletin of the Institute for the Study of the USSR*, Munich, Aug. 1961, pp. 10–16.

Kramish, Arnold. Great Chinese Bomb Puzzle, and a Solution. *Fortune*, June 1966, pp. 157–158.

Bibliography

————. The Organization of Atomic Energy in the USSR. *Bulletin of the Atomic Scientists,* Oct. 1959, p. 322+.

Lall, Arthur S. The Political Effects of the Chinese Bomb. *Bulletin of the Atomic Scientists,* Feb. 1965, pp. 21–24.

————. Mainland China and U.S. Security. *Bulletin of the Atomic Scientists,* Apr. 1964, pp. 24–27.

Lapp, Ralph E. 5:29 A.M. and the World Was Changed Forever. *Life,* July 16, 1965, p. 14.

————. Nuclear Power of China. *Life,* May 28, 1965, pp. 86–90.

Lear, John. Communist China: What Science Wants to Know about It. *Saturday Review,* Mar. 7, 1964, pp. 43–46. Discussion, Aug. 1, 1964, pp. 44–46.

Learning to Live with China: Symposium. *New Republic,* Sept. 5, 1964, pp. 13–16.

Lee, Rose Hum. Chinese Dilemma [the effects of the civil war in China on three groups of Chinese in the U.S.] *Phylon,* Second Quarter, 1949, pp. 137–140.

————. The Stranded Chinese in the U.S. *Phylon Quarterly,* July 1958, pp. 180–194.

Lindbeck, John M. H. Chinese Science: It's Not a Paper Atom. *New York Times Magazine,* Jan. 8, 1967, p. 38+.

————. The Organization and Development of Science in People's Republic of China. *China Quarterly,* Apr.–June 1961, pp. 98–132.

Look at Science in Red China; Interview with C. Wang [Dr. Wang Chi-hsiang]. *U.S. News,* Nov. 7, 1958, p. 107.

Making Nuclear Bomb Easier All the Time. *Science News Letter,* Oct. 31, 1964, p. 281.

Malina, Frank. Characteristics of the Rocket Motor Unit Based on the Theory of Perfect Gases. *Journal of the Franklin Institute,* Vol. 230, No. 4, 1940.

Mao Calls the "Boffins" Home; Appeal to Chinese Scientists in Exile to Return to Communist China. *Economist,* June 23, 1956, pp. 1175–1176.

Mao's Missile. *Saturday Review,* Dec. 24, 1966, p. 67.

Margolis, H. From Washington: The Bomb in China. *Bulletin of the Atomic Scientists,* Dec. 1964, pp. 36–39.

McNamara Minimizes Red China Atom Test. *Aviation Week,* Oct. 26, 1964, p. 29.

Missing Fissionist [Pontecorvo]. *Time,* Nov. 6, 1960, p. 30.

Modelski, J. A. Communist China's Challenge in Technology. *Australian Quarterly,* June 1958, pp. 57–68. Pub. by Australian Inst. of Political Science, Sydney.

Nanes, Allan S. The Armies of Red China. *Current History,* Dec. 1960, pp. 338–342.

———. Communist China's Military Strength. *Current History,* Sept. 1961, pp. 146–150.

New World Triangle, The. *Progressive,* Dec. 1964, pp. 17–20.

News Briefs [Pontecorvo's Defection]. *Science,* Oct. 21, 1955, p. 755.

Not-So-Backward China. *Science Digest,* Jan. 1965, p. 10.

Now Red China Makes the Bomb: What It Means; U.S. View: No Need to Panic. *U.S. News,* July 15, 1963, pp. 38–40.

Nuclear Club. *Commonweal,* Oct. 30, 1964, p. 148.

Nuclear Cutoff. *Newsweek,* Aug. 26, 1963, p. 45.

Nuclear Muscle; What the Snoopers Saw. *Newsweek,* May 23, 1966, pp. 53–54.

Nuclear Politics. *Scientific American,* Mar. 1963, p. 72.

Nuclear Progress in Red China. *Chemical Engineering Progress,* Mar. 1960, pp. 16–17.

Nuclear Thunder Out of China? *Newsweek,* Aug. 3, 1959, p. 33.

Number Five: Chinese Nuclear Explosion. *Nation,* Nov. 2, 1964, p. 289.

O'Ballance, Edgar. The Armed Might of Red China. *Military Review,* Nov. 1960, p. 33+.

———. The Chinese War Potential. *United Service Institution of India Journal,* July–Sept. 1959, New Delhi, pp. 243–252.

Parting the Veils over Red Rifts. *Saturday Review,* June 2, 1962, pp. 29–30.

Peake, A. Red China's Ambitions; the Pace of Her Economy and Propaganda En Route to Her Goals. *Magazine of Wall Street,* May 14, 1966, pp. 213–215.

Peking Joins the Club. *National Review,* Nov. 3, 1964, p. 942.

Peking Statement of 11/22/64. *Survival,* Jan.–Feb. 1965, pp. 4–7.

Peking Statement on Nuclear Test, October 16, 1964 (released by Hsinhua press agency). *Current History,* Feb. 1965, pp. 109–110.

People — Bruno Pontecorvo. *Time,* Mar. 14, 1955, p. 49.

Perkinson, W. J. Preview of Tomorrow's Nuclear Terror. *Science Digest,* Aug. 1963, pp. 50–53.

Polyot and Peking. *Newsweek,* Nov. 11, 1963, p. 73.

Pontecorvo Pops Up. *Newsweek,* Mar. 14, 1955, pp. 50–52.

Positive Proposal; Prevention Against Nuclear Threat. *National Review,* Dec. 1, 1964, p. 1045.

Powell, Ralph L. China's Bomb: Exploitation and Reactions. *Foreign Affairs,* July 1965, pp. 616–625.

Bibliography

——. Communist China as a Military Power. *Current History*, Sept. 1965, pp. 136–141.

——. Communist China's Military Potential. *Current History*, Sept. 1964, pp. 136–142.

——. Great Powers and Atomic Bombs are "Paper Tigers." *China Quarterly*, July–Sept. 1965, pp. 55–63.

——. Military Affairs of Communist China. *Current History*, Sept. 1966, p. 140+.

President Reports on Change in Soviet Leadership, Chinese Nuclear Test, and New British Government. *Department of State Bulletin*, Nov. 2, 1964, pp. 610–614.

Red Atom [Pontecorvo]. *Colliers*, Apr. 27, 1956, p. 36+.

Red China: Firecracker No. 2. *Time*, May 21, 1965, pp. 34–35.

Red China Gets Ready to Fire Its A–Bomb. *Business Week*, Aug. 1, 1964, p. 32+.

Red China in the Nuclear Race; Excerpts from Testimony of Robert McNamara. *U.S. News*, Feb. 7, 1966, p. 8.

Red China on Its Way to the H–Bomb. *Business Week*, May 29, 1965, pp. 49–50.

Red China: "Paper Tiger?" *U.S. News*, Oct. 25, 1965, p. 40+.

Red China Soon to Have the A–Bomb. *U.S. News*, Jan. 11, 1960, pp. 47–48.

Red China Trying to Beat France in the Race For an H–Bomb? *U.S. News*, May 23, 1966, p. 52.

Red China with the A–Missile; Meaning to the U.S. and Russia; Interview with C. Cheng. *U.S. News*, Nov. 14, 1966, pp. 50–52.

Red China's Atomic Shot — What It Means to the World. *U.S. News*, Nov. 7, 1966, p. 6.

Red China's Beehive of Science. *Business Week*, Mar. 14, 1959, p. 183+.

Red China's Bomb: How It Alters Things in the World. *U.S. News*, Oct. 26, 1964, pp. 48–50.

Red China's Drive. *Time*, Jan. 6, 1961, p. 53.

Red China's "Leap" Toward Science. *Business Week*, Nov. 24, 1962, p. 102+.

Red China's Nuclear Threat: The Time Grows Shorter. *U.S. News*, May 31, 1965, pp. 28–29.

Red Chinese Test Expected. *Senior Scholastic*, Oct. 14, 1964, p. 15.

Report on Khrushchev's Fall, China's Atomic Bomb: Oct. 18 Address on Nationwide Radio and Television. *Congressional Quarterly Weekly Report*, Oct. 23, 1964, pp. 2576–2577.

Review of L. Beaton and J. Maddox: *Spread of Nuclear Weapons*. Everybody's A–Bomb? *New Republic*, Feb. 16, 1963, p. 22.

The CHINA CLOUD

Review of R. De Toledano's *Greatest Plot in History: How the Reds Stole the A-Bomb. Bulletin of the Atomic Scientists*, Feb. 1964, pp. 29–30.

Rose, Jerry A. How Strong Is China's Army? *Reporter*, Mar. 11, 1965, p. 23.

Rusk and Bundy Interviewed on Red China's Nuclear Testing. *Department of State Bulletin*, Nov. 2, 1964, pp. 614–617.

Russia, China and England: Our Basic Policy Remains Unchanged (L. B. Johnson address on Oct. 18, 1964). *Vital Speeches*, Nov. 1, 1964, pp. 34–36.

Russia Has the Jump in Nuclear Research. *Business Week*, July 7, 1956, pp. 64–66.

Schneider, Fernand. Where Is Red China Headed? (condensed and translated from *Revue Militaire Générale*). *Military Review*, Dec. 1963, pp. 38–43.

Science — For Hypersonics [Tsien Hsue-shen Appointment at Caltech]. *Time*, Dec. 20, 1948, p. 57.

Science In Communist China (A.A.A.S. Symposium). *Scientific American*, Feb. 1961, p. 66+.

Science — Rockets Up and Down [Tsien Hsue-shen Speech at A.S.M.E.]. *Time*, Dec. 12, 1949, p. 46.

Scientific Enigma of Communist China [excerpts from *Scientific Revolution and World Politics* by C. P. Haskins]. *Saturday Review*, June 6, 1964, pp. 43–46.

Scientific Research in China. *Bulletin of the Atomic Scientists*, May 1966, pp. 36–43.

Scientific Revolution Brews in Red China. *Science News Letter*, Feb. 27, 1965, p. 133.

Scientist in China, The. *Time*, May 9, 1955, pp. 104–105.

Search for a Scientist [Pontecorvo]. *Newsweek*, Nov. 6, 1950, p. 35+.

Secretary [Rusk] Discusses Mainland China in Television Interview. *Department of State Bulletin*, Nov. 30, 1964, pp. 771–772.

Shackleton, N. A. The War-Making Potential of Communist China. *Canadian Army Journal*, No. 3, 1963, pp. 15–27.

Shannon, W. V. Optimists and the Pessimists — Shift in Power in Russia, and Explosion of the Chinese Nuclear Bomb. *Commonweal*, Nov. 13, 1964, pp. 217–218.

Should We Bomb Red China's Bomb? *National Review*, Jan. 12, 1965, pp. 8–10.

Slessinger, S. 600 Million Chinese + Communism + the Bomb = ? *Commonweal*, July 9, 1965, p. 506.

Spiritual A–Bomb. *Newsweek*, Aug. 28, 1961, p. 36.

Bibliography

Start of the Chain; Peking's Nuclear Firecracker. *Time*, Oct. 30, 1964, pp. 38–39.

Stowe, D. M. What about Mainland China? *Christian Century*, Jan. 13, 1965, pp. 44–46.

Summary of McNamara's Speech on 12/15/65 re China's Nuclear Development. *National Review*, Jan. 11, 1966, pp. 12–13.

Survey of Chinese Students in the U.S. *China and America*, Feb. 1949, pp. 10–17.

They Shot an Arrow in the Air [Chinese Set Off Guided Missile with Nuclear Weapon Attached]. *Economist*, Nov. 5, 1966, p. 567.

Thornton, Thomas P. Communist China and Nuclear Weapons. *Military Review*, Sept. 1964, pp. 31–38.

Tilting the Balance of A-Power: Red China's Progress in Nuclear Technology. *Business Week*, Oct. 31, 1964, p. 74+.

Trager, Frank N. and Hans Morgenthau. China Is (Is Not) an Aggressive Power. *New York Times Magazine*, Mar. 13, 1966, p. 28+.

Training of 20th-Century Lomonosovs: A Discussion by Dubna Scientists; Statements by Leading Scientists Who Participated [includes Pontecorvo]. Translated from *Izvestia*. Dec. 27, 1960. *Soviet Review*, Apr. 1961, pp. 15–27.

Truth about Red China — How Much of a Threat? *U.S. News*, July 4, 1966, pp. 40–43.

Truth about Red China's Bomb [interview with Chu-yuan Cheng]. *U.S. News*, Dec. 28, 1964, pp. 28–32.

Tsien San-tsiang [Chien San-chiang] and Ho Zah-wei [Ho Che-hui], et al. Ternary and Quaternary Fission of Uranium Nuclei. *Nature*, June 7, 1947, pp. 773–774. Pub. by British Association for Advancement of Science.

U.S. Comments on Peiping's Nuclear Capacity; Statement, Sept. 29, 1964, D. Rusk. *Department of State Bulletin*, Oct. 19, 1964, p. 542.

Waiting for Evolution. *Time*, Nov. 13, 1964, pp. 46–49.

War with China? *New Republic*, Jan. 29, 1966, pp. 7–8.

We've Been Asked . . . About Chinese Students Allowed to Leave the U.S. *U.S. News*, Apr. 15, 1955, p. 72.

Whither Red China's March on Science? *Newsweek*, Jan. 9, 1961, p. 76.

Wilson, Dick. China's Nuclear Effort. *Far Eastern Economic Review*, Aug. 19, 1965, p. 328.

With Red China Getting the Bomb. *U.S. News*, Oct. 12, 1964, pp. 38–39.

Wolfle, D. Chinese Embargo. *Science*, Aug. 4, 1961, p. 303.

World Reactions to the Chinese Nuclear Bomb. Published by Indian Council of World Affairs, New Delhi. *Foreign Affairs Reports* (India), Jan. 1965, pp. 3–14.

Wu, Y. L. Can Communist China Afford War? *Orbis,* Oct. 1962, pp. 453–464.

Young, Oran R. Chinese Views on the Spread of Nuclear Weapons. *China Quarterly,* Apr.–June 1966, pp. 136–170.

In addition to the books and periodicals listed above, the authors consulted some 250 newspaper stories for facts and editorial comment. Because of its invaluable index, the New York *Times* was the principal newspaper consulted (1949 through 1966), but scattered items were read also in the *Christian Science Monitor, Daily Worker,* Los Angeles *Times, Manchester Guardian Weekly,* New York *Daily News,* New York *Herald Tribune,* New York *Journal-American,* New York *World-Telegram,* and *Wall Street Journal.*

APPENDIX

Leading Chinese scientists who received their technical training in the United States include six of the top fifteen who worked on China's bomb, and four of the five leaders of the missile program, as well as a mathematician of world-wide reputation.

On the Bombs

Chien San-chiang, director of the Institute of Atomic Energy — University of Paris

Wang Kan-chang, deputy director — Universities of Berlin and California

Chao Chung-yao, deputy director — Caltech

Peng Huang-wu, deputy director — University of Edinburgh

Chang Chia-hua, deputy director — Washington University (St. Louis)

Hu Ning, physicist at Peking University — Caltech; Princeton University

Chu Hung-yuan, Institute of Atomic Energy — University of Manchester

Chou Kuang-chao, physicist at Peking University — USSR

Ho Tsu-hsiu, Institute of Atomic Energy — USSR

Chang Wen-yu, Institute of Atomic Energy — Cambridge and Princeton Universities

Ho Che-hui, Institute of Atomic Energy — Universities of Berlin and Paris

Tai Chuan-tseng, Institute of Atomic Energy — University of Liverpool

Chang Tsung-sui, Peking Normal University — Cambridge University

Yang Li-ming, physicist at Peking University — University of Edinburgh

Teng Chia-hsien, Institute of Atomic Energy — Purdue University

The CHINA CLOUD

On the Rockets

Tsien Hsue-shen, Institute of Mechanics	M.I.T.; Caltech
Kuo Yung-huai, deputy director of the Institute of Mechanics	Caltech
Shen Yuan, Peking Aeronautical Engineering College	London University
Chien Wei-chang, Chinese Academy of Sciences	Caltech
Wei Chung-hua	M.I.T.

The mathematician, Hua Lo-keng, of the Chinese Academy of Sciences, studied at the University of Illinois.

Over three thousand five hundred Chinese students were at colleges and universities in the United States at the end of 1949, when China fell under the control of Communist armies and Chiang Kai-shek's Nationalist government moved to Taiwan. The following eighty physicists, engineers, chemists, geologists and mathematicians are among the many American-trained scientists who subsequently returned to their homeland. In China, they reached positions of sufficient eminence to be included in Chu-yuan Cheng's survey of one thousand two hundred prominent scientists and engineers (*Scientific and Engineering Manpower in Communist China, 1949–1963*). Two scientists who were found in sources other than Cheng were included: they are Ying Cheng-fu and Wei Chung-hua. The scientists are listed according to the American universities they attended. The universities are given in alphabetical order.

Brooklyn Polytechnic Institute, Brooklyn, N.Y.

Huang Pao-tung: b. 1921. Ph.D. in chemistry, 1953. Research fellow, Institute of Applied Chemistry, Chinese Academy of Sciences

Brown University, Providence, R.I.

Lin Hung-sun: b. 1925. Studied mathematics at Brown, 1948–1950. Research fellow, Institute of Mechanics, Chinese Academy of Sciences; faculty member, Peking University

Wang Jen (alias *Alexander Jen Wang*): b. 1921. Ph.D. in physics, 1953. Associate professor, Department of Mathematics, Peking University

Ying Cheng-fu: Studied physics at Brown, 1952. Director of research in ultrasonics, Institute of Electronics

Appendix

Bryn Mawr, Pa.

Chih Chi-shang: b. 1919. Ph.D. in geology, 1949. Professor and chief, Teaching and Research Section of Petrography, Peking Geological Institute

California Institute of Technology, Pasadena, Calif.

Chao Chung-yao: b. 1902. Ph.D. in nuclear physics, 1930. He and four other Caltech students were arrested by U.S. military police in Japan, Nov. 1950, on their way home to China. One of Chien San-chiang's two top deputies on the atomic bomb project (Deputy Director, Institute of Atomic Energy, Chinese Academy of Sciences); board member and member of Standing Committee, Department of Physics, Mathematics and Chemistry, Chinese Academy of Sciences; directly involved in atomic bomb project. Deputy, Third National People's Congress

Chien Wei-chang (alias *Jimmy Chien*): b. 1914. Research engineer at Caltech, 1947, in physics (jet propulsion). Board member, Department of Physics, Mathematics and Chemistry, Chinese Academy of Sciences; Director of Institute of Automation and Remote Control (before 1958 and after 1960); Vice-president of Tsinghua University; member, Institute of Mathematics; directly involved in rocket project

Hsiao Chien: b. 1920. Ph.D. in nuclear physics, 1950. Research fellow, Laboratory of Cosmic Rays, Institute of Atomic Energy

Hu Ning: b. 1915. Ph.D. in nuclear physics, 1944 (then to Princeton). Board member, Department of Physics, Mathematics and Chemistry, Chinese Academy of Sciences; Research fellow, Institute of Atomic Energy; section head, Joint Nuclear Research Institute, Dubna, USSR; Professor, Department of Physics, Peking University; directly involved in atomic bomb project

Kuo Yung-huai: b. 1912. Ph.D. in aeronautical engineering, 1945. Board member, Department of Physics, Mathematics and Chemistry, Chinese Academy of Sciences; Vice-chairman, China Aeronautical Engineers Society; Deputy director, Institute of Mechanics; directly involved in rocket project. Deputy, Third National People's Congress

Li Cheng-wu: b. 1916. Ph.D. in nuclear physics (isotopic), 1951. Research fellow, Institute of Physics, Chinese Academy of Sciences. Member, Fourth National Committee, Chinese People's Political Consultative Committee

Meng Chao-ying: b. 1906. Ph.D. in physics, 1936: Board member, Department of Technical Science, Chinese Academy of Sciences. Professor and Chairman, Department of Radio, Tsinghua University

301

The CHINA CLOUD

Tang You-chi: b. 1920. Ph.D. in chemistry, 1950. Professor, Department of Chemistry, Peking University; Research fellow, Institute of Applied Chemistry, Chinese Academy of Sciences

Tsien Hsue-shen: b. 1909. Sc.D. in aeronautical engineering, 1939; professor of jet propulsion, 1949–1955. Deported from the U.S., 1955. Director, Institute of Mechanics; board member, Department of Physics, Mathematics and Chemistry, Chinese Academy of Sciences; member, National Committee of Chinese Science and Technology Association; Chairman, China Dynamics Society; Chairman, China Automation Society; Chairman, Department of Modern Mechanics, University of Sciences and Technology. Deputy, Third National People's Congress; member of Chinese Communist party

Carnegie Institute of Technology, Pittsburgh, Pa.

Shen Kuang-ming: b. 1923. Sc.D. in physics, 1954. Research fellow, Institute of Electronics, Chinese Academy of Sciences

Columbia University, New York, N.Y.

Hsu Kuang-hsien: Ph.D. in nuclear chemistry, 1951. Faculty member, Department of Atomic Energy and Department of Chemistry, Peking University. Deputy, Third National People's Congress

Peng Chi-jui: b. 1917. Ph.D. in mineralogy, 1952. Research fellow, Institute of Geology, Chinese Academy of Sciences

Tang Ao-ching: b. 1916. Ph.D. in chemistry, 1949. Board member, Department of Physics, Mathematics and Chemistry, Chinese Academy of Sciences; member of Academic Committee and research fellow, Institute of Applied Chemistry; Professor and vice-president of Kirin University. Deputy, Third National People's Congress; member of Chinese Communist party

Wang Tien-chuan: b. 1913. Ph.D. in nuclear physics, 1954. Member, Institute of Atomic Energy, Chinese Academy of Sciences

Cornell University, Ithaca, N. Y.

Huang Mao-kuang: b. 1921. Ph.D. in mechanics, 1951. Research fellow, Institute of Mechanics, Chinese Academy of Sciences

Li Wen-chu: Nuclear physics. Member of Institute of Atomic Energy, Chinese Academy of Sciences; member, Department of Physics, Chekiang University

Appendix

Tu Shan-cheng: b. 1923. Ph.D. in electrical engineering, 1953. Secretary general, China Automation Society, Chinese Science and Technology Assn.

Harvard University, Cambridge, Mass.

Chang Pao-kun: b. 1903. M.S. in meteorology, 1947–1949. Member of Academic Committee, Institute of Geophysics and Meteorology, Chinese Academy of Sciences

Chang Ping-hsi: b. 1903. Ph.D. in geology, 1950. Member of Academic Committee, Institute of Geology, Chinese Academy of Sciences

Huang Chang: b. 1927. Ph.D. in physics, 1953. Associate professor, Department of Physics, Peking University

Huang Wei-yuan: b. 1921. Ph.D. in chemistry, 1952. Research fellow, Institute of Organic Chemistry, Chinese Academy of Sciences

Ma Ta-yi: b. *c.* 1914. Ph.D. in physics, 1940. Board member, Department of Technical Science, Chinese Academy of Sciences; Deputy director, Institute of Electronics; member, National Committee of Chinese Science and Technology Association; Vice-chairman, Chinese Electronics Society. Deputy, Third National People's Congress

Yang Chia-chih: b. 1919. Ph.D. in automation, 1949. Member, Institute of Automation and Remote Control, Chinese Academy of Sciences. Deputy, Third National People's Congress

Yang Shih-te: b. 1917. Ph.D. in civil engineering (structural mechanics), 1949. Professor and vice-chairman, Civil Engineering Department, Tsinghua University

Indiana University, Bloomington, Ind.

Chen Ju-yu: b. 1919. Ph.D. in chemistry, 1952. Professor, Department of Chemistry, Nan-k'ai University.

Ho Ping-lin: b. 1918. Ph.D. in chemistry, 1952. Chairman, Department of Chemistry, Nan-k'ai University. Deputy, Third National People's Congress

Johns Hopkins University. Baltimore, Md.

Pien Yen-kwei: b. 1921. Eng.D. in mechanics, 1955. Research fellow, Institute of Mechanics, Chinese Academy of Sciences

The CHINA CLOUD

Louisiana State University, Baton Rouge, La.

Chang Hung-chi: b. 1916. Ph.D. in physics, 1953. Deputy director, Institute of Geology, Ministry of Geology

Chen Tien-chih: b. 1919. Ph.D. in chemistry, 1949. Research fellow, Institute of Petroleum, Chinese Academy of Sciences

Hung Chao-sheng: b. 1920. Sc.D. in physics, 1948. Member of Academic Committee and associate research fellow, Institute of Applied Physics, Chinese Academy of Sciences. Deputy, Third National People's Congress

Lu Yuan-chiu: b. 1920. Sc.D. in automation, 1949. Research fellow, Institute of Automation and Remote Control, Chinese Academy of Sciences. Deputy, Third National People's Congress

Tsao Chien-yu: b. 1917. Sc.D. in railroad engineering, 1950. Professor and chairman, Department of Electrical Engineering, Tang-shan Railroad College; executive director, China Electrical Engineering Society

Massachusetts Institute of Technology, Cambridge, Mass.

Tsien Hsue-shen: b. 1909. M.S. in aeronautical engineering, 1936 (before going to Caltech); professor of aeronautics, 1947–1949. Deported from the U.S., 1955. Director, Institute of Mechanics; board member, Department of Physics, Mathematics and Chemistry, Chinese Academy of Sciences; member, National Committee of Chinese Science and Technology Assn.; Chairman, China Dynamics Society; Chairman, China Automation Society; Chairman, Department of Modern Mechanics, University of Sciences and Technology. Deputy, Third National People's Congress; member of Chinese Communist party

Wei Chung-hua: Mentioned in a few sources as helping the rocket program

Wu Cheng-kang: At M.I.T. in 1957, studying mechanical engineering. Member, Institute of Power Engineers, Chinese Academy of Sciences

Wu Pao-chen: b. 1920. Sc.D. in chemistry, 1950. Member of Academic Committee, Institute of Petroleum, Chinese Academy of Sciences

Notre Dame University, Notre Dame, Ind.

Ho Kuo-chu: b. 1922. Ph.D. in nuclear physics, 1952. Professor, Department of Physics, Nan-k'ai University. Deputy, Third National People's Congress

Appendix

Ohio State University, Columbus, Ohio

Cheng Lin-sheng: b. 1921. Ph.D. in nuclear physics, 1952. Research fellow, Institute of Atomic Energy, Chinese Academy of Sciences

Ts'ai Ch'i-jui: b. 1914. Ph.D. in chemistry, 1950. Professor, Amoy University

Princeton University, Princeton, N.J.

Chang Wen-yu: b. 1910. Cosmic ray research at Princeton, 1945–1949 (after Ph.D. in nuclear physics from Cambridge University, England, 1938). Member, Department of Physics, Mathematics and Chemistry, Chinese Academy of Sciences; Chief, Cosmic Ray Laboratory, Institute of Atomic Energy; directly involved with atomic bomb project. Deputy, Third National People's Congress

Cheng Min-te: b. 1919. Ph.D. in mathematics, 1949. Professor, Peking University

Hu Ning: b. 1915. Research on quantum field theories, Princeton Institute for Advanced Studies (after Ph.D. in nuclear physics, Caltech, 1944); worked with physicists Pauli and Heitler. Board member, Department of Physics, Mathematics and Chemistry, Chinese Academy of Sciences; research fellow, Institute of Atomic Energy; section head, Joint Nuclear Research Institute, Dubna, USSR; professor, Department of Physics, Peking University; directly involved with atomic bomb project

Liao Shan-tao: b. 1919. Studied at Princeton Institute for Advanced Studies (after Ph.D. in mathematics, University of Chicago, 1955). Professor of mathematics, Peking University

Wang Hsiang-hao (alias *Wang Shiang-haw*): b. 1915. Ph.D. in mathematics, 1949. Board member, Department of Physics, Mathematics and Chemistry, Chinese Academy of Sciences; Professor, Kirin University. Deputy, Third National People's Congress

Purdue University, Lafayette, Ind.

Teng Chia-hsien: b. 1924. Ph.D. in nuclear physics, 1950. Research fellow, Institute of Atomic Energy, Chinese Academy of Sciences; directly involved with atomic bomb project. Member of Chinese Communist party

Wang Pu-hsuan: b. 1923. M.S. in mechanical engineering, 1949. Professor, Tsinghua University

Wang Shou-wu: b. 1919. Ph.D. in physics (semiconductors), 1949. Research fellow and member of Academic Committee, Institute of Applied Physics, Chinese Academy of Sciences. Deputy, Third National People's Congress

The CHINA CLOUD

Rutgers University, New Brunswick, N. J.

Hsiang Jen-sheng: b. 1917. Ph.D. in physics, 1949. Research fellow, Institute of Applied Physics, Chinese Academy of Sciences (a specialist in magnetism)

Stanford University, Palo Alto, Calif.

Hsieh Chia-lin: b. 1920. Ph.D. in nuclear physics, 1951. Research fellow, Institute of Atomic Energy, Chinese Academy of Sciences

Tu Ching-hua: b. 1919. Ph.D. in civil engineering, 1951. Professor, Department of Engineering Mechanics and Mathematics, Tsinghua University

University of California, Berkeley, Calif.

Chiang Shih-fei: b. 1924. Ph.D. in mechanical engineering, 1952. Research fellow, Institute of Computer Technology, Chinese Academy of Sciences

Kao Ting-san: b. 1917. M.S. in physics, 1952. Member, Institute of Applied Physics, Chinese Academy of Sciences

Ko Ting-sui: b. 1913. Sc.D. in physics (applied physics, specialized in metallurgy), 1944. Said to have worked on U.S. A-bomb project until late 1945. Board member and member of Standing Committee, Department of Physics, Mathematics and Chemistry, Chinese Academy of Sciences; Member of Academic Committee, Institute of Applied Physics and Institute of Metals; Professor, Tsinghua University. Member of Central Committee, Chiu-san Society; Deputy, Third National People's Congress

Wang Kan-chang: b. 1907. At Berkeley as research associate in physics, 1947–1948 (after Ph.D. in nuclear physics, University of Berlin, 1934). Returned to China, 1948. Board member, Department of Physics, Mathematics and Chemistry, Chinese Academy of Sciences; Deputy director, Institute of Atomic Energy; Deputy director, Joint Nuclear Research Institute, Dubna, USSR; directly involved in atomic bomb project. Deputy, Third National People's Congress

University of Chicago, Chicago, Ill.

Hsieh I-ping: b. 1917. Ph.D. in geophysics, 1949. Research fellow and member of Academic Committee, Institute of Geophysics and Meterology, Chinese Academy of Sciences; Professor of Meteorology, Peking University

Tang Ting-yuan: b. 1920. M.S. in physics (solid state physics and luminescent materials), 1950. Research fellow, Institute of Physics, Chinese Academy of Sciences (specialist in semiconductors)

Appendix

University of Illinois, Urbana, Ill.

Chu Chia-chen (alias *Kang Chu Chia-chen*): b. 1923. Ph.D. in nuclear physics, 1951. Faculty member, Department of Physics, Peking University

Hua Lo-keng: b. 1910. At Illinois until *c.* 1950 (after Sc.D. in mathematics, Cambridge University, England, 1936; Boxer fellow at University of Berlin). Board member and deputy director, Department of Physics, Mathematics and Chemistry, Chinese Academy of Sciences; Director, Institute of Mathematics; Director, Institute of Computer Technique; Member, National Committee, Chinese Science and Technology Association; Chairman, China Mathematics Society; Professor, Tsinghua University. Member of Standing Committee and Deputy, Third National People's Congress

Kuo Ke-chan: b. 1917. Ph.D. in mathematics, 1950. Professor, Mathematics Teaching and Research Laboratory, Tang-shan Railroad College

Tung Shih-pai: b. 1920. Ph.D. in electrical engineering, 1951. Professor, Department of Electrical Engineering, Tsinghua University

Wu Shih-shu: b. 1923. Ph.D. in physics, 1951. Professor, Department of Physics, Kirin University

University of Michigan, Ann Arbor, Mich.

Chu Kuang-ya: b. 1924. Ph.D. in nuclear physics, 1950. Professor, Peking University. Deputy, Third National People's Congress

Hou Yu-chun: b. 1922. Ph.D. in chemical engineering, 1955. Deputy, Third National People's Congress

Yu Tung-yin: b. 1917. Ph.D. in chemistry (high polymer), 1951. Director, Institute of High Polymers, Chinese Academy of Sciences; Professor, Futan University

University of Minnesota, Minneapolis, Minn.

Chiang Li-chin (alias *Hsu Li-chin Chiang*): b. 1919. Ph.D. in chemistry, 1951. Research fellow, Institute of Chemistry, Chinese Academy of Sciences. Member, Fourth National Committee, Chinese People's Political Consultative Committee

Ko Chun-lin: b. 1909. M.S. in chemistry, 1949. Member of Academic Committee, Institute of Applied Chemistry, Chinese Academy of Sciences

Tu Kuang-chih: b. 1920. Ph.D. in geology, 1949. Member of Academic Committee, Institute of Geology, Chinese Academy of Sciences

University of Missouri, Columbia, Mo.

Hsiao Chi-mei: b. 1920. Ph.D. in metallurgy, 1950. Research fellow, Institute of Metals, Chinese Academy of Sciences

Shih Sheng-tai: b. 1917. Ph.D. in metallurgy, 1954. Research fellow, Institute of Metallurgy, Chinese Academy of Sciences

University of Pennsylvania, Philadelphia, Pa.

Lin I: b. 1911. Ph.D. in chemistry, 1951. Research fellow, Institute of Chemistry, Chinese Academy of Sciences. Deputy, Third National People's Congress

Lin Lan-ying: b. 1919. Ph.D. in physics, 1955. Associate research fellow, Institute of Applied Physics, Chinese Academy of Sciences. Deputy, Third National People's Congress

University of Rochester, Rochester, N. Y.

Liu Chu-chin: b. 1919. Ph.D. in chemistry, 1951. Research fellow, Institute of Organic Chemistry, Chinese Academy of Sciences

Liu Ta-kang: b. 1905. Ph.D. in chemistry (applied chemistry and inorganic chemistry), 1949. Board member, Department of Physics, Mathematics and Chemistry, Chinese Academy of Sciences; Member of Academic Committee, Institute of Applied Chemistry; Director, Institute of Chemistry. Deputy, Third National People's Congress; member of Chinese Communist party

University of Southern California, Los Angeles, Calif.

Sun Hsiang (a woman): b. 1916. Ph.D. in physics, 1953. Returned to China, 1955. Associate research fellow, Institute of Physics, Chinese Academy of Sciences, noted for papers on plasma physics. Deputy, Third National People's Congress

University of Texas, Austin, Tex.

Li Shih-ngo: b. 1920. Ph.D. in chemistry, 1954. Professor, Department of Biochemistry, Chinese Academy of Medical Sciences

Appendix

University of Wisconsin, Madison, Wis.

Chang Wei-shen: b. 1909. Ph.D. in biochemistry, 1950. Director, Institute of Antibiotics, Chinese Academy of Medical Sciences. Member of Chinese Communist party

Hu Chih-pin. Studied chemistry, 1948–1950. Chairman, Department of Chemistry, Peking Normal University

Vanderbilt University, Nashville, Tenn.

Hsieh Yu-chang: b. 1915. Ph.D. in mathematics, 1949. Professor, Department of Mathematics, Tsinghua University

Washington University, St. Louis, Mo.

Chang Chia-hua: b. 1915. Ph.D. in nuclear physics, 1952. Deputy director, Institute of Atomic Energy, Chinese Academy of Sciences; directly involved with atomic bomb project

Yale University, New Haven, Conn.

Chen Neng-kuan: b. 1923. Eng.D. in metallurgy, 1950. Research fellow, Institute of Applied Physics, Chinese Academy of Sciences. Deputy, Third National People's Congress

Shi Ju-wei: b. 1903. Ph.D. in physics (applied physics, specialized in magnetics), 1934. Board member, Department of Physics, Mathematics and Chemistry, Chinese Academy of Sciences. Member, Academic Committee; Director, Institute of Physics. Deputy, Third National People's Congress

U. S. S. R.

• Novosibirsk

CASPIAN SEA

ARAL SEA

Lake Balkhash

Alma Ata • • Ili

• Urumchi

SINKIANG

Lop Nor

Tarim River

Takla Makan Desert

IRAN

AFGHANISTAN

KASHMIR

C H

PAKISTAN

New Delhi

NEPAL

SIKKIM

Lhasa •

BHUTAN

IND

PAKISTAN

INDIA

Calcutta •

1000 MILE RANGE

400 MILE RANGE

400 MILE RANGE

1000 MILE RANGE

INDIAN OCEAN

BAY OF BENGA

Madras •

CEYLON